THE MEDICINAL PLANTS OF THE PHILIPPINES

THE MEDICINAL PLANTS OF THE PHILIPPINES

T. H. PARDO DE TAVERA

GYAN

Published by

GYAN

Gyan Publishing House
5, Ansari Road
Daryaganj, New Delhi-110002
Phone: 011-47034999, 9811692060
E-mail: books@gyanbooks.com

Distribution Network
gyanbooks.com
India, USA, Canada, UK, Australia

ISBN: 978-93-7169-078-2 (PB)

First Published, 1901

2nd Impression 2025

Printed at: Gyan Press, Delhi.

THE MEDICINAL PLANTS OF THE PHILIPPINES
Author: T. H. PARDO DE TAVERA

THE MEDICINAL PLANTS OF THE PHILIPPINES

TRANSLATOR'S PREFACE.

This translation was undertaken with the especial object of facilitating the study of the native medicinal plants by the numerous medical officers stationed at small posts throughout the Philippines. In order to aid in the recognition of these plants, the botanical descriptions have been revised to the extent of adding, where possible, the size and shape of the plant, English name, length of leaves, color of flowers, etc., in many instances supplying the entire botanical description where it had been omitted on account of general familiarity with the plant. Comparing the few analyses that I have had an opportunity to make with corresponding ones in the native works from which Dr. Tavera has taken his botanical descriptions, I am impressed with the necessity for a revision of the Botany of the Philippines. However, as the therapeutic properties of the flora are of foremost interest to the medical profession I have not hesitated to publish the book in its present form as an entering wedge, leaving to those better fitted the great work of classifying the flora of these islands in accordance with modern botanical science.

Dr. Tavera has faithfully described the Malay and Hindu therapeutics of the present day, enriching his description by observations founded on a long practice in Paris and in his own native Luzon. From this potpourri of scientific therapeutics and ignorant, superstitious drugging the interested physician will elicit not a few useful data concerning the treatment of disease in the tropics, and at the same time gain a more intimate knowledge of both the people and plants of our new Asiatic possessions.

I take this occasion to gratefully acknowledge my obligations to Mr. A. P. Tonielli, stenographer and translator of the Supreme Court of the Philippines, for typewriting the manuscript of this translation.

JEROME B. THOMAS, JR.

MANILA, P. I.

PREFACE.

Commissioned by His Majesty's Government to study the medicinal plants of my native country, I returned there and spent two years in collecting data regarding the use that the Filipinos make of their plants in the treatment of disease. At the same time I collected and carefully preserved some with the purpose of taking them to Europe, to study their chemical composition in the laboratories of Paris under the direction of the eminent men who had been my instructors in medicine.

The work I did in the Philippines was preliminary, a preparation for the more extended study of the subject which I wished to make in Paris, where I went with my notes and collection. Unfortunately, upon leaving Manila, I confided the mounting and pressing of my plants to an inexperienced person who stupidly placed in the midst of them several succulent tubers which decomposed during the voyage and spoiled the other plants. At the same time I received in Paris an important collection of the vegetable drugs of the Philippines, sent by my friend the pharmacist, M. Rosedo Garcia, and destined for the World's Fair of 1889. I opened with great pleasure the wood and zinc box in which the collection came, anticipating that I should be able to carry out my plan of study and at the same time win for my friend, Garcia, a well-deserved premium. Imagine my disappointment upon finding that, by an unfortunate coincidence, his plants had arrived in the same condition as mine, having also been packed with tubers of ubi, gabi, etc., and several cocoanuts which had decomposed.

Many times since then I have tried to obtain from Manila, through exchange or payment of money, a similar collection, but have been unable to secure a single leaf of the plants I so desired. If in the future I have the good fortune to procure any, I shall make a study of those at hand and publish the results.

I herewith publish the results of my investigations and experiments in Manila, where, especially in the neighboring towns of San Mateo and San Miguel, I often had opportunities for using, with good results, the plants of which this volume treats. I may add that in spite of the limited means at my disposal in Manila and the short time left me by my regular occupations I was able to conduct a few laboratory experiments owing to which this work contains some personal observations reinforcing those quoted from medical literature.

The flora of the Archipelago is known to-day through the works of Fathers Blanco, Llanos, Fernandez del Villar and Naves, and of the engineers Jordano, the brothers Vidal and Soler and others who have brought such honor to Spanish science, preparing the way for the study of the therapeutic and industrial applications of that wonderfully rich plant life with which our islands have been endowed. Their works help us to recognize the plants whose medicinal virtues are herein described and it is to them I owe the botanical descriptions in this treatise.

Father Blanco, in describing certain plants, mentions their medicinal uses in the Philippines, but his descriptions are few and very deficient as one would expect in a work of the scope of his Flora. A Jesuit of some reputation, Father Clain, published in Manila in 1712 a book entitled "Remedios fáciles para diferentes enfermedades?" in which he speaks of the medicinal virtues of some of the indigenous plants, almost the same ones that appear in another work, a frank and pleasing little treatise written by Father Santa Maria. Father Mercado is the only one who has written a special treatise on the subject and his manuscript remained unedited until the Augustinian Fathers of Manila published it in the last edition of

Father Blanco's "Flora"; but neither this work nor those of Clain or Santa Maria are useful to a physician, nor are they as accurately written as works of a scientific character should be. From time to time superficial articles have appeared in the Manila papers regarding the virtues of some plant or other and these books and articles comprise the whole literature on the subject up to this time.

Some physicians regard with small favor the therapeutic application of plants by the Filipino "herb-doctors" (curanderos) as being entirely empirical. This disparagement is unjustified because in all the most rational and scientific remedies that we make use of, the first step towards the final development of their relative position among remedies is due to empiricism which is founded on daily experience, on observation of results obtained in specific cases, facts that are handed down from father to son for generations. The scientific explanation is lacking, but those first ideas frequently owing their origin to chance, or, perhaps, to superstition, have often been based upon the observation of facts which, although fortuitous, are none the less positive.

Many of the plants mentioned in this book are official in the Pharmacopœia of India and we see no reason why their use should be proscribed in the Philippines. Filipino physicians not only can but should employ many indigenous plants in their therapeutics; in many instances they would find them more useful than the exotics, which are not always fresh and are commonly reduced in strength by long keeping or damaged by some circumstance of voyage or climate. The price is another argument in favor of the use of native drugs. If the pharmacists would prepare extracts and keep on hand the crude drugs most in demand the public would gain a great advantage and the druggists be well repaid for their labor. Physicians and pharmacists will surely understand these advantages and when finally one considers that the patients generally prefer to be treated with native plants, I feel justified in the hope that their use will spread rapidly in the Philippines.

To employ therapeutically the drugs described in this work is not to experiment "in anima vilis," as some would have us believe. To experiment is to employ unknown remedies of unknown virtues and properties.

In this treatise I am not attempting to fix the indications for this or that product, but simply make known the diseases in which the Filipinos and the natives of other countries employ the products. Any physician has a perfect right to prescribe these drugs, as have also the "curanderos" and even the laity, with this difference, however, that the physician is capable of observing results and guiding himself by the physiologic action of the drugs. His knowledge of the physiologic and anatomo-pathologic problems of the human body, will enable the physician to make scientific inferences that would be hidden from the common "curandero."

As neither the Manila nor the provincial physicians keep these medicinal plants in stock, with the exception of those that are official in the European and American pharmacopœias, it will be necessary for the physician who wishes to use them, to busy himself with seeking them and laying in a sufficient stock to serve him when the opportunity presents itself. It is necessary to preserve them by drying and this is best done by exposing them several days to the fresh air in a dry place—for example, the corridors of the house—being careful not to expose them to the rays of the sun, in which latter event the fleshy and juicy plants which do not desiccate rapidly, putrefy or ferment.

A convenient way to get them is to visit the Binondo Square where there has been market for native drugs from time immemorial. The gardeners from the neighboring towns, especially those from Pasay and Singalon, regularly offer the plants for sale and will undertake to supply you with any that may not be on hand. Inasmuch as the common names of the plants lead to many mistakes and much confusion, it is indispensable to acquaint one's self with the description of the plant and be sure that the actual product conforms in all respects to the description. For this purpose it is well to obtain flowering specimens, and bearing this fact in mind I have been careful to indicate the flowering season of each plant. By making excursions to the towns of San Mateo and Angono I have obtained an abundance of whatever I sought and at the same time have learned by talking with the mountaineers and "curanderos," what uses they make of their plants. The "curanderos" know a great deal concerning these uses, but become very reticent as soon as they are questioned about them. Whether it is dread of ridicule or selfishness or fear that silences them, the fact remains that it is no easy matter to glean any useful facts from them. And yet by tact and friendliness one may elicit much more information from them than first impressions would lead one to hope.

Leaves should be gathered when fully developed, rejecting the old, dried and worm-eaten ones.

The best time to gather bark is one month before the period of inflorescence, when it is rich in sap. The flowers are best gathered when about half expanded. The fruit is gathered green or ripe according to the active principle sought. The seeds should always be mature.

Not all parts of the plant are equally provided with the active principle which may be localized in the root or the flower; or distinct principles may exist in different parts of the same plant. Therefore the part indicated, and only that part, should be employed.

In the root the active substance usually resides in the bark, sometimes in the parenchyma that envelopes the woody tissue and rarely in the woody tissue itself, as, for example, in "rhubarb" and "pareira brava."

The stem bark is also a frequent seat of the active principle, of which the outer portion contains the greater amount, according to the valuable experiments of Howard.

Some plants owe their therapeutic importance to their wood, others to their leaves or flowers, and regarding the localization of the active principle in these parts we have nothing especial to indicate. The fruit, however, may have a pericarp consisting of mucilage, starch, sugar and gum, etc., while the seeds contain fatty matter, fixed or essential oils or alkaloids, as is the case with coffee and cacao. In view of these facts, we repeat that it is indispensable to use that part of each plant which I have indicated as applicable to a determined case or condition.

I earnestly hope that the physicians and pharmacists practising in the Philippines may undertake investigations and experiments regarding the therapeutic properties of the plants of my native land, and that my endeavors may have acted as a stimulus or inspiration to the loyal and earnest study of the subjects that are now awakening such interest, not only in Europe and America, but in India and Japan.

I should be pleased to receive notes, plants or reports of researches from any one interested in the subject matter of this book, and I shall consider it a pleasure, as well as a duty, to devote my forces, small as they may be, to aiding any one who may do me the honor to claim my assistance.

T. H. P. de Tavera.

Paris, April, 1892.

CONTENTS.

DICOTYLEDONOUS, POLYPETALOUS.

DICOTYLEDONOUS, GAMOPETALOUS.

MONOCOTYLEDONS.

EXPLANATION.

For the common words of the different Filipino dialects I have adopted the orthography which in my various treatises on those dialects I have demonstrated to be the easiest, most rational and convenient. I should be inconsistent as to my own theories and convictions if I continued to follow the old form of spelling. For the benefit of those who are not familiar with the matter I will state that the consonants are pronounced as follows :

- g always as in get.
- h gutturalized aspirate.
- k as in English.
- w always as initial w in English, win, wan.
- ĝ as ng in sing, hung, etc.

ABBREVIATIONS.

Bic.—Bicol.
Eng.—English.
Iloc.—Ilocan.
Indo-Eng.—Indo-English.
Pam.—Pampango.
Pan.—Pangasinan.
Sp.—Spanish.
Sp.-Fil.—Spanish-Filipino.
Tag.—Tagalog.
Vis.—Viscayan.

MEDICINAL PLANTS OF THE PHILIPPINES

DICOTYLEDONOUS, POLYPETALOUS.

DILLENIACEÆ.

Tetracera macrophylla, Vall. (*T. monocarpa*, *T. sarmentosa*, Blanco.)

Nom. Vulg.—*Malakatmón*, Tag.

Uses.—The wood of *malakatmón* is one of the best known and popular drugs of the Binondo[1] market place. It is used as an infusion internally in the hæmoptysis of consumptives, and externally in the treatment of sore throat, its action being due to the large amount of tannin it contains. It is also employed in Malabar in the form of an infusion of the leaves of the species, *T. Rheedi*, to treat sore throat, mixing it with a decoction of rice called *cange*.

The Filipinos do not distinguish this species from the *T. Assa*. Both are called *malakatmón*, and are employed indiscriminately to accomplish the same results. The silicious concretion obtained from the leaves is used as a polish in the form of polish paper.

Dose.—In infusion for internal use, 4 grams of wood to 1 liter of water; as a gargle, 10 to 15 grams to the liter.

Botanical Description.—A shrub with leaves alternate, oval, serrate, finely dentate with very short and stiff hairs. Flowers of a strong, rather agreeable odor, axillary, in panicles. Calyx, 4 sepals. Corolla, 4 petals. Stamens indefinite, ex-

[1] A ward or Barrio of Manila.

panding at the upper end and bearing 2 anthers. Carpels 3, with ovules indefinite in two series. Seeds with red arils.

HABITAT.—In the vicinity of Manila. Blooms in July.

MAGNOLIACEÆ.

Magnolia Family.

Illicium anisatum, L.

NOM. VULG.—*Anis estrellado, Badiana,* Sp.; *Saĝki,* Tag.; *Star Anise,* Eng.

USES.—Although this plant does not grow in the Philippines, the use of its fruit is so common there that it demands a place in this work. It is employed chiefly as a condiment in the preparation of food, and its essential oil is used to prepare the native "anise cordial" by mixing it with alcohol obtained from the palm or from sugar cane.

The decoction of the fruit is given after meals as a tea-like beverage, to aid digestion or for its carminative effect in flatulent colic.

Star anise has an aromatic taste, slightly bitter and acrid, and a very marked perfume of anise which with its star-like form gives the plant one of its names. It is a very useful stimulant, tonic, stomachic and carminative.

It is official in all Pharmacopœias and the pericarp is the part employed.

The dose is from 1 to 2 grams to 100 of water in infusion, to be taken in one draught.

According to Schlegel it contains the following substances: An essential oil 4.675; a green waxy material which melts at 51°, a resin, a gum and saponin. The essential oil is (almost) identical with that of anise from which it is impossible to distinguish it chemically. The only difference is that the former has a blander odor and solidifies at 1°.25 instead of 10°, as does the oil of anise.

Botanical Description.—The plant grows in the mountains of Yunnan, China, and in Tonquin. The part used in the Philippines is the fruit, being indeed the only part known here. This is composed of 8 woody follicles arranged about a central column in the form of a star. These follicles open at maturity and reveal the seeds, which are shining, smooth, ovoid, hard, of a pretty chestnut-red color. In the Philippines they are sold even in the smallest food-vending shops.

Michelia Champaca, L.

Nom. Vulg.—*Tsampaka, Sampaka,* Tag.; *Champaca,* Fil.-Span.

Uses.—The bark of the trunk is well known as a febrifuge and emmenagogue in India. It is slightly bitter and aromatic. Dr. H. Folliat has used it with success in the Island of Mauritius in the treatment of the common intermittent fevers; he administered the infusion (bark 30 grams, water 600 cc.)—or the decoction (bark 30 grams, water 1,200 cc.); boil till reduced to 600 cc.—giving a wine-glassful every hour just before and after the paroxysm.

An astringent decoction made from the leaves is used as a gargle in sore throat. The root is emmenagogue and the seeds are used in the treatment of anal fissure.

Dr. Hooper has found the following substances in the bark of the *Champana:* a volatile oil with a pine-like odor; a fixed oil, insoluble in alcohol, melting at 15° and forming soap with soda; a resin extremely bitter, acrid, brown in color; tannin; sugar; a bitter principle, albuminoids, coloring matters, mucilage and starch.

Botanical Description.—A tree 15–18° high; leaves alternate, 6 x 2′, stipulate, simple. Flowers fragrant, saffron-colored, hermaphrodite, solitary and axillary. The receptacle, conical at its base, becomes narrow, lengthens and then enlarges, forming a column which is bare at its narrow part. At its base is inserted the perianth composed of 6 overlapping leaflets arranged in two series. Stamens indefinite, fixed in the base of the column of the receptacle on the superior portion of which are inserted the ovaries which contain many ovules arranged in two vertical series.

HABITAT.—Common in all parts (of the islands).

ANONACEÆ.

Custard-Apple Family.

Artabotrys odoratissimus, R. Br. (*A. hamatus*, Bl.; *Uvaria Sinensis* and *Unona uncinata*, Blanco.)

NOM. VULG.—*Ilaĝ-ilaĝ de China*, Sp.-Fil.; *Alaĝ-ilaĝ Sonson*, Tag.

USES.—A decoction of the leaves of this species is used to treat cholera in some of the islands of the Malay group; in the island of Java they use for the same purpose a decoction of the leaves of the species *A. suaveolens*, Bl., which is commonly called *Susoĝ Damulog* in the Pampanga dialect. The active principles of these plants are so powerful that one must beware of giving a large dose, as hemorrhages, nervous phenomena and abortion may follow.

BOTANICAL DESCRIPTION.—A tree 15–18° high with leaves alternate, lanceolate, glabrous, and petioles very short. Flowers very sweet, axillary, solitary. Petals 6, fleshy, concave at the base. Stamens indefinite, closely packed, overlapping. Peduncle curved like a crook.

HABITAT.—Cultivated in gardens.

Anona squamosa, L. (*A. tuberosa*, Rumph.)

NOM. VULG.—*Ates*, Tag.; *Custard Apple*, Eng.

USES.—The fruit of the mature ates is edible and is one of the most delicious that grows in the Philippines; its white and delicately perfumed pulp has a delicious flavor. The unripe fruit is exceedingly astringent. The fermented juice of the ripe pulp is used in certain parts of America to prepare a popular drink. The powdered seeds make a useful parasiticide especially when used on the scalp, but it is necessary to avoid getting any of the drug in the eyes on account of its irrritant effect.

BOTANICAL DESCRIPTION.—Tree 8 or 9° high with leaves alternate, oblong, the edges pubescent. Flowers greenish-yellow, axillary, solitary; peduncle not curved. Petals 6, convergent. Stamens crowded, indefinite. Fruit fleshy, covered with scales or rather rounded tubercles; beneath is the white and fragment pulp, covering the long-oval seeds.

A. reticulata, L.

NOM. VULG.—*Anonas*, Sp.-Fil.

USES.—The fruit of this species is neither as much prized nor as abundant in the Philippines as that of the ates. When unripe it possesses the same properties as the latter. The large proportion of tannin which both species contain in their unripe state, makes them very useful in treating diarrhœa and dysentery. They are administered in the form of a decoction, by enema. The sap of the trunk is very irritating. The roots are used by the American Indians to treat epilepsy. Lemon juice is the antidote for the sap of this species.

I wish to call attention to the similarity of the common name of this plant to another entirely distinct species commonly used in the Tagalo therapeutics; namely, the *anonag̃* (Cordia), with which it must not be confused.

BOTANICAL DESCRIPTION.—Tree 10° high with leaves lanceolate, pubescent. Flowers in a sort of umbel. Corolla like that of *A. squamosa*. Fruit without the plainly visible tubercles of the foregoing species, their presence being merely suggested by a sort of net traced on the surface.

A. muricata, L.

NOM. VULG.—*Guanábano*, *Goyabano*, Sp.-Fil.

USES.—The ripe fruit possesses antiscorbutic properties; the unripe fruit is used in treating dysentery. It is said that the ripe fruit is used in diseases of the liver.

BOTANICAL DESCRIPTION.—Tree with leaves oval, alternate and glabrous. Flower solitary, terminal, whitish. The fruit is much larger than that of the other species, is covered with scales that end in a soft point or thorn and has a very pronounced acid taste.

HABITAT.—All three species are common in all parts of the Archipelago.

MENISPERMACEÆ.

Moonseed Family.

Tinospora crispa, Miers. (*Menispermum crispum*, L.; *M. rimosum*, Blanco; *Cocculus crispus*, DC.)

NOM. VULG.—*Makabuhay*, Tag.

USES.—Makabuhay is one of the most widely known and used plants in the Philippines; a sort of panacea applied to all bodily afflictions. Its Tagalo name means literally "you may live." A shoot deprived of roots and dropped in some moist place is soon covered with bright green leaves and adventitious roots. This peculiarity of the plant made it possible for me to take a large number of sprouts from Manila to Paris where they arrived perfectly fresh after a voyage of forty days, during which they lay almost forgotten in the ship and the cars.

The stem is the part employed in medicine. A decoction is given internally in the various forms of malarial fever and of dyspepsia. Externally it is most useful as a wash for ulcers of all kinds, rapidly improving their appearance.

In India the species *T. cordifolia* is used; it differs but little from *T. crispa*. It is official in the Pharmacopœia and has been introduced into Europe. *T. cordifolia* has given excellent results in the mild forms of intermittent fever; in general debility following long and severe cases of illness; in chronic rheumatism, and in the second stage of syphilis. As the two species are so much alike we shall add the preparations and dose of *T. cordifolia* which we have used on several occasions with good results.

TINCTURE OF T. CORDIFOLIA.—Stems of the dried plant, 100 grams. Alcohol 21° (Cartier), 500 cc. Macerate seven days in a closed vessel stirring from time to time. After decanting add enough alcohol (21°) to bring the quantity up to 500 cc., and filter.

DOSE.—4–8 grams.

MACERATION.—Fresh stems cut in small pieces, 30 grams, water 300 grams. Macerate for two hours and filter.

DOSE.—30–90 cc. a day.

EXTRACT.—Dry makabuhay in small pieces 500 grams. Water 2½ liters. Macerate for twelve hours, filter the liquid and express the macerated drug which is then macerated a second time in 2½ liters of water. Express again, unite the two liquids and filter. Evaporate in a water-bath to the consistency of a pill mass.

DOSE.—½–1½ grams a day in fractional doses.

BOTANICAL DESCRIPTION.—A vine whose runners entwine themselves among the tops of the highest trees, giving off many adventitious roots which seek the earth. The stem is covered with projecting tubercles. Leaves heart-shaped, pointed, entire with five well-marked nerves. Flowers yellowish-green, diœcious, growing in axillary racemes. The male flowers have a corolla of six petals, the three smaller ones arranged alternately. In the female flower the stamens are represented by three glands situated at the base of the petals. Fruit, an elliptical drupe.

Anamirta Cocculus, Wight & Arn. (*Menispermum Cocculus*, (L.) Blanco; *M. lacunosum*, Famk; *Cocculus lacunosus*, *C. suberosus*, DC.)

NOM. VULG.—*Laktaĝ*, *Liktaĝ*, *Suma*, *Lanta*, *Lintaĝ bagin*, *Tuba*, *Balasin*, *Bayati*, Tag., Vis., Pam.

USES.—One of the uses to which the India berries (*Cocas de Levante*) are put in the Philippines, is to throw them into small sluggish streams or into lakes with the object of intoxicating the fish which soon come to the surface and float there as if dead. This custom is very extensive in Malaysia, in India and even in Europe, where, in order to avoid the cases of poisoning which this practice has occasioned in the consumers of fish taken in this way, it has been found necessary to forbid the sale of the berries except in the pharmacies. These restrictions are practiced in France.

In the Binondo market in Manila the root of this plant may be found in abundance; it is yellow and very bitter. The natives use the infusion (5–10 grams to 300 cc. of water) in fevers, dyspepsia and menstrual derangements. In India also the root is used in the same complaints.

The fruit contains the highly toxic principle *picrotoxin*, and others as follows:

Menispermin ($C_{18}H_{24}N_2O_2$) is an alkaloid which crystallizes in pyramidal prisms, is soluble in alcohol and ether and insoluble in water. Hot nitric acid converts it into oxalic acid and a yellow substance of a resinous appearance.

Picrotoxin ($C_{30}H_{24}O_{13}$) is not an alkaloid as may be seen from its formula. Its properties are not well known at the present time. It crystallizes in small quadrilateral prisms, white and transparent, or in needles grouped in stars. No odor, taste bitter, insoluble in water, partly soluble in alcohol and in ether, freely soluble in acids and alkalies. A solution in concentrated sulphuric acid has a saffron-yellow color. Nitric acid transforms it into oxalic acid.

Picrotoxinin exists in picrotoxin in the proportion of 32 to 100, and may be separated by boiling in benzine. It is bitter, poisonous, reduced by Fehling's solution and nitrate of silver. Sixty-six per cent. of picrotoxin consists of another bitter substance, non-poisonous—*picrotin*, which is insoluble in benzine and is reduced by Fehling's solution and nitrate of silver. Lastly, *anamirtin* is found in the mother water of picrotoxin; it is not bitter, not poisonous, and not reducible by the aforementioned reagents.

The fruit of the *anamirta*, the "coca de Levante" is an acrid, narcotic poison, which may not be employed internally; its uses are limited to external medication. In the Pharmacopœia of India is given the formula for a parasiticide ointment, highly recommended in the treatment of pediculi:

Unguentum anamirtæ:

4 grams Cocculus berries, powdered,
30 " Vaseline.
M. Fiat unguentum.

In applying this ointment it is necessary to make sure that there is no wound or abrasion of the skin through which absorption might take place.

Botanical Description.—A vine with leaves alternate, entire, glabrous, broadly oval, pointed, with 5 nerves which unite at the base, long petioles. Flowers diœcious, in compound racemes. Male flowers consist of a perianth without corolla, the sepals arranged by threes in two or three whorls. The end of the receptacle expanded like a bead, bears a large number of stamens in 6 vertical series, with anthers sessile and 4-lobed. Female flowers analogous as regards the perianth, with 6–9 sterile stamens. Carpels formed of 5 ovaries, free, unilocular, containing one ovule each. Fruit, a drupe of a purple color, the size of a filbert, kidney-shaped, the albumen horny.

Cissampelos Pareira, L.

NOM. VULG.—*Sansawsansawan*, Tag.; *Chinchaochinchauan*, Sp.-Fil.

USES.—Although this plant formerly bore the Portuguese name of *Pareira brava,* the U. S. P. and B. P. recognize now under this title only the root of *Chondrodendron tomentosum.* It is diuretic and tonic and apparently exercises an astringent and sedative action upon the mucous membrane of the genito-urinary organs. The root is used in acute and chronic cystitis.

In Brazil it is used as a diaphoretic and as such is employed in cases of venomous snake bites. It is also used there as an emmenagogue and diuretic, in intermittent fevers, dropsy and suppression of the lochia in women recently confined.

It is official in the Pharmacopœia of India.

DECOCTION.—Root of cissampelos, small pieces, 50 grams.
Water .... 600 "

DOSE.—30–100 grams.

Boil 15 minutes; filter and add enough water to bring the total bulk up to 600 cc.

EXTRACT.—Root of cissampelos in powder .... 500 grams.
Water .... 5 liters.

DOSE.—.5–1 gram.

Digest the powder for 24 hours in 500 cc. water, pour the mixture into a filter and add water gradually until the percolate amounts to 5 liters. Evaporate the percolate in a water-bath to the consistency of a pill mass.

FLUID EXTRACT.—This is prepared in the same manner as the extract and is allowed to remain in the bath until reduced in bulk to 400 grams. It is then removed and 100 grams of alcohol (36°) are added.

DOSE.—1.75–7 cc.

Chemical Composition.—Flückiger has isolated a bitter principle analogous to berberin; also *buxine* and *paracine*, which latter received the name *pelosine* from Wiggers in 1839. The former chemist proposed the name buxine for all these analogous principles. Pelosine or buxine is precipitated by a concentrated solution of HCl, by sal ammoniac, by potassium nitrate and potassium iodide. He also discovered a neutral substance, *deyamitin*, which crystallizes in microscopic tablets; sulphuric acid added to these gives a pretty dark blue color which changes to green.

Botanical Description.—A climbing shrub with cylindrical woody stem, with leaves simple, alternate, entire, petiolate, ovoid, broad at the base. The inferior surface of the leaf is pubescent, especially in the intervals between the ribs. Flowers diœcious, small, racemose. Calyx of 12 sepals arranged in 3 whorls, the inner ones broad and petaloid. Corolla of 6 petals arranged in 2 whorls. Stamens sterile or rudimentary in the pistillate flower, the staminate flower bearing 6; anthers innate, 2-celled. Drupes oval, 2 or 3 cm. long, black, closely resembling a grape seed.

NYMPHÆACEÆ.

Water-Lily Family.

Nymphæa Lotus, L.

Nom. Vulg.—*Lawas, Talaylo, Tunas, Gaway-gaway*, Tag., Vis., Pam.; *Water Lily*, Eng.

Uses.—The anaphrodisiac virtues attributed to this plant and to all the water-lily family are purely imaginary. Its juice being slightly bitter and astringent is used in decoction as an injection in gonorrhœa. It possesses mild narcotic properties, for which some use the juice of the whole plant, rubbing the forehead and temples with it to produce sleep.

Botanical Description.—An aquatic plant, with leaves

solitary, terminal, floating on the water, dentate, glabrous, broad, deeply cleft at the base, with a very long petiole. Flowers solitary, persistent in the ripe fruit, oval. Stamens indefinite in fine whorls or verticils.

HABITAT.—Common on the shores of the Laguna de Bay.

Nelumbium nucifera, Gaertn. (*N. speciosum*, Willd.; *N. Asiaticum*, Rich.; *Cyamus Nelumbo*, Sm.; *C. mysticus*, Salis.)

NOM. VULG.—*Bayno*, Tag.; *Sukaw*, Iloc.; *Sacred Lotus*, Eng.

USES.—An infusion of the flowers is used internally in dysentery. In India they use, for diarrhœa and vomiting, the viscid juice obtained from the petioles and the peduncles of the flowers. The rootstock contains a large quantity of starch which has been utilized for food in the periods of famine which have desolated India and Egypt. This flower was the Sacred Lotus of the Egyptians and the people of India have dedicated it to Lakshmi, the goddess of health and prosperity.

INFUSION.—Petals, dried.................... 5 grams.
Water..........................250 "
Sig. To be taken during 24 hours.

BOTANICAL DESCRIPTION.—An aquatic plant with fleshy rootstock which creeps along the muddy bottoms; from its nodes spring the stalks of the leaves and flowers. Its leaves are alternate, polymorphous, some above and some below the surface of the water, concave in the center whence ribs separate, shield-shaped. Petioles very long, bearing soft, short spines. The flowers white or pink, solitary; peduncle long and, like the petioles, covered with soft, short spines. Calyx of 4–5 unequal sepals, imbricated. Corolla with an indefinite number of unequal petals, the inner ones shorter. Stamens indefinite, inserted in the base of the receptacle. Receptacle expanded above the andrœcium, in the form of an inverted cone, containing a large number of alveoli with circular openings.

PAPAVERACEÆ.

Poppy Family.

Argemone Mexicana, L.

Nom. Vulg.—*Kasubhaĝ-āso*, Iloc.

Uses.—Padre Blanco says that the yellow juice of this plant "is used by the natives (Filipinos) to treat fissures of the corners of the eyes."

The negros of Senegal use the decoction of the root to cure gonorrhœa. The milky juice to which Blanco refers is used in different countries to treat various skin diseases, including the cutaneous manifestations of syphilis and leprosy; to remove warts, and as an eye wash in catarrhal conjunctivitis.

The English physicians of India state that it is dangerous to use the milky juice as an application to the eye, although Dymock claims the contrary.

The flowers are narcotic by virtue of a principle resembling morphine, perhaps identical with that alkaloid.

The seeds yield a fixed oil on expression, which is laxative and relieves the pains of colic, probably by virtue of its narcotic properties. Physicians in India praise this oil highly; not only is it a sure and painless purgative, but it is free from the viscidity and disgusting taste of castor-oil; besides it has the advantage of operating in small doses, 2–4 grams. Its activity is proportionate to its freshness. Dr. W. O'Shaughnessy does not value this oil highly, but the experience of many distinguished physicians of India has proved the purgative and other properties that have just been mentioned. Possibly the differences of opinion may arise from the fact that oils from different plants were used in the trials.

The seeds yield a fixed oil, yellow, clear, of sweet taste, density 0.919 at 15°; it remains liquid at − 5°; is soluble in an equal volume of alcohol at 90°; characterized by an orange-red color on adding nitric acid. From its soap Frolicher has obtained acetic, valerianic, butyric and benzoic acids. Charbonnier claims to have found morphine in its leaves and capsules. Dragendorf has isolated from the seeds an alkaloid which presents the principal characters of morphine. It is, then, probable that morphine is the narcotic principle possessed by this plant, which is not hard to believe when one considers the family to which it belongs.

BOTANICAL DESCRIPTION.—A plant of American origin nowadays acclimated in almost all warm countries. Its stem is green, pubescent, 30–40 centimeters high. Leaves alternate, thin, sessile, lanceolate, covered with rigid green thorns. Flowers hermaphrodite, terminal, yellow. Calyx, 3 sepals with conical points. Corolla, 6 rounded petals. Stamens indefinite, free, hypogynous. Ovary free, triangular. Capsule expanded, oblong, angular, thickly set with prickles : it opens inferiorly by 5 valves.

CRUCIFERÆ.

Mustard Family.

Brassica juncea, Hook. & Thom. (*Sinapis juncea*, L.)

NOM. VULG.—*Mostaza*, Sp.; *Mustard*, Eng.

USES.—The seeds are used in the same way as those of white or black mustard (*Sinapis alba* and *S. nigra*, L.).

BOTANICAL DESCRIPTION.—Plant with a glabrous stem, leaves sessile, glabrous, lanceolate, the upper ones serrate, the lower ones almost entire. Flowers in racemes. Calyx, 4 sepals. Corolla, 4 rounded, unguiculate petals. Stamens 6, two of them short and the other four longer and united in pairs. Ovary flattened. Seed vessel quadrangular, nodular, glabrous, containing many oval seeds.

Raphanus sativus, L.

NOM. VULG.—*Rábano*, Sp.; *Radish*, Eng.

USES.—Used principally as food ; it possesses the antiscorbutic properties common to the greater part of the Cruciferæ.

It is an herbaceous plant, the root of which is so commonly known that its description would be useless.

CAPPARIDACEÆ.

Caper Family.

Cleome viscosa, L. (*C. icosandra*, L.; *Polanisia viscosa*, DC.)

Nom. Vulg.—*Balabalanoyan*, *Apoyapoyan*, Tag.; *Wild Mustard*, Eng.

Uses.—The seeds possess the same properties as those of mustard and are used in place of the latter in Manila. In America the leaves are used as a poultice in otitis, their action being rubefacient. In India the seeds are given internally for their anthelmintic and carminative effect; the dose is one teaspoonful twice a day. The juice of the leaves mixed with cocoanut oil is used in the form of eardrops in suppurative otitis.

The natives give the same common name to the *Gynandropsis pentaphylla*, DC. (*Cleome pentaphylla*, L.; *C. altiacea* or *C. alliodora*, Blanco), which is distinguished from the former by its six stamens inserted on the pistil and its violet-colored stem. Its therapeutic properties are identical with those of the *Cleome viscosa*. Dr. Sir W. Jones believes that the plant possesses antispasmodic properties, basing his belief on its odor, which resembles *asafetida*, though not so disagreeable. In India the juice of the leaves is a popular remedy for earache. It is also used there as a rubefacient.

Botanical Description.—An annual, the stem channeled and bearing glandular hairs. Leaves compound, alternate; leaflets lanceolate with glandular hairs. Calyx, 4 sepals. Corolla, 4 petals, yellow. Stamens 14–16, encircling the pistil. Seed vessels cylindrical, with channels and glandular hairs. The whole plant is sticky and emits a garlicky odor.

Cratæva religiosa, Forst.

Nom. Vulg.—*Saliĝbobog*, Tag.; *Balay-namuk*, Iloc.

Uses.—It is in common use in India as a tonic and stomachic. It seems also to possess laxative and diuretic properties. In Concan the juice of the leaves mixed with cocoanut oil is used as a liniment in rheumatism.

Infusion.—Leaves, fresh .... 50 grams.
Water .... 500 "

Dose.—50–100 grams a day as a tonic or stomachic.

Botanical Description.—A shrub 15–20° high with compound trifoliate leaves with long petioles; leaflets lanceolate, acuminate, smooth, dark green. Calyx of 4 imbricated sepals. Corolla of 4 unguiculate petals, between white and straw color, 1′ long. Stamens indefinite, violet-colored. Ovary unilocular, many-ovuled. Berry spherical with many seeds buried in pulp.

Habitat.—Blanco has seen the plant growing in Ilocos and Imus.

BIXINEÆ.

Bixa Orellana, L.

Nom. Vulg.—*Atsuiti*, *Achuiti*, Tag.; *Achiote*, *Achuete*, Sp.-Fil.; *Annatto*, Eng.

Uses.—The principal use of the seeds is in cookery and everybody knows the yellow color which Filipino cooks impart to almost all their dishes. In medicine the fine powder that covers the seeds is used as a hæmostatic and internally as a stomachic. On account of the astringent qualities of the coloring matter it is used in some countries to treat dysentery, a fact which suggests its possible therapeutic or rather hygienic usefulness as a condiment. It seems to effect a cure in dysentery in the same manner as ipecac.

In India, Brazil and the Antilles the natives make a sort of paste of achuete known under the name of *rocu*. There is a hard, odorless form of rocu and another soft, unctuous, of a delicate red color and an odor rendered highly disagreeable by the urine added to it to keep it soft. Rocu is the preparation of achuete that has been subjected to chemical analysis. Its composition is as follows: Two coloring matters, *bixin* ($C_{28}H_{34}O_5$), of a red color, resinous, soluble in alcohol, ether, alkaline solutions and benzine, crystallizing in microscopic laminæ, quadrangular, red, of a metallic violet lustre; *orellin*, yellow in color, soluble in alcohol and in water.

BOTANICAL DESCRIPTION.—A well-known tree growing to a height of 5–7 meters, with leaves alternate, simple, oval, heart-shaped at the base, sharply pointed, glabrous, short petioles. Flowers in panicles. Calyx, 5 rounded sepals, tuberculate at the base, imbricated, caducous. Corolla of 5 rose-colored petals. Stamens very numerous, free, inserted on the receptacle. Capsule round, dark red, bristling with stout hairs of the same color. The seeds are covered with a fine, yellowish-red powder.

Pangium edule, Reinw. (*Hydonocarpus polyandra*, Blanco.)

NOM. VULG.—*Pangi*, Tag.

USES.—All parts of this tree are anthelmintic. The seeds, fruit, leaves and bark all possess narcotic properties dangerous to man and the symptoms following an excessive dose are sleepiness, headache, a sort of intoxication or an attack of delirium that may end in death. These narcotic properties have been utilized in Java to stupefy the fish in the rivers by throwing the bark in the pools and quiet portions of the stream. The juice of the leaves is used in the treatment of chronic skin diseases. In Amboina the natives eat the seeds, the toxic quality of which is removed by brushing and macerating in pure water for a certain time. After such treatment they may be eaten with impunity and an oil may be extracted from them which is useful as a food.

BOTANICAL DESCRIPTION.—A tree with leaves 5′ long, alternate, ovate, broad, entire, glabrous, palmately nerved. Petiole long with 2 persistent lateral stipules. Flowers diœcious, the male ones in panicles, the female solitary. Calyx gamosepalous, dividing unequally when the flower opens. The male flower has a corolla of 5–7 petals, violet-colored, concave, half oval, with pubescent borders; at its base a flat scale. Stamens free, numerous, thick filaments, anthers bilocular. In the female flower the perianth is the same as in the former, the stamens sterile. Ovary unilocular, with 2–4 parietal placentæ with many ovules. Fruit as large as a man's head, with thin woody pericarp and many seeds embedded within its pulp.

PORTULACACEÆ.

Purslane Family.

Portulaca oleracea, L.

Nom. Vulg.—*Verdolagas*, Sp.; *Olasiman*, *Kolasiman*, Tag.; *Purslane*, Eng.

Uses.—The entire plant is edible, in the form of a salad or as a condiment with meat or fish. The leaves are succulent and acid, and the juice expressed from them is used as an eye-wash to remove corneal opacities; it is also used in superficial erysipelas and other skin affections. The bruised leaves are used as a poultice for abscesses, contusions and on the temples for headache. The juice is given internally to check hæmoptysis and in diseases of the lungs and bladder; the seeds also are used in these complaints.

Botanical Description.—A plant with prostrate stem. Leaves fleshy, wedge-shaped. Flowers small, sessile, terminal, pale yellow. Calyx of 2 large teeth, deciduous. Corolla, 4–5 petals with a notch at the end. Stamens 9–14. Style of equal length with the stamens. Stigma in 4–6 divisions. The seed vessel, which dehisces horizontally, contains many small, heart-shaped seeds.

Habitat.—It grows in all parts of the islands.

GUTTIFERÆ.

Gamboge Family.

Garcinia mangostana, L.

NOM. VULG.—*Mangostán*, Sp.; *Mangosteen*, Eng.

USES.—The seed of the fruit is astringent and is given internally as an infusion in dysentery and chronic diarrhœa. The decoction is very useful as an injection in leucorrhœa.

The following potion has given excellent results to Dr. Ed. J. Waring in chronic dysentery and the diarrhœas of tropical countries:

Dried peel of mangosteen............	60	grams.
Cumin seed.......................	5	"
Coriander........................	5	"
Water............................	1,200	"

Boil till reduced to 600 grams. Take 120 grams twice a day. Tincture of opium may be added.

An analysis of mangosteen peel by W. Schmidt demonstrated a large quantity of tannin, a resin and a crystallizable principle named *mangostin* ($C_{20}H_{22}O_5$) which exists in the form of fine, golden yellow laminæ, tasteless, soluble in alcohol, ether and the alkalies, insoluble in water. With the perchloride of iron it gives a blackish-green color, and sulphuric acid colors it red.

BOTANICAL DESCRIPTION.—The mangosteen grows only in the southern islands of the Archipelago and its delicious fruit is the part of the plant known in Manila. The peel is at the present time almost universally employed in medicine. The fruit is about the size of a small Manila orange, the pericarp a dark red or chocolate color, tough and thick, crowned with the remains of the calyx. On breaking it open the edible portion of the fruit is seen, consisting of 6–18 seeds covered by a white, sweet pulp, cottony in appearance, of a delicious slightly acrid flavor.

1. **Garcinia venulosa**, Choisy. (*Cambogia venulosa*, Blanco.)

2. **G. Cambogia**, Desrouss. (*Cambogia binucao*, Blanco.)

Nom. Vulg.—*Binukaw*, Tag., applied to both trees, though the first is also called *Gatasan pulá* in Tagalo and *Taklaĝ-anak* in Pampango.

Uses.—The fruit of the second species, the true name of which is *binucaw*, is acid and edible. The fruit and the trunk of both species, when cut, exude a gum-resin very much like gamboge which is obtained from the *G. morella* or *G. pedicellata*, Desr. These gum-resins, however, seem to be much inferior to gamboge; they contain an essential oil which does not exist in the latter and their color is paler.

Botanical Description.—The *G. venulosa* is a tree with leaves opposite, lanceolate, acute, entire and glabrous, the inferior surface covered with nervelets which converge at the apex. Petioles short and flattened. Flowers tetramerous. Calyx, 4 persistent sepals. Corolla, 4 petals, overlapping, fleshy, ovate, of the same color as the calyx. Stamens numerous; no filaments; anthers round and very small. Style very short and thick, stigma peltate, divided into 10 parts. Fruit globose, depressed, no well-marked ridges when ripe.

G. Cambogia differs from the foregoing in the leaves which present no nervelets on the lower surface and the fruit which presents 8 angles or rounded ridges.

Habitat.—Very common throughout the islands, abounding in the mountains of San Mateo and Morong. Blooms in August.

Garcinia morella, Desr.

Nom. Vulg.—I do not know the name given by the Filipinos to this tree, which Vidal and Soler have seen in Montalván, Tiwi (Albay) and San Mateo (Province of Manila); but it is highly important in medicine as the true gamboge is obtained from it. *Gamboge Tree*, Eng.

The Gamboge of the U. S. P. and B. P. is obtained from

G. Hanburii which differs somewhat botanically from *G. morella.*

Uses.—All parts of the plant contain a thick, yellow, milky juice which constitutes the gamboge. In Malabar, Ceylon, Canara and Singapore the following method of extraction is followed: At the beginning of the rainy season a spiral incision is made around the bark of about half the tree trunk, and a piece of bamboo is fixed in place to collect the juice which slowly exudes from the cut for several months, soon becoming viscid and then solid after contact with the air. One tree, as a rule, yields enough sap to fill three internodal segments of bamboo, each 50 cm. long by 3–5 cm. in diameter.

Gamboge is a laxative in doses of 10–15 cgm., produces abundant evacuations with violent colicky pains in doses of 30–50 cgm., and is an irritant poison in large doses. In other words it is a highly energetic hydragogue cathartic, especially indicated when we wish to drain off the fluid element of the blood, as in dropsy, asthma, pulmonary and cerebral congestion. It is also used as a vermifuge.

It is rarely given alone, but is combined with calomel, aloes, jalap, rhubarb, etc.

It is official in all pharmacopœias.

Botanical Description.—A tree 10–20 meters high, with leaves opposite, elliptical, lanceolate, narrowed at both extremities, acuminate, entire, coriaceous, glabrous, 10–12 cm. long by 3–4 cm. broad, with short petioles. Flowers diœcious. Male flower axillary, solitary or in groups of 3–6, pedunculate with small bracts. Calyx, 4 sepals. Corolla, 4 petals, orbicular, thick, fleshy. Stamens 30–40, sessile, adherent at the base. Anthers unilocular. Female flower sessile, solitary, axillary, larger than the male; calyx and corolla equal; staminodia 20–30, jointed at the base, forming a membranous corolla from the upper edge of which spring a few short filaments which support each a suboval sterile anther. The ovary is superior and almost spherical, with 4 cells each containing 1 ovule. The fruit, almost spherical, is 2½ cm. in diameter, corticate, bearing at its base the persistent calyx; each of its 4 cells contains a seed.

Ochrocarpus pentapetalous, Blanco. (*Tovomita pentapetala*, Blanco.)

Nom. Vulg.—*Namakpakan*, *Tagudin*, Iloc. (?).

Uses.—An oil expressed from the fruit is used in Ilocos for illuminating purposes. The flowers are astringent and are used in infusion in cases of diarrhœa. The oil of the fruit is also used locally in rheumatism, tumefactions and other painful conditions. In some countries of Malaysia the oil is used in the same way especially in beriberi and the periarticular inflammations incident to puerperium.

Botanical Description.—Straight trunk about 8′ in diameter, with milky sap. Leaves 1½′ long, sessile, opposite, ovate, expanded, minutely notched and glabrous, with a small downy swelling at the base, superior and glued to the branch. Flowers terminal, in racemes, with opposite pedicels. Calyx white, of 2 rounded leaflets bent downwards. Corolla white, 5 petals (not 4), oval, concave, twice as long as the calyx. Stamens numerous, joined to the receptacle. Filaments slightly longer than the corolla. Anthers oval, 2-celled. Ovary superior, oval. Style longer than the stamens. Stigma peltate, sometimes bilobed, sometimes 4-lobed. Fruit about the size of an acorn, oval, fleshy, containing a milky juice; it is 2-celled and each cell contains a solitary, hard seed; of these one aborts.

Habitat.—It grows near the sea. Blooms in December.

Calophyllum Inophyllum, L.

Nom. Vulg.—*Palo Maria*, Sp.-Fil.; *Bitanhol*, *Tamawian*, *Dunkalan*, *Dinkalin*, Tag.; *Dankalan Bitaog*, Vis., Pam., Bik.

Uses.—From the seeds of the fruit there exudes a yellowish-green oil, bitter and aromatic. It is used in some districts for illuminating purposes. Its density is 0.942 and its point of solidification 5° above zero. In India it is used by innunction in rheumatism and in the Philippines locally over the stomach in indigestion and colic. The bark of the tree when incised exudes a green resin of a very agreeable odor, which is used as an application to wounds and old sores. In India it is used in the same way. This resin is fusible and dissolves completely in alcohol. It has been mistaken for the *tacamahaca* of India, which, however, is a product of the *C. calaba*, L. Mixed with equal parts of pitch and wax it is applied to the chest as a plaster in bronchitis. A decoction of the leaves is used for purulent ophthalmia in some parts of India and Mauritius. The pounded bark is applied locally in orchitis and epididymitis. We have had occasion to use a mixture of equal parts of the resin with white vaseline spread on linen and applied between the shoulder blades; in the persistent cough of senile bronchitis the relief was marked.

Botanical Description.—A large tree with beautiful, dark green leaves 4–5′ long, opposite, entire, large, oval with nerves numerous, fine and perpendicular to the midrib. Petioles very short. Flowers large, white, sweet-scented, axillary, in racemes of 7–9. Calyx white, of 4 sepals. Corolla white, of 4 petals. Stamens numerous, polyadelphous. Ovary rudimentary in the male flower; unilocular and uniovulate in the female. Style single and large. Drupe superior, with a hard, bony pit, containing a thicker, softer substance which envelopes a seed of like consistency.

Habitat.—It is found in central Luzon and in the Provinces of Tayabas, La Union and Ilocos. Blooms in November.

Mesua ferrea, L. (*Calophyllum apetalum*, Blanco.)

Nom. Vulg.—*Malabukbuk* (?), Tag.

Uses.—We do not know to what use the Filipinos put this plant, but in India the sweet flowers are dried and sold in the bazars under the name of *Nag-Kasar* or *Nagesur*, which is used as a mild stimulant, but especially as a perfume.

A dark oil is expressed from the seeds, its density 0.954 and its solidifying point 5° above zero. In northern Canara it is used locally in rheumatism. The incised root bark exudes a resinous sap which is a good bitter tonic. The infusion of the wood is equally good. The dried flowers, finely powdered and mixed with oil or lard make a useful ointment for acute hemorrhoids. The fruit is acrid and purgative.

BOTANICAL DESCRIPTION.—A tree with leaves long-petioled, oblong, lanceolate, acuminate, rounded at the base, thick, coriaceous, upper surface lustrous, lower surface greenish or covered with a waxy, ash-colored powder. Flowers terminal or axillary, solitary, yellowish. Calyx 4 imbricated sepals, orbiculate, slightly pubescent. Corolla 4 persistent petals, wedge-shaped, short, with rounded points. Stamens indefinite, free, in 5–6 series. Ovary free, 2-celled, each cell containing 2 ovules. Style bilobed. Fruit nearly unilocular, ovate, acuminate, encompassed at its base by the sepals, the lower part of the petals, and crowned by the style. Pericarp woody, dehiscent at the tip by 2–4 valves ; contains 1–4 seeds, slightly orbiculate, coriaceous.

HABITAT.—Common in the forests.

DIPTEROCARPEÆ.

Dipterocarpus turbinatus, Gaertn. (*D. Indicus*, Bedd.; *D. Mayapis*, Blanco.)

NOM. VULG.—*Mayapis*, Tag.; *Gurjun*, *Kanyin*, Indo-Eng.

USES.—This tree yields an oleo resin, used in medicine and known under the name of *bálsamo de gurjun*. Other species of *Dipterocarpus* (*D. alatus*, Roxb.; *D. incanus*, Roxb.; *D. trinervis*, Bl., etc., etc.) produce the same substance. Balsam of Gurjun is a stimulant of the mucous membranes, especially those of the genito-urinary tract, and is diuretic. It is also indicated in bronchial catarrh and as a local application in ulcer. The first to recommend the use of gurjun as a substitute for copaiba was Sir W. O'Shaughnessy in 1838, and in 1852 this property was confirmed by Waring with highly satisfactory results. Dr. Enderson of Glasgow employed it in cases that received no benefit from copaiba, giving a teaspoonful t. i. d. in emulsion. Dr. Rean also classed it as equal to copaiba in efficiency.

The daily dose ranges from 5–20 grams, in liquid or pill.

The following is an excellent formula for an emulsion :

Cinnamon water	125	grams.
Sodium carbonate, crystals	2	"
Balsam of gurjun	25	"
Syrup of gum	25	"
Sulphuric ether	2	"

Mix and shake.

DOSE.—6–12 large spoonfuls each day, for the declining stage of gonorrhœa.

In Burmah they extract the balsam by the following method : A large hole is cut in the trunk of the tree and a fire is built in this cavity and kept up till the wood of the trunk begins to burn, by which time the oleo resin has collected in abundance in the segments of bamboo placed to receive it. When the exudate diminishes, fire is again placed in the cavity and one tree may tolerate 2, 3 or even 4 of these cavities. The exudate on standing separates into 2 parts ; a solid called "guad" which forms the lower layer, and a supernatant liquid which is the balsam. It is dense, viscid and very fluorescent ; opaque and gray-green by reflected light. It has an odor similar to that of copaiba, is bitter and aromatic. Its density is 0.964. It is soluble in benzine, in bisulphuret of carbon, chloroform, the essential oils and less so in ether and acetic acid. It becomes turbid and coagulates if it be kept at 100° for some time and it solidifies at 200°, while copaiba remains liquid at this temperature.

A specimen of the balsam examined by Flückiger consisted of 54.44 parts semifluid resin and 45.56 volatile material. Upon distillation it yields an essential oil, of slight odor, straw-colored; formula $C_{20}H_{32}$ (Werner). If purified its density is 0.915. It is soluble in amylic alcohol, scarcely so in absolute alcohol. Hydrochloric acid colors it a beautiful blue. The resin remaining after distillation, dissolved in alcohol 0.838 with the addition of ammonia, yields as a precipitate a crystalline acid (gurjunic acid), $C_{44}H_{64}O_8$, soluble in alcohol 0.838, in ether, in benzol and bisulphide of carbon. It melts at 220° (Werner), solidifies at 180° and is decomposed at 260°.

BOTANICAL DESCRIPTION.—A very large, handsome tree with leaves about 5′ in length, alternate, ovate, broad and lanceolate, entire, glabrous and membranaceous. Petioles very short. Flowers terminal, paniculate, handsome, fragrant. Calyx free, 5 lanceolate sepals, of which 2 are slightly longer than the others. Corolla, 5 yellow oblong petals longer than the sepals. Stamens numerous, attached to the receptacle. Filaments very short. Anthers of 2 divisions each ending in a long beard. Ovary half buried in the receptable. A single thick style. Three simple stigmas. Seed vessel of 3 cells, seeds in pairs.

HABITAT.—In Luzon in the mountains of Tala, Angat and San Mateo; in Mindanao, Paragua, Balabac and Negros. Blooms in June.

MALVACEÆ.

Mallow Family.

Sida carpinifolia, L. (*S. acuta*, Burm.; *S. stipulata*, Cav.; *S. frutescens*, Blanco.)

NOM. VULG.—*Wawalisan, Eskobaĝhaba, Pamalis, Higotbalato, Mamalis*, Tag., Vis., Pam.

USES.—The root is emollient and bitter. The decoction is used as a lotion for ulcers, and internally as a sudorific and tonic-astringent. The physicians of India prescribe the powdered root with milk for fevers and for nervous and urinary diseases. The leaves are used locally in ophthalmia.

The juice of the root is employed as a wash for all kinds of sores and ulcers and the juice of the entire plant is given for spermatorrhœa. After experimenting with the root, the compilers of the Bengal Dispensatory announced their uncertainty as to whether or not it possessed antipyretic properties; however, they pronounce it diaphoretic, an exciter of the appetite and an excellent bitter tonic. In Goa the Portuguese consider it diuretic and use it especially in rheumatic affections.

The root of *S. carpinifolia* gives a blue color with the salts of iron. It does not precipitate gelatin and contains asparagin.

BOTANICAL DESCRIPTION.—A plant 2–4° high with woody, branching stem, leaves alternate, oblong, pointed, serrate, under surface neither hoary nor tomentose as in some other species of *Sida*. Petioles very short, curved near the leaf, 2 stipules near the base. Flowers axillary, solitary. Calyx simple, in 5 parts. Corolla, 5 petals notched obliquely. Stamens numerous, inserted on the end of a column. Anthers globose. Styles 5, mingled with the stamens. Stigmas globose. Cells of the same number as the styles, verticillate, with solitary seeds.

HABITAT.—Common in Luzon, Panay, Mindanao, Paragua, Cebú and Balabac.

Abutilon Indicum, Don. (*Sida Indica*, L.)

NOM. VULG.—*Kuakuakohan*, *Gilig̑-gilig̑an*, Tag.; *Iabig̑*, *Malis*, *Dulupag*, *Pilis*, Vis.; *Malvas de Castilla*, Sp.-Fil.

USES.—The trunk bark is slightly bitter, and in decoction is used as a diuretic. An infusion of the leaves and flowers is used as an emollient in place of mallows. The infusion of the root it used for the same effect, as a lotion or injection. I have often had occasion to employ this plant and would never use the *Philippine mallow* in place of it.

Botanical Description.—A plant 3–4° high, all its parts covered with hairs, simple and tomentose. Leaves heart-shaped, angular, obtuse, unequally serrate, smooth, soft, the lower surface hoary and bearing 9 well-marked nerves. Petioles longer than the leaves, with 2 stipules at the base. Flowers yellow, axillary, solitary. Peduncles long, with a node near the end. Calyx, 5 sepals, as in all the Malvaceæ. Corolla, 5 petals with a small notch at the end. Stamens very numerous as well as the styles. Both arise from the summit of a very short column and twist in all directions forming a tassel or tuft. Fruit much higher than the calyx, of 10–20 cells or carpels which are broad, compressed, hairy, the walls united toward the center, each containing 2–3 seeds.

Habitat.—Common in Luzon, Panay, Mindanao and other islands. Blooms in September.

Urena sinuata, L. (*U. morifolia* and *muricata*, DC.; *U. multifida*, Blanco.)

Nom. Vulg.—*Kulutan, Kulutkulutan, Molopolo,* Tag., Vis., Pam.

Uses.—The infusion of the root is used internally as an emollient and refrigerant; externally in skin diseases accompanied by smarting and inflammation. The boiled and pounded leaves are used as a poultice in inflammation of the intestines and bladder.

Botanical Description.—A spreading plant 4–6° high, with straight stem, leaves cleft at the base, serrate and hairy; the larger ones have 5–6 lobules which subdivide into smaller ones and bear a small gland in the inferior surface of the midrib. Petioles short. Flowers terminal and racemose. Calyx double, composed of 5 narrow sepals externally, and 5 colored sepals internally alternating with the outer ones. Corolla, 5 petals. Stamens numerous, inserted about a small column. Styles 10, on the end of the column. Stigmas thick, covered with little spheres. Five united carpels, kidney-shaped, bristling with short stiff hairs, containing solitary seeds.

HABITAT.—Common in all parts of the Archipelago.

Hibiscus Abelmoschus, L.

NOM. VULG.—*Kastuli, Kastio, Kastiogan, Dalupan,* Tag.; *Marikum, Dukum, Marukum, Marapoto,* Vis.;[1] *Marsh Mallow,* Eng.

USES.—The bruised seeds emit an odor of musk, and for this reason the plant has received the name *Kastuli,* signifying musk in Sanscrit. They possess antispasmodic and stimulant properties, and the infusion is diuretic. Bonastre[2] analyzed Kastuli seeds as follows:

Water and parenchyma	52.00
Gum	36.00
Albumin	5.60
Fixed oil, resin, crystals and odorous principles	6.40
Total	100.00

The fixed oil is greenish-yellow, fluid, but gradually solidifying in the air. The crystalline material is white, of an agreeable odor, soluble in ether, where it crystallizes in rays, fusible at 35°. The odorous principle is a bright green, non-volatile liquid of the odor of musk.

BOTANICAL DESCRIPTION.—A plant 5–6° high, the stem hairy and with few branches. Leaves heart-shaped, cleft at the base, with 5 large pointed lobes, serrate, pubescent. Petioles long with two awl-shaped stipules at the base, and a large vio-

[1] In the U. S. P. and P. G. Marsh Mallow is a synonym for *Althæa officinalis,* the root being the part of the plant which is used.

[2] Journal de Phar. et de Chim., XX., p. 3811.

let spot in the axil. Calyx double; the outer sepals 8–9 in number, awl-shaped; the inner ones are larger and separate unequally when the flower expands. Both sets are deciduous. Corolla very large, yellow. Stamens very numerous, inserted around a column. One pistil. Five stigmas. Ovary very large, downy, ovoid, 5-angled, with 5 compartments, each containing many kidney-shaped seeds with numerous grooves concentric at the hilum.

HABITAT.—Common in all parts of the islands.

Hibiscus tiliaceus, L.

NOM. VULG.—*Balibago*, Tag., Pam.; *Malabago*, Vis.

USES.—An infusion of the leaves is used as a wash for ulcers and indolent sores. The flowers boiled in milk are used to relieve the pain of earache (Blanco), the warm milk being dropped into the external canal. The powdered bark in dose of 3 grams is emetic (?) (Blanco).

BOTANICAL DESCRIPTION.—A small tree 6–12° high with leaves 4–6′ long, alternate, 7-nerved, cleft at the base, abruptly acute, scalloped, pubescent. Petioles long. Flowers axillary, in panicles of very small flowerets. Calyx double, the outer portion divided into 8–9 teeth, the inner into 5 longer parts. Stamens numerous, inserted about a column. Style 1. Stigmas 5. Ovary of 5 cells, each containing 2 seeds.

HABITAT.—Abounds in all parts of the islands.

Hibiscus Rosa-Sinensis, L.

NOM. VULG.—*Takuragan, Arogganan, Kayaĝa, Tapulaĝa, Gumamila*, Tag., Vis., Pam.; *Rose of China*, Eng.

USES.—The flowers are emollient and are widely used by the Filipinos as a domestic remedy; they are bruised and applied to boils, tumors and all sorts of inflammations. The decoction is much used internally in bronchial catarrh for its sudorific effect.

The Chinese use the trunk bark as an emmenagogue, calling it Fu-yong-pi.

BOTANICAL DESCRIPTION.—A small tree about 7° high commonly called *Gumamela* in Manila; the leaves are ovate, acute, with about 5 nerves, serrate from the middle to the apex, hairs growing sparsely on both surfaces, with a small group of dark-colored, deciduous hairs growing on the lower part of the midrib. Petioles short with 2 stipules at the base. Calyx double, the outer part divided almost to the base into 6–8 parts; the inner cylindrical, divided in 5. Corolla large, splendid scarlet-red, often double, on slender peduncles. Styles numerous. Fruit identical with that of the *Hibiscus tiliaceus*.

HABITAT.—Universally common in the Philippines.

Thespesia populnea, Corr.

NOM. VULG.—*Babuy* or *Bobuy gubat*, Tag.; *Bulakan*, Vis.

USES.—The fruit yields a yellow juice which is used locally in the itch and other cutaneous troubles, after first washing the affected part with a decoction of the roots and leaves. The bark is astringent and is used as a decoction in the treatment of dysentery and hemorrhoids.

BOTANICAL DESCRIPTION.—A tree of the second order with leaves 4–5′ long, sparse, 5-nerved, heart-shaped, broad, acute, entire, glabrous, 6 small glands on the lower face of the base. Petioles of equal length with the leaves. Flowers large, axillary, solitary. Calyx double, the outer portion deciduous, consisting of 3 small, acute leaflets inserted on the base of the inner calyx; the inner is bell-shaped, larger than the outer, with 5 inconspicuous, persistent teeth. Corolla four times longer than the calyx, of 5 fleshy, fluted petals, their borders overlapping, much broader above. Stamens very numerous, arranged around and along a column. Filaments long. Anthers of half-moon shape. Style 1, very thick. Stigma cleft in 5 parts, which are twisted in spiral form. Seed vessels about the size of a filbert, 5-sided, with 5 apartments each containing 5 ovoid seeds attached by separate seed stalks to the central axis of the ovary. Seeds not woolly.

HABITAT.—Mandaloya Tayabas, Iloilo.

Gossypium herbaceum, L. (*G. Indicum*, Lam.; *G. Capas*, Rumph.)

NOM. VULG.—*Algodón*, Sp.; *Bulak*, Tag.; *Cotton*, Eng.

USES.—The root bark is antiasthmatic, emmenagogue, and according to Daruty[1] is a substitute for ergot in uterine hemorrhage. The leaves are used in bronchial troubles and the seeds are sudorific. The negroes in the United States use the root bark in large doses as an abortifacient; but a dose of 60 grams to 1,200 of water in decoction is proper and useful in treating dysmenorrhœa.

For a long time the seeds went to waste but industry has learned to obtain from them a brownish-red oil which is used as a substitute for olive oil, from which it is hard to distinguish it, if the latter is adulterated by mixing the two; for both have the same density and a very similar odor and taste. For this reason the production of cottonseed oil is very considerable nowadays. It is cheap and excellent for domestic, industrial and pharmaceutic use.

The seeds are used in North America in dysentery and as a galactagogue, and the juice of the leaves as an emollient in diarrhœa and mild dysentery. The pulp of the seeds, after the oil is extracted, yields a sweet material called *gossypose*, which is dextrogyrous and has the formula $C_{18}H_{32}O_{16} + 5H_2O$.

The cotton itself, the part used in commerce as a textile, is also the portion of the plant most widely employed in therapeutics; not only the fiber from this species is used, but also that of others that grow in the Philippines, the *G. Barbadense*, L.

[1] Daruty, loc. cit., p. xxvi.

(nom. vulg. *Pernambuko*, Tag.), and the *G. arboreum*, L. (*Bulak na bundok*, *Bulak na totoo*, Tag.).

Cotton is used extensively in bacteriological laboratories as a filter of liquids and gases. This property possessed by cotton, of retaining in its fibers the germs of the air was utilized by the famous French surgeon Guérin in the treatment that bears his name. The denuded surfaces exposed to infection by air-borne bacteria are completely protected against them when, according to the Guérin treatment, they are enveloped in large masses of fresh, raw cotton, presumably free from microörganisms. To avoid the possibility of infection by the cotton itself, it is now the practice to sterilize it either by means of chemicals such as carbolic acid, iodoform, etc., or by physical means such as high temperatures.

Raw cotton is used in compounding gun cotton or explosive cotton, also named *pyroxylin*, and this is used to make collodion, so extensively employed in medicine.

Pyroxylin is made by treating cotton with equal parts of nitric and sulphuric acids, then washing with water till the latter ceases to give a precipitate with chloride of baryta; then dry in the air.

Collodion is made by dissolving 5 grams of pyroxylin in the following mixture:

Sulphuric ether, rectified.............. 75 grams.
Alcohol at 95°....................... 20 "

Filter.

Elastic collodion:

Canada Balsam.................. 1.50 grams.
Castor oil.... .... .50 "
Collodion...................... 30.00 "

Mix.

Botanical Description.—A plant 2–3° high, of herbaceous stem, branches sparsely covered with small, black points;

leaves cleft at their base, with 5 lobules and a small gland on the midrib. Petiole long with 2 stipules at the base. Flowers axillary, solitary. Calyx double; the outer portion divided in 3 parts, heart-shaped, and each with 5–9 long, acute teeth. Corolla bell-shaped, of 5 petals, pale yellow or turning rose color, purple at the base. Stamens many, inserted on a column. Stigma in 4–5 parts. Ovary of 3–5 compartments. Seeds enveloped in the fiber.

HABITAT.—Batangas, Ilocos.

Bombax malabaricum, DC. (*B. Ceiba*, Blanco.)

NOM. VULG.—*Taglinaw, Bobuy gubat*, Tag.; *Talutu*, Vis.

USES.—In India the roots are used to obtain an astringent and alterative effect and form part of a well-known aphrodisiac mixture called *Musla-Samul.* If the trunk is incised, an astringent gum exudes and this they use in diarrhœa, dysentery and menorrhagia. Dose of the gum 2½–3 grams.

BOTANICAL DESCRIPTION.—A large tree covered with sharp, conical and tough spines. Leaves alternate, compound, digitate, caducous; leaflets 5–7 with long common petiole. Flowers solitary or in axillary cymes, hermaphrodite, regular. Calyx gamosepalous, cup-shaped, with 5 acute lobules. Corolla violet, with 5 deep clefts; æstivation convolute. Stamens numerous, united at the base in 5 bundles, free above, bearing unilocular anthers. Ovary of 5 many-ovulate compartments, with a style ending in 5 short branches. Capsule woody, ovoid, loculicidal, with 5 valves. Seeds numerous, black, covered with cottony fibers.

HABITAT.—Angat, Iloilo. Blooms in February.

Eriodendron anfractuosum, DC. (*Bombax pentandrum*, L.)

NOM. VULG.—*Boboy*, Tag.; *Doldol*, Vis.; *Bulak kastila*, Pam.

USES.—The principal use made of this plant in the Philippines is to stuff the pillows with the cotton that it yields. The leaves, pounded with a little water, yield a mucilaginous juice highly prized by the natives as a wash for the hair, mixing it with *gogo*. The root bark is emetic in dose of 1.25 grm. The cotton yielded by this tree should be used for the same therapeutic purposes as that of gossypium, and being of an exceedingly fine fiber it would give better results. The Filipinos use it to treat burns and sores. I have often used it, being careful always to impregnate it thoroughly with some antiseptic solution. In the treatment of burns it has been my custom to envelope the part in a thick layer of this cotton, after bathing it with a tepid 1–2,000 solution of corrosive sublimate and dusting with a very fine powder of boracic acid.

Botanical Description.—A tree 40–50° high. Trunk somewhat thorny, the branches horizontal, arranged in stars of 3–4. Leaves compound with 7 leaflets, lanceolate, entire, glabrous. Flowers in umbels of 8 or more flowerets. No common peduncle, the individual ones long. Calyx, 5 obtuse sepals, slightly notched. Corolla, 5 fleshy petals, obtusely lanceolate and bent downwards. Stamens 5. Anthers of irregular shape, peltate, with the borders deeply undulate. Stigma in 5 parts. Pod 4–6′ long, spindle-shaped. Seeds enveloped in very fine cotton fiber.

Habitat.—Exceedingly common in all parts of the islands. Blooms in December.

STERCULIACEÆ.

Sterculia Family.

Sterculia fœtida, L. (*S. polyphilla*, R. Br.; *Clompanus major*, Rumph.)

Nom. Vulg.—*Kalumpaĝ*, Tag.; *Baĝar*, Iloc.

Uses.—A decoction of the leaves is used as a wash in suppurative cutaneous eruptions. The fruit is astringent and is used in Java as an injection for gonorrhœa. In western India and in the Philippines it is an article of diet. The seeds yield an oil that is used for illumination and as a comestible.

BOTANICAL DESCRIPTION.—A large tree of the first order with digitate leaves of 6–8 leaflets, broad, oval, very acute, tough, glabrous, growing on a long common petiole. No petiole proper. Flowers of a fœtid or feculent odor, hermaphrodite, in compound racemes. Calyx fleshy, soft pubescent internally, bell-shaped, in 5 parts. Corolla none. Nectary 5-toothed, on the end of a small column. Stamens 15, inserted on the border of the nectary by threes, forming a triangle. Filament almost entirely wanting. In the midst of the stamens is visible a small, hairy body of 5 lobules which are the rudiments of the ovaries. The style protrudes and twists downwards. Stigma thick, compressed, of 5 lobules. Fruit, five woody pods, semicircular, joined to a common center, each enclosing many oval seeds inserted in the superior suture.

HABITAT.—Luzon, Mindanao, Cebú, Iloilo. Blooms in March.

Sterculia urens, Roxb. (*S. cordifolia*, Blanco; *Cavallium urens*, Schott. & Endl.)

NOM. VULG.—*Banilad*, Tag.

USES.—The root bark is pounded up and applied locally in orchitis and in severe contusions with supposed fracture of the bones; native charlatans pretend to cure the latter condition by this treatment.

The trunk exudes a sort of gum, which with water forms a sort of colorless, odorless gelatin which dissolves at the boiling point. I do not know to what use this gum is applied in therapeutics, but it is often found mixed with the Senegambian gum acacia.

Botanical Description.—A tree with leaves bunched, 7–9-veined, heart-shaped, ovate, broad and entire, glabrous upper surface, short white down on lower surface. Petioles of same length as the leaves. Flowers small, yellow, numerous, polygamous, growing in large, terminal panicles covered with a fine, sticky down. Calyx bell-shaped, 5 acute papyraceous divisions, each bearing a small gland near its base. No corolla. Stamens 10, united in a column, the upper ends free. Five pods joined at one point, half-moon shaped, with woody shell, glabrous within and with a short down on the outer surface. Three or four kidney-shaped seeds, the testa thin and crustaceous.

Habitat.—Cebú, Iloilo.

Kleinhovia hospitata, L.

Nom. Vulg.—*Tanag*, Tag., Vis.; *Hamitanago*, Vis.; *Panampat*, Pam.; *Bitnoĝ*, Iloc.

Uses.—The decoction of the leaves is used, according to P. Blanco, to cure the itch. It is also used locally in all forms of dermatitis, and the tender leaves and sprouts are cooked and eaten.

Botanical Description.—Tree 25° high or more, with leaves alternate, heart-shaped, pubescent, almost entire. Petioles long with 2 stipules at the base. Flowers red, axillary, in large panicles. Calyx, 5 sepals, almost linear. Corolla the same size as the calyx, 5 linear petals, the lower shorter and curved. Nectary bell-shaped, of 5 parts, each 3-toothed; set on a column; at its base a wavy fringe with dentate edge. Stamens 15. No filaments. Anthers seated on the 15 teeth of the nectary. Ovary within the nectary, 5-angled, 5 apartments each containing an almost spherical seed.

Habitat.—Luzon, Mindanao, Panay, Cebú, Joló. Flowers in March and September.

Helicteres Ixora, L. (*H. chrysocalyx*, Miq.; *H. Roxburghii*, G. Don.)

NOM. VULG.—(?); *Indian Screw Tree*, Eng.

USES.—I am ignorant of the use that the Filipinos make of this plant, though it is very possible that they do not employ it at all in medicine, which is usually the case with those plants to which they have given no name. In India the peculiar spiral form of the fruit has suggested its application, according to the theories of the doctrine of symbolism. Ainslie says that the Hindoos use it to treat diseases of the external auditory canal. On account of its emollient properties and probably on account of its twisted form, it is used internally as a decoction, in flatulence and the intestinal colic of children. It is indispensable in the marriage ceremonies of the caste of Vaisya, among whom it is customary for the groom to wear on his wrists in the form of bracelets, strings of this fruit combined with that of *Randia dumetorum*.

The root yields a juice which is employed in skin diseases, in abscess, and in cardialgia. In Jamaica the juice of the leaves is sometimes used for constipation.

BOTANICAL DESCRIPTION.—A small tree with leaves alternate, simple, entire, irregularly nerved or veined at the base, petiolate. Flowers of a handsome red color, hermaphrodite, regular, axillary. Calyx gamosepalous, tubular, of 5 parts. Corolla, 5 free petals slightly dentate at the point. Stamens numerous, united on a free column on the cusp. Compound nectary of 5 unilocular, many-ovuled ovaries. Styles 5, joined at the base. Fruit of 5 carpels, thin, twisted on themselves in spirals, forming a cone, pubescent, of a greenish-brown color, each containing a single row of angular seeds.

HABITAT.—Luzon, Panay.

Abroma fastuosa, R. Br. (*A. angulata*, Lam.; *A. communis*, Blanco; *A. augusta*, L.)

Nom. Vulg.—*Aniboĝ*, Tag.; *Anabo*, Vis.; *Perennial Indian Hemp*, Eng.

Uses.—The root bark is used in India as an emmenagogue in the congestive and neuralgic forms of amenorrhœa. It seems to act as a uterine tonic. The dose is 2 grams of the juice of the fresh root mixed with pepper which also acts as a carminative and stomachic.

Botanical Description.—A shrub 3–4 metèrs high with hairy branches. Leaves opposite, oval, oblong, serrate, tomentose. Flowers purple, solitary, terminal. Calyx, 5 sepals. Corolla, 5 petals. Stamens 5, united in the form of a tube. Ovary sessile, with 5 many-ovuled compartments. Styles 5, united in the form of a tube which divides into 5 stigma-bearing branches. Capsule membranous, 5-angled, truncate, dehiscent at apex. Seeds albuminous, covered with filaments of cotton.

Habitat.—San Mateo, La Laguna, Batangas, Iloilo.

Theobroma Cacao, L.

Nom. Vulg.—*Cacao.*

Uses.—The roasted bean ground with sugar constitutes chocolate, one of the most generally used foods of the Philippines.

It is very nutritious by virtue of the fat and sugar it contains, but all stomachs do not bear it well and its use is the unsuspected cause of much dyspepsia. The custom of drinking it very hot and following with a large quantity of cold water is a very common cause of dilatation of the stomach in the Philippines. The seed of the cacao contains several substances: cacao butter, albumin, theobromine, starch, glucose, gum, tartaric acid, free or combined, tannin, and mineral substances. Of these the butter and theobromine are the most important.

Theobromine ($C_7H_8N_4O_2$) is a weak alkaloid, crystalline, slightly bitter, slightly soluble in cold water, more soluble in hot water, less soluble in alcohol and ether; stable in the air up to 100° ; sublimes without decomposition at 290° in microscopic crystals of the form of rhomboid prisms ending in an octohedric point (Keller).

This alkaloid is very little used in therapeutics and its physiological action is said to be analogous to that of caffeine but weaker. It is better to use the salt of the alkaloid, and that most frequently employed is the salicylate of soda and theobromine in doses of from 2 to 6 grams daily in solution or pill. Lately, however, Dr. Gram has maintained that theobromine is a powerful diuretic operating when other diuretics fail and further that this effect is produced without injuring the heart. The double salt is non-toxic, though sometimes in exceedingly weak patients it produces vertigo. Dr. Gram administers 6 grams a day in one-gram doses.

Cacao butter is a white substance, slightly yellowish, unctuous to the touch, brittle ; with the agreeable odor peculiar to cacao, and a sweet and pleasant taste. Its density is 0.961, it melts at 30°–33°, and solidifies at 25°. It dissolves in 20 parts of boiling alcohol, in 100 parts of cold alcohol and in twice its weight of benzin. Cacao butter is obtained by grinding or mashing the roasted seeds in a hot apparatus and mixing the mass with a fifth or tenth of its weight of boiling water. It is then pressed between two hot iron plates and the butter thus obtained is refined by boiling water. It is then put aside in earthen pans, or still better, in moulds, where it solidifies. It does not easily become rancid and, for this reason, enters into the composition of many ointments and pomades, or is used alone. It serves as the base for suppositories and is, finally, a highly valued cosmetic. A common substitute is made by mixing oil of almonds, wax and animal fat.

Before going further let us describe the composition of

Spanish chocolate according to the French chemist Boussingault:

Cane sugar	41.40	grams.
Cacao butter	29.24	"
Starch, glucose	1.48	"
Theobromine	1.93	"
Asparagin	a trace	
Albumin	6.25	"
Gum	1.42	"
Tartaric acid	1.98	"
Tannin and coloring matter	0.022	"
Soluble cellulose	6.21	"
Ash	2.34	"
Water	4.36	"
Undetermined material	3.27	"
	100.00	

Botanical Description.—A small tree about 10° high, with leaves broad, 6–12′ long, hanging or drooping, lanceolate, entire, and somewhat pubescent on both surfaces. Petioles very short with 2 deciduous stipules at the base. Flowers in clusters on the roots, trunk and branches. Peduncle very long. Nectary divided in 5 parts, straight, awl-shaped and 2-nerved. Calyx, 5 sepals. Corolla, 5 petals curved upward in the form of a bow as far as the middle, where they form a hollow with two little horns; then curving downwards, then upwards, widening at the end, the edge finely dentate. Stamens 5, inserted on the nectary, and alternating with the lobes of the latter. Anthers 2 on each filament, concealed in the hollows of the petals. Ovary globose. Style awl-shaped. Stigma cleft almost to the middle, 5-parted. Fruit broad, spindle-shaped, 4′ or more long, dark reddish, warty, 10-ribbed, with 5 compartments each containing many compressed, ovoid seeds.

Habitat.—Common in orchards and gardens throughout the islands.

GERANIACEÆ.

Geranium Family.

Oxalis corniculata, L. (*O. Acetosella*, Blanco.)

NOM. VULG.—*Taiĝan dogá*, *Susokayoli*, Tag.; *Darasig*, Vis.; *Malabalugbug dagis*, *Ayo*, *Kongi*, *Yayo*, Pam.; *Indian Sorrel*, Eng.

USES.—The part of the plant used in medicine is the leaf which is acid by virtue of the potassium oxalate which it contains. The decoction is used internally as an antipyretic in fevers and in dysentery. Mistaking the properties of the plant it is given for vesical calculus which, if composed of oxalates, would be increased instead of diminished by the treatment. In fact the salt of sorrel in the leaves contains a large quantity of oxalic acid mixed with potassium oxalate. In China, India and the Philippines the entire plant is used as an antiscorbutic.

The cold infusion of the leaves is given internally in doses of from 30 to 60 grams, but it is not a medicine to be given indiscriminately, because in addition to its power of adding to the bulk of calculi of the oxalates, the contained potassium oxalate is poisonous in doses of 25 to 30 grams. If a concentrated solution is taken, it operates as a corrosive poison, producing violent pains in the stomach, vomiting, faintness and great weakness. If the solution is dilute its absorption is rapid and it operates very energetically. When a patient is poisoned by a concentrated solution, the stomach-pump is contraindicated, because the mucous membrane of the organ is corroded and ulcerated; if by a dilute solution, use the pump to remove as much of the poison as possible. The best antidote is a watery solution of a soluble salt of lime, *i. e.*, the saccharate, which forms an insoluble salt with oxalic acid.

The juice of the leaves is an antidote for the *Datura* (Stramonium). In India they make a decoction of the plant, mix it with onion juice and apply it to the head as a fomentation in hemicrania.

BOTANICAL DESCRIPTION.—A plant 1° high, with a creeping, glabrous stem, leaves horizontal, ternate with common long petiole. Leaflets sessile, obcordate, with downy borders. Flowers axillary or terminal, from 1 to 3 in number on a common long peduncle. The pedicel is also long. Calyx common to the family. Corolla, 5 petals ending in small claws. Stamens 10, monadelphous, the 5 shorter ones bearing each a small gland on the outer surface of the base. Ovary large, fluted. Styles 5, short. Stigmas hemispherical. Seed vessel pyramidal, containing many seeds enveloped in an elastic aril by which they are ejected when the fruit opens.

HABITAT.—Abundant in Luzon, Panay and Cebú.

Biophytum sensitivum, DC. (*B. cumiagianum*, Turcz.; *Oxalis sensitivum*, Blanco.)

NOM. VULG.—*Makahiya*, *Damoĝhiya*, Tag.; *Mahihiin*, Iloc.

USES.—A decoction of the leaves is used internally as an expectorant. The bruised leaves are used as an application to wounds and contusions. In Java the decoction is used internally in asthma, phthisis and snake bites.

The peculiar property which this plant possesses of closing its leaves when touched, has caused the natives of India to attribute to it mysterious virtues. Symbolism has determined its therapeutic application and the Hindoos pretend that it endows with delicacy and modesty women who lack these virtues and that it restores virginity.

BOTANICAL DESCRIPTION.—A plant about 7′ high. Stem straight, nodose and without branches. Leaves abruptly pinnate, the place of the odd leaflet taken by a stylet. The leaflets nearly linear with a small point at the apex, 11–13 pairs, 2 stipules to each pair. Common petioles long, cleft at the base and disposed in whorls around and on the end of the stem.

Flowers sessile, verticillate, on the ends of several very long peduncles which rise from the midst of the petioles. Calyx, 5 sepals. Corolla, 5 petals, clawed, rounded at the end and slightly notched, forming a tube. Stamens 10, free. A small gland on the outer surface of the base of each short stamen. Styles 5. Seed vessels ovate, 5-angled, containing many seeds.

HABITAT.—Common in all parts of the islands.

Averrhoa Bilimbi, L.

NOM. VULG.—*Kamias*, *Kalamias*, Tag.; *Kilingiwa*, Vis.; *Pias*, Iloc.

USES.—The small fruit of the camia springing from the branches and trunks of the trees is widely known in the Philippines, where they eat it green, pickled, and in salad; and when ripe fresh and preserved. Its qualities and therapeutic applications are the same as those of the following species.

BOTANICAL DESCRIPTION.—A tree 4–5 meters high with odd-pinnate leaves. Leaflets 12 pairs, ovate, linear, acute, soft and downy. Flowers small, pinkish or purplish, on trunk and branches. Stamens 10, five alternately longer. Pistils divergent. Fruit oblong, obtuse at the end, with five broad ribs.

HABITAT.—Very common throughout the islands.

Averrhoa Carambola, L.

NOM. VULG.—*Bilimbin*, *Balimbin*, Tag.

USES.—The common name of this tree, whose fruit is so common, causes it to be confused with the name which Linnæus gives to the former species. Balimbin is a fruit of an acid taste, agreeable when ripe, serving the same uses for food as the camia. Its acidity is due to the presence of oxalic acid, which makes the green fruit useful for removing ink and rust stains from clothes. The juice of the fruit is refreshing and is given internally mixed with water and sugar as a refreshing drink in fevers and as an antiscorbutic. For the latter the ripe fruit is eaten uncooked.

In Mauritius the juice is used to treat dysentery and hepatitis. Padre Blanco says that the natives use a decoction of camias and unthreshed rice in diarrhœa and bilious colic. In connection with the subject of camias and balimbins we should mention the fruit treatment of the bilious diarrhœa of the tropics, spoken of by the French physicians of Cochin China. Dr. Van der Burg of the Dutch Indies also strongly recommends the treatment of diarrhœa by fruits; in temperate regions using fruits like peaches, pears, etc., and in the tropics, lychies, mangosteens, etc. In regard to the mangosteens we must not forget that, while the bark is given because of the amount of tannin it contains, the composition of the pulp is very different. The fruit acids seem to exercise great influence in the cure of this obstinate disease and I do not hesitate to recommend for this purpose the camia and the ripe balimbin.

Botanical Description.—A tree much like the former. Leaves odd-pinnate. Leaflets, 3–4 pairs, obliquely ovate, acute, the terminal leaflet nearly lanceolate. Flowers on the trunk, branches and in the axils of the leaves. Fruit oblong, with 5 very prominent acute-angled ribs.

Habitat.—It grows, like the former plant, in all parts of the islands.

RUTACEÆ.

Rue Family.

Ruta graveolens, L. (*L. angustifolia*, Pers.)

Nom. Vulg.—*Rudu*, Sp.; *Rue*, Eng.

Uses.—The rue of the European, American and Indian pharmacopœias is emmenagogue, antispasmodic, anthelmintic, excitant, diaphoretic, antiseptic and abortive. It contains an essential oil, and rutinic acid ($C_{25}H_{28}O_{15}$, Borntrager), starch, gum, etc. The essential oil is greenish-yellow, thick, acrid and bitter; specific gravity 0.911. It boils at 228°, is slightly soluble in water, and soluble in absolute alcohol. It is promptly oxidized by nitric acid, and is converted into pelargonic acid and other fatty acids.

Rutin (or rutinic acid), according to Weiss, is a glucoside which exists in the form of fine needles, bright yellow in color. It is slightly soluble in cold water and more so in boiling water. It melts at 190°, and solidifies at freezing point, forming a resinous mass. Its physiological properties are as yet unknown. The part of the plant employed is the leaves, which owe their property, apparently, to the essential oil they contain, from which they also derive their strong and disagreeable odor and their bitter, acrid and nauseous taste.

It is used principally as a uterine stimulant or emmenagogue, for which purpose it is given in doses of 0.10–0.15 centigrams of the freshly powdered leaf and 0.05–0.10 centigrams of the fresh leaves infused in a liter of water. The dry powder of the leaf should not be used because the essential oil volatilizes and a large proportion of it is lost, which is the most active principle of the drug. It is an agent which should be prescribed with the greatest prudence for large doses are poisonous even to the point of causing death. The symptoms following such doses are colic, vomiting, bloody diarrhœa and tenesmus.

It is also used as an antihemorrhagic after childbirth, but its action is slow, not being felt for several hours after the administration of the drug; for this reason it cannot take the place of ergot, though it seems to be superior to the latter in passive hemorrhages. The essential oil is given internally in doses of 2–6 drops on a piece of sugar. It is sometimes used as an antispasmodic in hysteria, epilepsy and chorea.

The Chinese make extensive use of this drug and it is one of their principal abortives. In Hindostan the dried leaves are burnt and the smoke inhaled as a cure for catarrh in children. They are careful not to administer it to pregnant women.

Botanical Description.—A plant, 1 meter high, with leaves alternate, compound, the inferior ones 2–3-cleft; leaflets narrow, oblong, slightly fleshy. Flowers greenish-yellow, hermaphrodite, arranged in corymbose terminal cymes. Corolla, 4–5 free, concave petals. Calyx deeply divided, persistent. Stamens 8–10, free, in two whorls, inserted beneath a thick disc. Ovaries 5, unilocular, many-ovuled. Styles 5, first free, then united, forming a column terminating in a small stigma. Follicles 5, united at the base, 1 centimeter long, free superiorly, hard, rounded, rugose, opening on top. Seeds ovoid, angular, blackish, albuminous.

Habitat.—Common everywhere in the Philippines.

Xanthoxylum oxyphyllum, Edgew. (*X. violaceum*, Wall.; *Fagara piperita*, Blanco.).

Nom. Vulg.—*Kayutana*, Tag.; *Salay*, *Saladay*, Vis.

Uses.—The trunk bark is stimulant and is used as a sudorific in the treatment of fevers. The fresh bark is quite irritating, for which reason it is best to use bark taken from the more mature parts of the trunk, powdered and desiccated. The dose is $\frac{1}{2}$–2 grams 2–3 times a day. Its stimulating properties render it useful in colic and in India it is used as a stomachic and digestive. Is seems also to possess diuretic properties.

Botanical Description.—A tree 30–35° high, with trunk thickly set with large spines. Leaves odd-pinnate. Leaflets ovate, acute, obtusely serrate, small transparent vesicles on the surface, spines on the midrib and common petiole. Calyx very small, monophyllous. Corolla twice as large as the calyx, 4 petals. Stamens 4, inserted on the receptacle, the same length as the petals. Ovary superior, 4-angled. No style. Stigmas 2.

Habitat.—Batangas, Morong, Manila.

Murraya exotica, L. (*M. paniculata*, Jack.; *Connarus fœtens*, and *C. santaloides*, Blanco.)

NOM. VULG.—*Kamuniĝ*, Tag.

USES.—The leaves are stimulant and astringent, and are used in infusion (15 grams, to water one liter) to treat diarrhea and dysentery. The root and trunk barks are used for the same treatment and they as well as the leaves owe their properties to an essential oil and a bitter principle present in all parts of the plant. Vry has demonstrated the presence of a glucoside which he has named *murrayin* ($C_{18}H_{22}O_{10}$) ; it crystallizes in small, white needles, is slightly bitter, soluble in hot water and alcohol, insoluble in ether, slightly soluble in cold water. It melts at 170°, and dissolves in alkaline solutions coloring them green. Boiled in dilute acids it splits into *murrayetin* and glucose. *Murrayetin* ($C_{12}H_{12}O_{10}$) crystallizes in white needles, inodorous, tasteless, slightly soluble in cold water and in ether, soluble in hot water and alcohol. Heat destroys its green color in solutions ; alkalies, in the presence of cold, increase it. The leaves and the bark of the plant contain an essential oil.

The foregoing description of this species applies equally well to the following species.

BOTANICAL DESCRIPTION.—A small tree 12° high with leaves alternate, odd-pinnate. Leaflets lanceolate, almost entire, rigid with small dots on each surface. Flowers in axillary, very short, compound racemes. Calyx very small, monophyllous, 5 lanceolate lobules. Corolla much longer than the calyx, 5 lanceolate petals. Stamens 10, joined, but not entirely united at the base ; 5 alternate stamens longer than the others. Anthers sessile, regular. Ovary superior, compressed and borne on a disc. Style 1, same length as the stamens. Stigma thick, depressed, apparently 4-angled. Fruit fleshy, ovoid, acute and somewhat curved at the end enclosing a seed with coriaceous, downy testa.

Murraya Koenigi, Spreng. (*Bergera Koenigi*, L.; *Connarus* sp., Blanco.)

Nom. Vulg.—(?)

Botanical Description.—Leaves alternate, odd-pinnate. Leaflets obliquely ovate, acute, entire and glabrous. The testa of the seed bears no down, and may be divided into two parts. The decoction of the leaves of this species as well as the former is used to allay toothache.

Citrus acida, F. (*C. notissima*, Blanco.)

Nom. Vulg.—*Limón*, Sp.; *Dayap*, Tag.; *Lemon*, Eng.

Uses.—The essence (essential oil) and juice of the fruit are the parts of the plant used in therapeutics. The essence extracted from the rind is yellow, fragrant, slightly bitter; density, 0.856; boiling point 165°. The juice which is turbid and pale yellow in color contains 9% citric acid, 3–5% gum and sugar and $2\frac{3}{10}$% inorganic salts. The essence is used to flavor certain pharmaceutical preparations, and is a diffusible stimulant which may be given internally in doses of 3–6 drops on a little sugar. The bitter rind is occasionally used in infusion as a stomachic and stimulant. The juice is most commonly used in lemonade, a cooling drink which, used intemperately in the Philippines, is apt to cause gastro-intestinal trouble, so commonly attributed to "irritation," but really the result of a general atony of the digestive organs. Lemon juice is also used with very good results as a local cleansing application for sore throat, as well as externally on fetid ulcers. In some forms of malarial fever it seems to have given satisfactory results, administered internally.

In many navies lemon juice forms a part of the sea ration as a preventive of scurvy, upon which it exercises a real and noteworthy action. The Danish navy adopted it for this purpose in 1770, the English navy followed, then the French and possibly others. The English call it lime-juice, and its preventive dose is 30–40 grams a day. Its curative dose is 100–150 grams a day. To preserve the lime-juice it was bottled with a layer of oil, which, floating on the surface kept it from contact with the air; but this process gave it a bad taste as did also the addition of sulphate of calcium, and at present the English add, to each liter of juice, 60 grams of alcohol, which preserves it perfectly. Fonssagrives says that the antiscorbutic action of lemon juice is due rather to the vegetable juice itself than to the citric acid which it contains.

Botanical Description.—A most familiar tree 11° or more high, trunk with solitary thorns. Leaves ovate, obtuse, acute-toothed, the petiole bearing serrate wings. Calyx 4–6-toothed. Corolla, 4 thick petals. Filaments 10–25 on the receptacle, some joined and bearing 2–3 anthers. Fruit thin-skinned, globular, about 1′ in diameter; the rind adheres closely to the pulp.

(This fruit closely resembles, if it is not identical with the lime fruit, *C. Limetta*, or *C. Bergamia*, Risso, though Gray states that the leaf of the latter has a wingless petiole.—J. B. T.)

Habitat.—Common to all parts of the islands.

Citrus Bigaradia, Hook. f. (*C. vulgaris*, Risso; *C. aurantium*, Blanco.)

Nom. Vulg.—*Naranjas del país*, Sp.; *Kahel*, *Kahil*, Tag.; *Native Orange*, Eng.

Uses.—The rind of the *cagel* is the so-called bitter orange peel, the best of which comes from Curaçao and Barbadoes. It is tonic and is used in decoction and in syrup. The infusion of the leaves, 5–10 grams to the liter, is useful as a sedative and diaphoretic in hysterical and nervous attacks; the infusion of the flowers is similarly used. When distilled the flowers yield a very sweet essential oil called *neroli*, which is used as a perfume only.

Botanical Description.—A tree 15–20° high, trunk

bearing solitary spines. Leaves medium lanceolate, serrate, the apex notched, petioles winged. Flowers usually solitary. Calyx 4–5-toothed. Corolla 4–5 petals. Filaments joined or separate. Anthers about 20. The fruit, a small orange 2′ or more in diameter, the peel closely adherent.

The *C. aurantium verum* or *C. reticulata* (Blanco) has a yellow pulp and the rind is readily separated from it, a thin net of fibers intervening.

Citrus decumana, L.

Nom. Vulg.—*Suha, Lukban,* Tag.; *Toronjas* Penins.; *Naranjas,* Sp.-Fil.

Uses.—The fruit, which is handsome and large, and the leaves and flowers, are used for the same purposes as those of *C. bigaradia.*

Habitat.—The above species are cultivated in all parts of the islands, and, like the variety *C. aurantium verum,* H. f. (*C. reticulata,* Blanco), commonly called *naranjita,* are among the most abundant of native fruits.

Ægle decandra, Naves. (*Feronia ternata,* Blanco.)

Nom. Vulg.—*Malakabuyaw,* Tag.; *Tabog,* Pam., Tag. (A species of Bael-Fruit Tree.)

Uses.—We do not know the medicinal use of this plant in the Philippines. Probably it has none, but we may give those of the species. *R. marmelos,* Cor., the fruit of which is almost identical with that of our species and is called *Bela* or *Bael* in India. The fruit of the Malakabuyaw is ovoid and full of a mucilaginous pulp, aromatic and acid, the same as that of the Bael. The uses of the latter are the following: The pulp acts as an astringent, but it would be more correctly called a tonic of the intestinal mucosa, for it has been experimentally proved that, although it checks diarrhœa, it also acts as a laxative in chronic constipation. In both conditions it seems to operate by toning and regulating the functions of the intestine.

Martin, an English physician, was the first to call attention to the properties of Bael, and according to Dr. Green one dose of the pulp of the ripe fruit, prepared with sugar and given every morning, is an efficient remedy in the treatment of the dyspepsia of Europeans in India, especially in the form characterized by constipation and flatulence. The green fruit is a powerful astringent used by the Hindoos for diarrhœa. In cholera epidemics Dr. Bose advises the daily use of an ice made from the pulp of the ripe fruit, the object being the regulation of the functions of the intestine.

The Pharmacopœia of India contains the following preparations:

Mixture.—Pulp of the ripe fruit	60	grams.
Water	120	"
Sugar	60	"

Mix, and if desired add chopped ice. This forms a very agreeable drink which has the aroma of the fruit itself, and may be repeated 2–3 times a day. When the fruit is ripe, this preparation is not only astringent in cases of diarrhœa, but possesses the additional property of increasing the appetite. If the patient's stomach is very weak, the preparation may produce vomiting in which event it is necessary to give it in small doses or to employ the extract.

Extract of Bael.—Pulp of the ripe fruit is placed in a vessel and sufficient water added to cover it. It is then heated and evaporated to the consistency of a soft extract. The dose is 2–4 grams, 2, 3 or 4 times a day.

Fluid Extract of Bael.—

Pulp of Bael	500	grams.
Water	3	liters.
Rectified alcohol	60	grams.

The Bael is macerated in a third of the water and at the end of 12 hours the liquid is decanted and another third of water is added; the maceration is repeated and the same process followed till the last third of water is used. Express the residuum, put all the liquid into one vessel, filter and evaporate till reduced to 800 grams, then cool and add the alcohol. Dose, 4–8 grams.

The fluid extract is less active than the freshly prepared solid extract.

According to Dr. G. Bidie, the fruit of the *Feronia elephantum*, Correa (the species that grows in the Philippines), possesses the same properties as Bael. Its leaves are astringent, aromatic and carminative, and the gum with which the trunk of the tree is covered is a good substitute for gum arabic.

BOTANICAL DESCRIPTION.—A tree 7–8 meters high, the trunk covered with large, solitary spines. Leaves alternate, ternate. Leaflets lanceolate, scalloped and glabrous, the middle one larger than the others. Calyx 5-toothed. Corolla, 5 thick petals, linear, much longer than the calyx. Stamens 10. Ovary cylindrical. Style and stigma thick. Fruit oblong, more than 3′ long and 2′ thick, with a surface irregular with prominences and grooves; 10 or more compartments, each containing several ovoid, compressed seeds, ending with a woolly tuft.

HABITAT.—San Mateo, Montalbán (Manila); Arayat (La Pampanga).

Feronia elephantum, Correa. (*Murraya odorata*, Blanco.)

NOM. VULG.—*Panoan, Pamunoan,* Vis.; *Wood-apple,* Eng.

USES.—The pulp of the ripe fruit has an agreeable odor and is edible. In India the green fruit is used as an astringent in diarrhœa and dysentery; the ripe fruit is given in diseases of the gums and as a gargle. Mir Muhammad Husain states that the ripe fruit is a refrigerant, astringent, cardiac and general tonic, and is very efficacious in the treatment of salivation and ulcers of the throat, strengthening the gums and operating as an astringent. A sorbet made of the ripe fruit whets the appetite and the pulp is used locally for bites of venomous animals. In the latter case the pulverized bark may be used if the fruit cannot be obtained.

The fruit of Ferona is a substitute for Bael (*Ægle Marmelos*), and is used as such by the English physicians in the hospitals of India. The tender leaves have an agreeable aroma similar to that of anise and are used internally in decoction as a stomachic and carminative.

The incised trunk exudes a gum which is used in India as a substitute for gum arabic and there is an active trade in this gum in the bazars of Bombay and Calcutta. According to Pereira, it was at one time imported into England from the east of India under the name of gum arabic. It exists in the form of irregular, semitransparent pieces, of a brownish-red color. With water it forms a mucilage as adhesive as gum arabic, and this solution reddens litmus paper. It is dextrogyrous and is precipitated by the neutral acetate of lead and by caustic baryta.

BOTANICAL DESCRIPTION.—Tree 3–4 meters high. Leaves fragrant, opposite, odd-pinnate. Leaflets, 2 pairs, lanceolate, entire, and glabrous. Common petiole flattened above. Flowers terminal, white, racemose, with 2 flattened peduncles. Calyx inferior, with 5–6 divisions. Corolla, 5–6 petals. Anthers oval. Ovary oblong, 5-lobuled. Style short, caducous. Stigma spindle-shaped. Ovules numerous, compressed, in several series. Fruit pulpy, globose, with woody rind, one compartment and many compressed, oblong seeds.

HABITAT.—Mountains of Angat. Woods of Catugán (Iloilo).

SIMARUBACEÆ.

Quassia Family.

Samadera Indica, Gaertn. (*Niota tetrapela,* DC. & Blanco; *Manungala pendula,* Blanco.)

Nom. Vulg.—*Manungal,* Tag., Pam., Bicol.; *Manunagl, Linatoganak, Palagarium, Daraput,* Vis.

Uses.—The wood and seeds contain an intensely bitter principle. The Filipinos make cups and vases of the wood and allow water to stand in them 6–12 hours, thus preparing a solution of the bitter principle of the plant which they use in various stomach disorders.

Vrij has extracted from the seeds a 33 % oil of a bright yellow color, composed, according to Oudermans, of 84 parts olein to 16 of palmitin and stearin.

The bitter principle contained in the root, wood and bark was discovered by Blunse who named it *samaderin;* it is a white, crystalline, foliaceous substance, more soluble in water than in alcohol, fusible. Nitric and hydrochloric acids color it yellow. Sulphuric acid immediately forms a violet red color which disappears as iridescent, feathery crystals are precipitated. (D. Beaumentz et Egasse.)

The Filipino "herb-doctors" concoct an oil of manungal that in reality contains none of the ingredients of the seeds; it is simply cocoanut oil in which chips of the wood have been soaked. They use it in doses of 30–60 grams as a purgative, externally as an application to the abdomen in colic or indigestion and with friction in rheumatism or contusions. In India the oil extracted from the seeds is used locally with friction in rheumatism.

The decoction of the wood and the powdered wood are given in fevers, in dyspepsia and as a general tonic.

Infusion.—Chips of the wood........ 20 grams.
Water.................. 500 "

A wineglassful several times a day in cholera, fevers, diarrhœa, etc.

BOTANICAL DESCRIPTION.—A small tree, trunk straight, the wood white and very light in weight. Leaves 4–5′ long, alternate, acute, oval, entire, glabrous, coriaceous, veined. Petioles very short, no stipules. Flowers in terminal umbels, each composed of 4–6 flowerets with moderately long pedicels. Common peduncle, very slender, very long, drooping. Calyx of same color as corolla, inferior, very small, 4-lobuled. Corolla purplish, very long, 4 straight, linear petals. Stamens 8, inserted on the receptacle. Filaments of equal length with the petals, with 1–2 appendices at the base. Anthers spiral. Ovary 5-lobuled, borne on small stalk. One style of equal length with the stamens, situated above the center of the 5 lobules of the ovary which develop into 5 future pods. Stigma simple. Fruit 5 woody pods, short, united centrally above a small base, semilunar in form, medianly expanded, venate, containing a small wrinkled, kidney-shaped seed attached by a seed-stalk to the superior suture.

HABITAT.—Very common and well known everywhere in the Philippines. Blooms in February.

BURSERACEÆ.

Myrrh Family.

Garuga pinnata, Roxb. (*G. Madagascarensis*, DC.)

NOM. VULG.—*Bugo*, Tag.

USES.—The fruit is slightly acid and edible. The trunk exudes an abundant gum, of the odor of turpentine, translucent, greenish-yellow, forming small masses slightly soluble in alcohol, soluble in water, with which a mucilage is formed. The juice of the leaves is used for asthma. The sap is used in Bombay to remove opacities of the cornea. There is another species in the Philippines, *G. floribunda*, Decsne (*Icica Abilo*,

Blanco), *abilo*, Tag., the root of which furnishes a decoction used for phthisis. This species also produces a gum-resin similar to that of the *bugo*.

BOTANICAL DESCRIPTION.—A tree, with leaves alternate, odd-pinnate, without stipules, bunched on the ends of the branches, with opposite, serrate leaflets. Flowers yellowish-white in panicles, compound, polygamous. Calyx bell-shaped, 5-toothed. Corolla, 5 petals. Stamens 10, free, in 2 series. Ovary inferior, 5-lobuled. Fruit, a globose, greenish-yellow drupe with numerous bony seeds.

HABITAT.—Everywhere in Luzon, Panay and Balabac.

Canarium commune, L. (*C. album* and *C. Luzonicum*, Blanco.)

NOM. VULG.—*Pili*, Tag.; *Java Almond Tree, East Indian Elemi*, Eng.

USES.—The ripe pili nut is edible and sold in confectioneries. It yields a fixed oil, an excellent sample of which was sent by the Manila pharmacist D. A. del Rosario to the Paris Exposition of 1889. "It is an oil very similar to oil of almond and owing to its physical properties may be used as a substitute for the latter for all the requirements of pharmacy. The only inconvenience connected with its use is the slight one that it solidifies at 3° C. It could furthermore be very advantageously used in the manufacture of fine grades of soap." (D. A. del Rosario.)

The incised trunk exudes a gum-resin called *brea blanca* (white pitch) in the Philippines and *elemi* in Europe. Until recently it was not known in Europe what tree yielded the gum elemi, some authors stating that according to Blanco it was the resin of the *Icica abilo*, Blanco (*Garuga floribunda*, Decsne); it is not true, however, that Padre Blanco ever attributed such origin to that product or named his Icica the "pitch-tree." On the contrary in speaking of the Canarium, Blanco states that it yields a resin called "pili-pitch." I do not know the reason for this confusion of terms, but presume it to be due to imperfect knowledge of Spanish on the part of those who thus quote Blanco.

Pili-pitch, or elemi, as they call it in Manila, is a substance existing in soft masses, slightly yellowish or gray, resembling old honey in appearance. Its odor is strong and agreeable, somewhat like that of lemon and turpentine. Its taste is acrid and bitter.

The French pharmacist Meaujean demonstrated in 1820 that elemi contains two resins, one soluble in the cold, and the other in hot spirits of wine. Other chemists, among them Baup, Flückiger and Hanbury, have found elemi to be composed of a resinous substance and a colorless essential oil; the proportion of the latter Flückiger gives as 10% and further states that it is dextrogyrous. Sainte-Claire Deville found the essential oil levogyrous, a fact that emphasizes the probability of there being different products in the market bearing the name of elemi.

Baup obtained several principles from it: (1) A resin, *brein*, fusible at 187°, soluble in cold alcohol, crystallizable in oblique rhombic prisms; (2) another crystalline substance, *bryoidin*, soluble in 360 parts water at 10°, and melting at 13°; (3) a small amount of *breidin*, a body soluble in 260 parts water and melting at 100°+; (4) another resin soluble in boiling alcohol, called *amyrin*.

White pitch is used in the Philippines to make plasters which they apply to the back and breast of patients suffering from bronchial or pulmonary complaints; it is also applied to indolent ulcers. We believe that elemi possesses the same properties as copaiba, and that its indications for internal use are the same.

Botanical Description.—A tree 30–40 meters high, with leaves alternate, odd-pinnate; leaflets opposite, coriaceous. Flowers yellowish-white in axillary, compound panicles, hermaphrodite. Calyx 3-toothed. Corolla, 3 oblong, concave petals. Stamens 6, inserted on the base of the disc. Ovary free, of 3 lobules each containing 2 ovules. Style simple. Stigma, 3 lobules. Drupe oblong, size of large prune, fleshy, containing a hard, 3-sided pit.

HABITAT.—Very common in all Philippine woods especially in Camarines.

MELIACEÆ.

Melia Family.

Melia Azedarach, L.

NOM. VULG.—*Paraiso* (*Paradise*), Sp.-Fil.; *Pride of India*, *China Tree*, Eng.

USES.—The root was official in the U. S. P., 1880, as an anthelmintic; it is administered in the following form:

Fresh root bark........................120 grams.
Water............................ 1 liter.

Boil till reduced one half.

DOSE.—For a child 1 soup-spoonful every 15 minutes till nausea is produced.

In view of the narcotic effects produced by this drug, the foregoing method of administration seems to us imprudent; we prefer to give 30–70 grams of the decoction and follow with a purgative such as castor oil.

This drug is also tonic, febrifuge and astringent, and a decoction of its leaves and flowers is used as a wash for ulcers. Some believe that the leaves and fruit contain toxic principles, which may well be true considering the effects of large doses of their preparations. It has also been observed that the bark collected in March and April may cause dilatation of the pupil, stupor, etc.; this may be explained by the fact that at this season the sap is rising in the tree and the bark contains an increased amount of active ingredients.

The fruit yields a fixed oil, and by fermentation and distillation produces alcohol.

The root bark referred to is bitter and nauseous, if taken from the superficial roots—the part usually employed; the bark of the deeper parts is astringent by virtue of the contained tannin.

Jacobs analyzed the bark and isolated an amorphous resin of yellowish color and very bitter taste. It is soluble in alcohol, ether and chloroform, slightly soluble in sulphuret of carbon, insoluble in turpentine or benzin. He believes that it is the active principle of the root, and produces the anthelmintic action already mentioned; the proper dose is 0.20 centigrams to a child of 4 years, followed by a purge of calomel.

BOTANICAL DESCRIPTION.—A tree, 30–40° high, with leaves alternate, compound, odd-pinnate; leaflets opposite, ovate, pointed, dentate. Flowers in large axillary compound panicles. Calyx, 5 sepals. Corolla, 5 petals, rose-colored within, lilac-colored without. Stamens 10, united into a cylindrical tube, expanded at both ends, the mouth 15-toothed. Anthers inserted near the apex of the tube, short, fleshy, bilocular. Ovary free, of 5 biovuled cells. Style of equal length with the tube. Stigma button-shaped. Fruit a drupe, about the size of a small olive, yellow when ripe, with a dark brown pit of 5 one-seeded cells.

HABITAT.—Native of China; is cultivated in most gardens in the Philippines.

Dysoxylum Blancoi, Vidal. (*D. salutare*, F. Villar; *Turroea virens*, Blanco.)

NOM. VULG.—*Igiw, Agiw, Taliatan*, Tag.; *Ananaĝtaĝ, Bakugan, Makasili*, Vis.; *Malabaĝaw*, Pam.; *Basiloag*, Iloc.

USES.—The bark of the trunk, dry and finely powdered, is used in doses of 1½–2½ grams as an emetic, and, according to Padre Blanco, its effect is very certain.

It is also a febrifuge, and Padre Mercado states that it cures "all forms of asthma, suffocative affections of the chest, and griping pains of the belly." He also states that it yields marvelous results in malarial fevers, given during the cold stage in doses of 4–8 grams in water or wine in which it has macerated 12 hours. He also recommends its use before breakfast as an anthelmintic in lumbricoids, and finally attributes to it virtues as an emmenagogue.

Padre Blanco calls attention to the species *D. schizochitoides*, Turcz. (*Turroea octandra*, Blanco), *Himamaw*, Tag., as a substitute for *D. Blancoi.*

The Tagalo "herb-doctors" pretend that the part of the bark near the earth is doubly efficacious, for which reason they administer only that portion which is within one meter of the ground, giving it in the doses already mentioned.

Botanical Description.—Tree 16–20 meters high. Leaves glabrous, odd-pinnate, petioles very long; leaflets entire, opposite, short-petiolate, acute, oblique at the base. Flowers in axillary panicles. Calyx, 5 imbricated sepals. Corolla, 5 linear, lanceolate petals united at the base. Staminal tube, 10-toothed and 10-anthered. Ovary 5-celled, each cell containing two ovules. Style somewhat longer than the stamens. Stigma thick and depressed. Seed vessel globose, depressed, somewhat downy, 5-angled; with 5 compartments each containing 2 seeds.

Habitat.—Batangas and Laguna.

Sandoricum Indicum, Cav.

Nom. Vulg.—*Santol*, Tag.

Uses.—The santol is doubtless one of the best known fruits in Manila. The most savory portion is the center, which consists of seeds covered with a white pulp of a delicious flavor in the ripe fruit of good quality. The fleshy covering is edible only in the center of the fruit and only a very thin layer of that, the rest having very little flavor. The whole fruit is used in making a confection often prescribed as an astringent.

Padre Mercado compares it very appropriately to the quince. The root of the santol is aromatic, stomachic and astringent, by virtue of which latter property it is used in Java in the treatment of leucorrhœa.

Botanical Description.—A tree, 30–40° high, well known in the islands. Leaves ternate; leaflets 4–5′ long, half-ovate, obtuse, entire, stiff and downy, the middle one elliptical. Flowers in panicles. Calyx 5-toothed. Corolla much longer than the calyx, 5 greenish petals, linear and curved downwards. Nectary a cylindrical tube attached to the corolla for half its length, mouth 10-toothed, containing 10 sessile anthers. Style somewhat longer than the stamens. Stigma 5-parted. Fruit about size and form of a small apple, thick, brown, pericarp indehiscent, 5 or more one-seeded compartments.

Habitat.—Grows in all parts of the islands, commonly along the roads.

Carapa Moluccensis, Lam. (*Xylocarpus granatum*, Blanco.)

Nom. Vulg.—*Tabigi, Nigi, Kalumpañ̃ sa lati*, Tag.; *Migi*, Pam.

Uses.—The seeds contain a yellow oil, bitter and astringent, with a characteristic odor, having a taste somewhat resembling the odor. In decoction they are used for diarrhœa and dysentery, on account, doubtless, of the tannin they contain. The dose is 1–2 seeds dried, pounded and infused with 200 grams of sweetened water.

The bark, also bitter, is said to be useful in fevers.

In America they extract an oil from the species of the *C. Guianensis*, Aubl., with which the negroes anoint themselves to keep away stinging insects. Wood soaked in this oil is also proof against insects.

Botanical Description.—This tree, 20° high, grows in swampy districts. Leaves opposite, abruptly pinnate. Two pairs of wedge-shaped leaflets, entire and glabrous. Petiole very short. Calyx inferior, 4–5-toothed. Corolla, 4–5 concave petals, slightly notched at the end. Nectary notched, ovate, 8–9-toothed. No filaments. Anthers equal in number to the teeth of the nectary and inserted between them. Ovary very thick, globose. Stigma shield-shaped. Drupe globose, resembling a very large orange, 5 chambers, each containing 1, 2 or more seeds, convex on one side and concave on the other, angular and much crowded. Testa hard and porous.

HABITAT.—Common throughout the Archipelago.

Cedrela Toona, Roxb. (*C. odorata*, Blanco.)

NOM. VULG.—*Kalantas*, Tag., Pam.; *Lanigpa*, Vis.

USES.—The infusion of the flowers is antispasmodic. The trunk bark is an excellent astringent, and Dr. Waitz recommends it in extract as a treatment for infantile diarrhœa, for which I also have found it very useful. Blume says that it contains marked antispasmodic virtues, and Dr. G. Kennedy confirms it. Other physicians of India, among them Ros and Newton, have recommended the bark as a substitute for cinchona, given dry in doses of 30 grams.

INFUSION.—

Bark dry, pounded.................... 30 grams.
Water ....150 "

Filter and add:

Syrup of cinnamon.................. 20 grams.

DOSE.—Several dessert-spoonfuls a day.

The powdered bark is very useful as an application to indolent ulcers which it instantly deodorizes; like powdered quinine it is used in the treatment of superficial gangrene.

BOTANICAL DESCRIPTION.—A large tree. Leaves odd-pinnate. Leaflets oval, lanceolate, acuminate, entire, glabrous, 5–6 pairs. Flowers yellow, in terminal panicles. Calyx 5-toothed. Corolla, 5 oblong petals. Stamens 5, free, inserted on the apex of a disk. Ovaries sessile, 5 many-ovuled cells.

Style short. Stigma on a disk. Seed vessel coriaceous, 5 compartments, septicidal, 5-valved. Seeds compressed, pendulous, prolonged in a membranous wing.

HABITAT.—Very common in the islands.

CELASTRACEÆ.

Staff-Tree Family.

Celastrus paniculata, Willd. (*C. alnifolia*, DC.; *C. Rothiana*, Roem.; *Diosma serrata*, Blanco.)

NOM. VULG.—*Bilogo*, Tag.

USES.—I am not acquainted with the medicinal uses of this plant in the Philippines. In India, by means of a primitive system of distillation, they extract from the seeds a dark-colored oil of empyreumatic odor, which under the name of Oleum nigrum was once proclaimed by Dr. Herklots as the sovereign remedy for beriberi.

This oil in doses of 10–15 drops a day is a very powerful stimulant, the action of which is manifested by profuse perspiration several hours after its administration. Malcolmson reports that it has given him good results in several cases of beriberi, particularly in recent cases and those in which nervous and paralytic symptoms predominated. In Concan, the juice of the leaves is given in doses of 30 grams as an antidote for opium. The bruised seeds made into a paste with cow urine are used locally in treatment of itch. They are also used in the treatment of leprosy, gout, rheumatism, and other diseases which according to their medical theories, are derived from "cold humors." For these purposes they give the seeds internally, beginning with one and increasing daily until 50 are taken. At the same time they make external applications of the oil or of another compound prepared in the following way:

Place in an open pot with one opening, seeds of *C. paniculata*, cloves, benzoin, nutmeg and mace. The pot having been previously heated, is covered with another, inverted over the opening. On the sides of the latter a thick black oil condenses which Herklots very appropriately named *Oleum nigrum.*

BOTANICAL DESCRIPTION.—A climbing shrub, 6–9° high, without spines. Leaves 6–7′ long by 5′ broad, alternate, petiolate, entire, glabrous, half-ovate. Flowers small and paniculate. Calyx, 5 divisions. Corolla, 5 petals. Stamens 5, inserted in a disc. Anthers oblong. Ovary 3-celled. Stigma 3-lobulate. Style short. Seed vessel the size of a pea, globose, 3-celled, loculicidal, with pulpy seeds.

HABITAT.—Tayabas, Laguna, Ilocos North, San Mateo, Albay. Flowers in April.

RHAMNACEÆ.

Buckthorn Family.

Zizyphus Jujuba, Lam. (*Rhamnus Jujuba,* L. & Blanco; *Z. Mauritania,* Wall.)

NOM. VULG.—*Manzanitas,* Sp.-Fil.; *Jujube Fruit,* Eng.

USES.—The small fruit known commonly as *manzanitas* has an agreeable taste, although ordinarily offered for sale before they are quite ripe. They are among the most popular dainties at the fairs and festivals in the provinces of Manila and are the only part of the plant used in medicine. They possess emollient qualities and are official in the codex. They enter in the composition of the so-called pectoral remedies (composed of equal parts of figs, dates, Corinthian raisins and manzanitas).

BOTANICAL DESCRIPTION.—A shrub, with hooked thorns, leaves alternate, petiolate, coriaceous, entire, 3-nerved, 2 thorny stipules, one of them crooked. Flowers small, greenish, axillary. Calyx, 5 oval divisions. Corolla, 5 petals. Stamens 5, free. Ovary bilocular, situated on the disc. Styles 2–3, divergent; small papillary stigmas. Drupe pulpy, globose, resembling a crab-apple in size and taste, enclosing a hard, 2-celled seed.

HABITAT.—Common in all parts of the islands.

Rhamnus Wightii, W. & Arn. (*Ceanothus Wightiana*, Wall.; *R. Carolianus*, Blanco.)

Nom. Vulg.—*Kabatiti*, Tag.

Uses.—The dried trunk bark is the part employed in medicine. Hooper analyzed it in 1888 and found a crystalline principle (0.47 %), a brown resin (0.85), a red resin (1.15), a bitter principle (1.23), sugar, starch, calcium, oxalate, etc.

As the active principles exist in the resins, an alcoholic tincture of the latter is the best preparation for administration. In India it is used as a tonic and an astringent.

Botanical Description.—A small tree that grows near the sea coast. Trunk 9–12° high, straight, many-branched, devoid of thorns. Leaves alternate, ovate, acutely serrate, glabrous, short-petioled. Flowers greenish-white, axillary, perfect. Calyx 5-toothed, inversely conical. Corolla, 5 petals, smaller than the teeth of the calyx, oval, without claws, notched at the apex. Disc fleshy, smooth, slightly concave. Stamens 5, hidden within the petals. Filaments flattened. Anthers rounded. Ovary fleshy, inserted at the bottom of the calyx tube. Style short. Stigmas 3, divergent. Fruit oval, its base adherent to the calyx, 3 seeds.

Habitat.—Batangas. Blooms in July and October.

ANACARDIACEÆ.

Cashew Family.

Mangifera Indica, L.

Nom. Vulg.—*Manga.*

Uses.—The dried and pulverized kernel of the seed is used as an anthelmintic in doses of 1½–2 grams both in India and Brazil. The same preparation is used in the Philippines in the treatment of dysentery and diarrhœa and its effect is doubtless due to the large quantity of tannin it contains. It is administered as follows: The pounded kernels of 20–25 seeds are brought to a boil in 2 bottles (sic) of water. When the liquid has evaporated a third, it is removed from the fire, cooled, decanted, and again placed on the fire after adding three to four hundred grams of sugar. This time it is allowed to boil till reduced to one bottle. The dose is 50–60 grams 2–3 times a day. Incisions in the trunk exude a brownish resin which solidifies in the air, is slightly acrid, bitter, dissolves in alcohol and partially in water. In Malabar it is given internally in the treatment of diarrhœa and dysentery, mixing it with white of egg and opium. But the curative value of the combination is more likely due to the albumen and opium than to the resin. Dissolved in lemon juice it is a useful application in the itch. The trunk bark is astringent and is employed in decoction as a wash for ulcers and eczema and as an injection in leucorrhœa.

The fruit is one of the most highly prized in the Philippines, and resident Europeans are able to eat large quantities of it without ill effects unless the fruit is over-ripe, in which case it often causes transient diarrhœa, which should be treated with a mild purge.

In Mauritius the following compound powder is used in dysentery:

Dried slices of manga fruit	30	grams.
Dried manga kernels	60	"
Plantain seeds	15	"
Dried ginger	8	"
Gum arabic	15	"
Pulverize each ingredient separately; add powdered candy sugar	30	"

Mix.

Dose.—For an adult one dessert-spoonful every 4 hours; may be given in cange or arrowroot.

The flowers, testa and bark are, in Hindoo therapeutics, considered "cold," and "astringent," and are used especially in diarrhœa. In certain throat affections the Hindoos employ the burning leaves for inhalation. They also use the gum made by evaporating the juice of the ripe fruit, as a confection and an antiscorbutic. Dr. Linguist recommends the bark as a local astringent in uterine, intestinal and pulmonary hemorrhage and employs the following:

Fluid Extract.—

Fluid extract of manga bark	10 grams.
Water	120 "

Mix. Dose, 1 teaspoonful every 1 or 2 hours.

BOTANICAL DESCRIPTION.—A noble tree, 30° to 40° high, dome-like or rotund in outline. Leaves dark green, lustrous, alternate, lanceolate, entire; short petioles. Flowers racemose, in verticillate panicles. Calyx, 4, 5 or 6 sepals. Corolla white, fragrant, 4, 5 or 6 petals. Stamens 5, of which perhaps 1, 2 or 3 are fertile. Style on one side of the ovary. Stigma simple. Fruit large, reniform, fleshy, yellow when ripe; contains a large, flattened, reniform pit. Blooms from January even till June. The natives force the fruit by building fires under the trees when but little air is stirring.

HABITAT.—Common throughout the islands.

Anacardium occidentale, L. (*Cassuvium reniforme,* Blanco.)

NOM. VULG.—*Kasuy,* Tag.; *Caskew Nut,* Eng.

USES.—The pericarp of the nut contains an essential oil which is very irritant and used by the Hindoos as a vesicant; it severely blisters the lips and tongues of imprudent persons who break the nut without taking the precaution of cleansing it of the oil before opening it. In addition to the oil called *cardol,* the pericarp contains an especial acid *anacardic,* a little tannin and ammonia. Cardol ($C_{21}H_{31}O_2$) is an oleaginous, yellow liquid very unstable, neutral, soluble in alcohol and ether, insoluble in water, volatile, and vesicant if applied to the skin. "Anacardic" acid is white, crystalline, odorless, with a burning, aromatic taste. It melts at 26° and decomposes at 200°

forming a colorless oil; it is not vesicant, burns with a dark flame, and has the odor of rancid oil. A tincture of the pericarp has been made (1 part to 10 of alcohol) and given internally as a vermifuge in doses of 2–10 drops. Cardol, according to some authors, does not exercise a vesicant action in the gastro-intestinal canal, because it is not dissolved by the gastro-intestinal juices; I am sure, however, that I have seen a choleraic diarrhœa brought on by swallowing, in fun, the pericarp of one nut and a half. Cardol is eliminated by the urine.

The kernel is edible and has a very agreeable taste when roasted. By expression it yields a sweet, yellowish oil, density 0.916.

The trunk exudes a gum resin in masses varying in color from red to yellow.

The fleshy part, called the fruit, is edible but contains a certain quantity of cardol not only evidenced by the odor but by the smarting of the mouth and throat after eating. It is very juicy and the expressed liquid is fermented in Bombay and distilled to make a very weak alcohol which sells for the very low price of 4 annas (5 cents gold) a gallon. This alcohol is again distilled and a stronger obtained which sells for 1½ rupees a gallon. The Portuguese of India make a sort of wine from the fermented juice of the fruit, which, like the weak alcohol we have mentioned, is a well-known diuretic and is used as a liniment.

The gum resin of the trunk contains 90% of anacardic acid and 10% cardol. Wood soaked in it is preserved from the ravages of insects, especially of white ants, for which purpose it is used by bookbinders also. Therapeutically it is used externally in leprosy, old ulcers and to destroy corns, but on account of its rubefacient and vesicant qualities it is necessary to use it cautiously.

Botanical Description.—A tree, 18° high, with leaves cuneiform, glabrous, stiff, short-petioled. Flowers polygamous in terminal panicles. Calyx with 5 erect segments, imbricated, caducous. Corolla, 5 linear, lanceolate petals, curved and imbricated. Stamens 8–10, all fertile. Filaments united to one another and to the disc. Ovary heart-shaped. Style filiform and eccentric. Stigma defective. Ovule solitary. Fruit a reniform nut enclosed in a pulpy pyriform body, formed by the matured disc and extremity of the peduncle. Seed reniform, testa membranous.

HABITAT.—Common throughout the Archipelago. Blooms in February.

Odina Wodier, Roxb.

NOM. VULG.—*Amugis*, Tag. and Vis.

USES.—The bark is very astringent and in decoction is used for chronic ulcers. In India Dr. Kirkpatrick has used it as a lotion in impetigo. It has also given good results as a gargle in affections of the pharynx and buccal cavity.

The trunk exudes a gum called in India "kanni ki gond," an article of commerce. It is almost odorless and has a disagreeable taste. It is only partially soluble in water, forming a viscid mucilage. It is used in the treatment of contusions and sprains and is edible when mixed with cocoanut milk.

BOTANICAL DESCRIPTION.—A tree, with leaves bunched at the extremities of the branches, oblong, oval, acuminate, odd-pinnate, 3–4 pairs of opposite leaflets. Flowers greenish-white, polygamous, in terminal panicles. Calyx gamosepalous, 4 rounded lobules. Corolla, 4 imbricated petals. Stamens 8, free. Ovary 4-parted. Pistillate flowers; ovary sessile, oblong, unilocular. Style 4-parted, thick. Drupe oblong, compressed, unicellular. Testa hard, with 1 non-albuminous kernel.

HABITAT.—San Mateo.

MORINGEÆ.

Moringa pterygosperma, Gaertn. (*M. oleifera*, Lamk.; *M. poligona*, DC.; *Guilandina Moringa*, Blanco.)

NOM. VULG.—*Malugay*, *Kamalugay*, *Kalugay*, Tag.; *Dool*, *Malugit*, Vis. and Pam.; *Horse Radish Tree*, Indo-Eng.

Uses.—The root is vesicant and the Filipinos bruise it and use it for sinapisms. I have often observed, however, that it is quite painful used in this way. Dr. Waitz states that it is a good plan to add a few drops of the root juice to mustard sinapisms, a proceeding which seems to me superfluous, especially in the case of children as he advises it.

The Bengal pharmacopœia contains the following official preparations:

Compound Spirit.—

Small pieces of moringa root Orange peel	āā 600 grams.
Nutmeg	20 "
Spirit of wine	4½ liters.
Water	1 "

Mix and distil 4 liters.

Dose.—8–30 cc. as a stimulant and diuretic.

Compound Infusion.—

Moringa root, small pieces, bruised Mustard seed	āā 30 grams.
Boiling water	½ liter.
Let stand 2 hours, filter and add compound spirit	30 grams.

Dose.—30–60 grams a day, as a strong stimulant.

The expressed seeds yield a fixed oil, which is irritating and in my opinion should not be used internally.

The green pods, the flowers and the tender shoots of the leaves are eaten stewed. The juice of the leaves is given internally in India, as an emetic, in doses of 30 grams.

Botanical Description.—A well-known tree, 5–6 meters high. Leaves 3-pinnate, their terminal divisions odd-pinnate. Leaflets oval, glabrous, entire. Calyx, 5 unequal petaloid segments, imbricated, caducous. Corolla white, 5 unequal petals. Stamens inserted on the border of a disc, unequal, 5 opposite the petals bearing anthers, 5 alternate without anthers. Anthers dorsal, unilocular. Ovary pedunculate, lanceolate, unilocular, with many ovules in 2 series, inserted on the parietal placentæ. Fruit a pod terminating in a beak, 3-valved. Seeds numerous, very large, winged, embedded in a spongy substance.

HABITAT.—Common throughout the islands. Blooms in November.

LEGUMINOSÆ. (PAPILIONACEÆ.)

Pulse Family.

Agati grandiflora, Desv. (*Sesbania grandiflora*, Pers.)

NOM. VULG.—*Katuray*, Tag.

USES.—The flowers are edible. They and the leaves are purgative and are given in decoction for this purpose, 30–40 grams to 200 of water. The juice of the flowers is a popular remedy in India, for migraine and coryza. The trunk bark is bitter and tonic.

BOTANICAL DESCRIPTION.—A tree, 4–6 meters high, with drooping limbs; leaves long, very narrow, abruptly pinnate; many caducous leaflets, linear, elliptical. Flowers large, white, fragrant, in axillary racemes. Calyx bell-shaped with two indistinct lips. Corolla papilionaceous, white. Standard oval, a slight notch at the apex. Wings almost as large as the keel which is strongly arched. Stamens 10, diadelphous. Anthers uniform. Style and stamens equally long. Stigma a small head. Pod 1–2° long, linear, 4-sided, containing many oval seeds, separated by filamentous partitions.

HABITAT.—Grows in all sections of Luzon and Panay.

Abrus precatorius, L.

NOM. VULG.—*Saga*, *Sagamamin*, *Bag̃ati*, Tag.; *Bag̃ati Gikosgikos*, Vis.; *Kanaasaga*, Pam.; *Bugayon*, Iloc.; *Jequiriti*, *Prayerbeads*, Eng.

Uses.—The part of the plant most important in therapeutics is the seed, the size of a small pea, bright red with a black spot, hard and shining. The Filipino children use them to make rosaries and other decorations. In the distant past the Filipinos used these seeds to weigh gold, a practice followed even to-day by the Hindoos. The famous Susrutas, author of the "Ayur Veda," recommends them internally for nervous diseases; modern therapeutics, however, limits their use to one disease, though that is frequent and stubborn enough, namely chronic granular conjunctivitis.

Some physicians state that these seeds are poisonous and others the contrary, but the fact that they are used as food among the poor classes of Egypt, demonstrates their harmlessness in the digestive tract at least; when introduced into the circulation they undoubtedly exercise a toxic effect. We have already mentioned that their use is limited nowadays to the therapeutics of the eye; the decoction of the seeds known in Europe under the name of "Jaqueriti"—so named in Brazil—produces a purulent inflammation of the healthy conjunctiva and it is precisely this counter-irritant effect which makes it useful in chronic granular conjunctivitis, the persistence of which has defied the most heroic measures of therapeutics. The French oculist, Dr. de Wecker, was the first to employ jequirity for this purpose, in the form of a 24 hours' maceration of the seeds, 10 grams to 500 grams of water. It is necessary to use a product recently prepared and with this several applications a day are made. It is now known that the inflammation of the healthy conjunctiva is not caused by germ-life contained in the solution but by an inorganic ferment discovered by Bruylans and Venneman and named jequiritin; they state that it is produced during the germination of the seeds or of the cells in the powdered seeds. Warden and Waddell, of Calcutta, have isolated an essential oil, an acid named "ábric" and an amorphous substance called abrin, obtained by precipitation with alcohol from a watery infusion of the pulverized seeds. Its action is identical with that of "jequiritin."

The infusion appears to possess considerable value as a stimulating application to indolent ulcers.

The root is a good substitute for licorice, is emollient and has an agreeable taste. The extract is useful in catarrhal diseases of the bronchi and in dysuria. The leaves contain the same properties as the root and an extract prepared from them is used as a substitute for licorice.

Botanical Description.—A vine, with leaves opposite, abruptly pinnate, a stylet taking the place of the terminal leaflet. Leaflets linear, entire, glabrous, tipped with a small point. Common petiole with 2 awl-shaped stipules at the base. Flowers in small racemes. Calyx gamosepalous, caducous, 4–5 short teeth. Corolla papilionaceous, wings horizontal. Stamens 9, monadelphous with bilocular anthers. Style very short. Stigma globose. Pod 4–5 cm. long, truncate at the ends, with 5–6 red seeds, each with a black spot.

Habitat.—Common in all mountainous regions of the islands. Grows near houses and roads.

Mucuna pruriens, DC. (*M. prurita*, Hook.; *M. utilis*, Wall.; *Dolichos pruriens*, L.; *Carpopogon pruriens*, Roxb.)

Nom. Vulg.—*Nipay*, *Lipay*, Vis.

Uses.—The pods are official as an anthelmintic in the Pharmacopœia of India. They are used in the form of an electuary triturated to the proper consistency with honey or syrup. The dose for adults is one soupspoonful, and for children a teaspoonful, given every morning for 3–4 consecutive days. The last day a purge is given to expel the lumbricoids.

Botanical Description.—A vine with ternate leaves. Flowers red, keel larger than the standard and wings. Pods about as thick as the little finger, lacking transverse grooves, curved in the form of the letter f, covered with bright red down, which causes an unendurable itching. They are divided into 3 or 4 oblique cells each containing a brown, shiny seed.

HABITAT.—Luzon and Panay.

Erythrina Indica, Lam. (*E. corallodendron*, L.; *E. carnea*, Blanco.)

NOM. VULG.—*Dapdap, Kasindik*, Tag.; *Dapdap, Kabrab*, Vis.; *Dapdap, Sulbaĝ*, Pam.; *Indian Coral Tree*, Eng.

USES.—This tree is well known on account of the beauty of its crimson flowers. The decoction of the leaves is a useful cleansing and deodorizing application for ulcers. The bruised leaves are used locally in painful affections of the joints and to abort syphilitic buboes and abscesses of all kinds. The juice of the tender leaves is used in Concan to destroy maggots in ulcers, and the powder has a similar use. A decoction is used locally in ophthalmia.

The root and the leaves are used as a febrifuge in the Philippines and in India, according to Wight. In Brazil the bark is given in small repeated doses as a hypnotic and in the Philippines as a diuretic and purgative; a decoction of the leaves is similarly used. The bark contains an alkaloid discovered by Rochefontaine and Rey, called *erythrin*, which acts upon the central nervous system, diminishing its normal functions even to the point of abolishment, without modifying motor excitability or muscular contractility. W. Young isolated a glucoside, *migarrhin*, similar to saponin, but possessing the additional property of dilating the pupil.

In bronchitis with dyspnœa the following infusion of bark is very useful:

Fresh bark, Freshly bruised leaves,	āā	2 grams.
Water	1,500	"

Boil till reduced one-half, filter and add:

Simple syrup	200	"

Dose: Wineglassful every two hours.

Botanical Description.—A large tree, 20^c high, thorny, with ternate leaves. Leaflets rhomboid, broad, entire, glabrous. Secondary petioles: that of the middle leaflet long, bearing 2 glands, those of the others short, bearing 1 gland each. The leaves fall at the end of the rainy season and the flowers bloom. They are a handsome scarlet color, large, in terminal racemes. Calyx half-cylindrical, oblique, truncate, entire. Corolla papilionaceous; standard elongated, lanceolate. Wings short. Keel very short, 2-lobuled. Stamens diadelphous. Anthers large. Ovary woolly. Stigma thick. Pod curved, rounded, furrowed in parts corresponding to the seeds which are numerous, oval, pointed at the ends.

Habitat.—Common throughout the islands. Blooms in February.

Clitoria ternatea, L.

Nom. Vulg.—*Kolokantiĝ*, *Pukingaĝ*, Tag.; *Kolokatiĝ*, Vis.; *Butterfly-pea*, Eng.

Uses.—The pounded seeds mixed with oil are used locally for painful joints. They possess purgative and emetic properties and Dr. J. Shartt has employed a mixture of the powdered roasted seeds, 8 grams, with double the quantity of acid tartrate of potassium. Its action is gentle, but sure. The alcoholic extract of the root, a soft, brown, resinous substance with an odor recalling that of jalap, is a very active cathartic, producing sharp effects in doses of 30–60 centigrams; in fact it produces such severe tenesmus that its use in such doses should not be recommended.

The root bark is used internally in an infusion (4–8 grams to 1 liter of water) as an emollient in irritability of the bladder and urethra and has been recommended for such a purpose by Mooden Sheriff. It is a diuretic which frequently acts as a purgative, a fact that is not surprising in view of the above-mentioned properties of the alcoholic extract.

The roasted seeds used as a purgative are so trustworthy that they deserve the further attention of physicians.

Botanical Description.—A vine very well known by its blue flowers. Leaves alternate with 3 pairs of oval leaflets. Stipules persistent. Flowers axillary, solitary, 1–1½′ in long diameter. Calyx in 5 acute divisions, the two upper ones smaller. Corolla papilionaceous. Standard open, notched at the end. Keel shorter than the wings and covered by them. Stamens 10, 9 united and 1 free. Stigma downy, thick. Pod full of short hairs, with more than 6 surrounded with a tow-like substance, reniform, with black spots.

Habitat.—Common along the roads and in gardens. Flowers in July and November.

1. Pterocarpus santalinus, L.[1]

Nom. Vulg.—*Narra*, *Naga*, Tag.; *Apalit*, *Daytanag*, Pam.; *Red Saunders* or *Red Sandalwood Tree*, Eng.

2. P. Indicus, Willd. (*P. pallidus*, Blanco.)

Nom. Vulg.—*Asana*, Tag.; *Naga*, Vis.

3. P. erinaceus, Poir. (*P. echinatus*, Pers. & DC.)

Nom. Vulg.—*Asana*, *Narra*, Tag.

Uses.—The wood of the first is the so-called "red sandalwood." It is used for building purposes and, in medicine, as an astringent. In decoction it is used as a gargle for sore throat. The second is also an excellent building material and is used medicinally for its astringent properties. A decoction of sufficient strength to color the water a light blue is used as a mouth wash in toothache and has some reputation as a solvent of vesical calculi. All three species yield a resin known in pharmacy under the name of "kino." The true gum kino is really

[1] Official in the U. S. P. under the name of *Santalum rubrum*, and used only for coloring alcoholic solutions.

produced by the *P. marsupium*, Roxb., but the Philippine product, especially that of the second and third species, has for a long time been exported to Europe under the name of "red astringent gum" or "kino." This name is given to the sap of these trees dried without the aid of artificial heat. The bark is the part which produces it and the following extractive process is employed in Madras: a vertical incision is made in the trunk and lateral incisions perpendicular to it and a receptacle is placed at the foot of the tree. This soon fills and when the gum is sufficiently dried by air and sun it is packed in boxes and exported.

In respect to appearance, solubility and chemical composition, Flückiger and Hanbury were unable to discover any difference between the kino of *P. marsupium*, Roxb., and that of *P. erinaceus*, Poir. It is therefore interesting to consider a product that is identical with that described in the pharmacopœias as produced by the *P. marsupium*, Roxb., though the latter does not grow in the Philippines.

Kino is at present used but little in therapeutics and its action is analogous to that of tannin and catechu. It is given internally for its astringent effect in chronic diarrhœa, leucorrhœa, blenorrhœa and hemorrhages. The dose of the powder is 1–4 grams, and of the alcoholic tincture, containing 20 parts kino to 100 of alcohol, 5–10 grams. In prolapse of the rectum and anal fissure the following solution is used by enema:

Kino........................... 3 grams.
Water.......................500 "

For vaginal injections a solution of 20 to 250 water.

Botanical Description.—The "pterocarpus," L., is a tree of the first order with odd-pinnate leaves. Leaflets alternate and coriaceous. Flowers yellow, in racemes, with caducous bracts and bractlets. Calyx turbinate, with short teeth. Petals exserted, markedly unguiculate. Standard and wings curled. Keel obtuse with its petals slightly or not at all coherent. The staminal tube, cleft above and below or above only. Stamens superior, often almost, and at times entirely, free. Anthers versatile. Ovary pedunculate, with 2 ovules. Style curved. Stigma terminal. Pod orbicular, smooth or spiny, usually containing one seed, encircled by a broad, rigid wing, the point curved downward.

HABITAT.—In the mountains of Luzon, Panay and Mindoro. Blooms in March.

Pongamia glabra, Vent. (*Robinia mitis*, L.; *Gadelupa maculata*, Blanco.)

NOM. VULG.—*Balikbalik*, Tag.; *Butoĝ*, Vis.

USES.—The oil expressed from the seeds is used in India for lighting purposes, and in addition is of notable therapeutic value. It is an excellent local remedy for the itch, for herpes and especially for pityriasis versicolor, used alone or emulsified with lemon juice. In stubborn cases Dymock recommends the addition of oil of *hydrocarpus*, camphor and powdered sulphur. Dr. Gibson states that he knows of no plant in the vegetable kingdom possessing more notable curative properties in itch, herpes and other cutaneous diseases than the plant under consideration. It is also used as an embrocation in articular rheumatism.

The powdered leaves mixed with common salt and pepper are given internally with a little milk, as a remedy for leprosy.

The juice of the root makes a useful wash for gangrenous ulcers and a good injection for fistula.

BOTANICAL DESCRIPTION.—A tree, 18° high, with leaves opposite, odd-pinnate. Leaflets in 3 pairs, ovate, lanceolate, entire, glabrous and membranaceous. Flowers slightly spotted, racemose. Calyx bell-shaped, with 5 scarcely visible toothlets. Corolla papilionaceous, petals equal, clawed. Standard with 2 callosities athwart the base. Stamens 10, diadelphous. Pod with one seed, which is flat, smooth, veined, bright red.

HABITAT.—Luzon and Panay. Blooms in October.

LEGUMINOSÆ.

Brasiletto Family.

Cæsalpinia Bonducella, Flem. (*Guilandina Bonducella*, L.)

NOM. VULG.—*Bayag-Kambiĝ, Kalambibit*, Tag.; *Dalugdug*, Vis.; *Fever Nut, Physic Nut, Bonduc Seeds*, Indo-Eng.

USES.—The seed is the part of the plant employed and is official in the Pharmacopœia of India. It is used as a tonic and antiperiodic in intermittent fevers and in general where tonic treatment is indicated. It has given good results in the malarial fevers of India, according to English physicians. The Pharmacopœia of India contains the following preparation under the name of "Compound Powder of Bonduc" (Pulvis bonducellæ compositus).

Seeds of Bonduc, powdered............30 grams.
Pepper..............................30 "

Mix and keep in a well-corked flask.

DOSE.—1–2 grams 3 times a day.

In the Philippines the powdered seed is given in affections of the digestive tract, especially in diarrhœa and feeble digestion. The same name of Bonduc is given to the seeds of another species that grows in the Philippines, *C. Bonduc*, Roxb.; *Kamot-Kabag, Bayan-Kambiĝ*, Tag. The seeds are identical in chemical composition and therapeutic indication.

The two principal substances contained in the seeds are an oil, 24% and a resin, 1.88%. The former is straw-colored and slightly bitter by virtue of the presence of a resin that may be precipitated by alcohol. The resin or bitter principle exists as an amorphous powder, white, bitter, not acrid, soluble in chloroform, alcohol, acetone, crystallizable acetic acid, fixed and essential oils; slightly soluble in ether and bisulphide of carbon, insoluble in water and petroleum ether. The alkalies do not affect it. It melts at 140°, decomposing and leaving only a carbon. Its discoverers, Heckel and Schlagdenhaussen, have given it the name *bonducin* ($C_{14}H_{15}O_5$). Hydrochloric acid colors it red; sulphuric acid, a maranthin red in half an hour.

Bonducin seems to be the active principle of the seeds and is given internally in doses of 10–20 centigrams; according to Dr. Isnard, of Marseilles, this dose has given as good results in fevers as the same quantity of quinine.

BOTANICAL DESCRIPTION.—A shrub with prostrate stem bristling with thorns. Leaves twice abruptly pinnate, a thorn taking the place of the terminal leaflet. Leaflets in 10–14 pairs, ovate, expanded, with a spine at the apex. Common petioles thorny, with 4 leaf-like stipules at the base. Flowers yellow, in racemes. Calyx 5-parted, curved downward. Corolla inserted on the calyx, 5 petals, 4 nearly equal, the uppermost broader and shorter. Stamens 10. Filaments very unequal in height, inserted on the calyx, united and woolly at the base. Pistil very short. Stigma thick. Pod rhomboidal before maturity, prickly, containing 2 semi-globose seeds with testa hard, mottled and tough.

The other species, *C. Bonduc*, Roxb., is distinguished by leaflets unequal at the base, by the absence of stipules, and by the bright orange yellow seeds.

HABITAT.—Common in Luzon, Panay and Joló. Blooms in December.

Cæsalpinia Sappan, L.

NOM. VULG.—*Sibukao, Sapag*, Tag.; *Palo del Brasil*, Sp.; *Sappan Wood*, Eng.

USES.—The decoction of Sibukao is given in hemorrhages, especially of the lungs. It is probably the red color of this decoction which originated the idea of giving it to check bleeding, and this is the practice of the native Filipino doctors, as well as of the Arabs and Hindoos. The natives of Cochin China, reasoning in an opposite manner, prescribe it as emmenagogue. Some authors recommend Sibukao as a substitute for logwood. The decoction is administered in chronic diarrhœa, especially that of children. A few cases of phlebitis have been reported as occasioned by its use. The extract is made as follows:

Sibukao in small pieces..............500 grams.
Boiling water..................... $4\frac{1}{2}$ liters.

Macerate for 24 hours, boil until reduced by half, filter and evaporate the filtrate to a syrupy consistency. Do not use iron vessels.

Sibukao contains much tannin and gallic acid, and a peculiar substance which distinguishes it from logwood, *brasilin* ($C_{22}H_{20}O_7$), which gives a red color to alkaline solutions instead of blue or purple. It is a crystalline pigment which may be considered a compound of hematoxylon and fenol.

BOTANICAL DESCRIPTION.—A very common tree, 12–15° high, with spiny trunk, leaves twice abruptly pinnate. Leaflets linear, notched at the apex. Flowers racemose. Calyx boat-shaped. Corolla, 5 petals, the uppermost broad, short, spotted red. Stigma bifid. Pod sabre-like, woody, with 3–4 seeds separated by partitions. The wood is well known everywhere in the Philippines, being a very important article of commerce, and there is no fear of logwood being substituted for it, as the latter is more expensive, and substitutions are not ordinarily made under such circumstances. In commerce it occurs in large pieces of all shapes and forms, since the branches and trunks are cut into pieces which vary from $\frac{1}{2}$–2 meters in length. Its color is reddish-yellow or white with more or less red grain. Blooms in September.

Cæsalpinia pulcherrima, Swartz. (*Poinciana pulcherrima*, L. & Blanco.)

NOM. VULG.—*Flores y Rosas Caballero, Caballero*, Sp.-Fil.; *Barbadoes Flower-Fence*, Eng.

USES.—The leaves are emmenagogue, purgative like those of senna, and excitant. The bark especially is a powerful emmenagogue, used in some countries for criminal purposes. The decoction of the flowers is pectoral and febrifuge and is given in bronchitis, asthma and malarial fever. The flowers contain a bitter principle. The roots are acrid and poisonous. The seeds of the green fruit are eaten frequently by children; when ripe they contain gallic and tannic acids, by virtue of which they are used in tanning hides and to dye yellow combined with alum, and black combined with salts of iron. They also contain a pigment and a resin.

INFUSION OF THE FLOWERS.—

Flowers of the caballero, dry	20	grams.
Water	500	"
Sugar	70	"

Mix. Dose, a wineglassful several times a day.

BOTANICAL DESCRIPTION.—A shrub, with prickly trunk, Leaves twice abruptly pinnate. Leaflets 5–8 pairs, glabrous. ovate and elliptical, bearing a spine at the extremity, 3 stipules to each pair of leaflets. Flowers yellow and red, in racemes on the ends of the branches. Calyx divided almost to the base, with 5 concave parts. Corolla, 5 petals 1′ long with short claws, one petal very small and straight, the others larger, with wavy edges. Stamens 10, crimson, 3′ long, free, woolly, united at the lower end. Pistil the same length as the stamens. Stigma somewhat concave. Ovary sessile, unilocular, many-ovuled. Pod compressed, with 7 or more seeds inserted on the superior suture and separated from each other by fleshy divisions.

HABITAT.—Very common in gardens where it is cultivated for its beautiful flowers. Blooms throughout the entire year.

Cassia fistula, L.

NOM. VULG.—*Cañafístula*, Sp.; *Lombayoĝ, Ibabaw, Baloyoĝ*, Vis.; *Purging Cassia*, Eng.

USES.—The pod known in pharmacy under the name of "Cañafistula" contains a blackish, sweet pulp, which is a mild purgative if combined with carminatives, but it produces severe colic if given alone. The urine sometimes takes on a dark color after taking it. The laxative dose is 4–8 grams, the purgative 30–60.

EXTRACT OF CASSIA.—

Pulp and seeds of ripe pods .... 1 kilo.
Water .... 1 liter.

After mixing the pulp with water the liquid is strained through a woolen cloth; the material which remains in the strainer is washed with a little more cold water which is added to the other liquid and the two are evaporated to the consistency of the extract.

DOSE.—15–30 grams.

Dr. Irving states that the root is a very energetic purgative. In Concan the juice of the tender leaves is used in the treatment of impetigo.

BOTANICAL DESCRIPTION.—A tree with trunk about as thick as the human body, with leaves opposite and abruptly pinnate. Leaflets, the lower ones smaller, 5 pairs, ovate, lanceolate, glabrous and rather tough. Common petiole, cleft at the base, lacking glandule. Flowers bright yellow, in long, pendulous racemes. Calyx, 5 ovate sepals. Corolla, 5 unequal petals. Stamens 10, free, 3 longer than the rest. Ovary unilocular, many-ovuled. Pod cylindrical, pointed at the end, woody, black, 1–2° long, with many circular seeds, surrounded by a blackish pulp and separated by partitions.

HABITAT.—Common in Luzon and Panay. Blooms in March.

Cassia occidentalis, L.

NOM. VULG.—*Tighiman*, *Balotagaso*, Tag.; *Tambalisa*, Vis.; *Western Senna*, *Styptic Weed*, Eng.; *Negro Coffee*, Indo-Eng.

USES.—In Brazil they use an infusion of the root as a tonic and diuretic, 4 grams of the root bark and 180 of boiling water to be taken in one day. In Dahomey the leaves are used as a febrifuge. Thirty grams of fresh leaves are boiled in 300 grams of water till the liquid is reduced to 250 grams. The patient takes this decoction hot the first day of the fever and a profuse perspiration promptly breaks out. As a rule the effect is immediate and the fever does not recur. This treatment of fevers is more common in that country than that by quinine and they claim that it has the advantage over the latter of acting as a stomachic tonic. By adding a small quantity of the roots to the decoction it is rendered diuretic. The seeds possess the same properties and are used in decoctions of 30 grams to 300 of water. According to De Lanesan the roasted seeds are used in La Réunion in infusion similar to coffee in the treatment of gastralgia and asthma. In some countries they mix them with coffee just as chicory is used in Europe.

Heckel and Schlagdenhaufen have made a very complete study of the plant and we quote the following from their works:

Chemical composition of the seeds.—

Water	8.850
Fats and pigments soluble in petroleum ether	1.600
" " " " " chloroform	1.150
Odorous material and traces of tannin	5.022
Glucose	0.738
Gummy, mucilaginous and pectic matter	15.734
Soluble albuminoids and aleuron	6.536
Cellulose	7.434
Insoluble albuminose	2.216
Lignose	32.727
Fixed salts	17.976
Lost material	.017
	100.000

Previous to the studies of the above authors the seeds had been therapeutically tested by Delioux de Savignac and Professor Clouet. Heckel and Schlagdenhauffen have confirmed the febrifuge virtues of the seeds and are uncertain as to the active principle since they found no glucoside or alkaloid in their analysis. The antiperiodic properties are comparable with those of quinine and have even proved effective in some cases in which quinine failed. It seems quite clear that the tannin is the active principle which is the more probable because its antiperiodic virtues are now recognized by all therapeutists.

It is given in maceration or infusion, 2–15 grams of the seeds to 3 or 400 of water to be taken several times a day. The treatment causes no very marked physiological effects. It seems to act as a sedative to the nervous system.

Botanical Description.—An annual plant, .60–1 meter high. Root central with lateral rootlets. Stem straight, ramose. Leaves opposite, abruptly pinnate with a stylet in place of the odd leaflet. Leaflets, 5–6 pairs, the lower ones smaller, ovate, oblong, margins and lower face downy. Common petiole swollen at the base, 2 stipules and 1 glandule. Calyx, 5 unequal sepals. Corolla, 5 nearly equal petals, sulphur yellow, concave, the posterior one further developed. Two verticils of 5 stamens each. Of the 5 stamens superior to the sepals, 2 are fertile, larger and arched; of the other 5 stamens 4 are fertile and small. Pod compressed, linear, smooth, 5′ long, containing many compressed, heart-shaped seeds, separated by thin partitions.

Habitat.—Common in Luzon. Blooms in October.

Cassia alata, L.

Nom. Vulg. — *Acapulco*, Sp.-Fil.; *Katandá, Gamut sa Buni, Sontiĝ*, Tag.; *Suntiĝ, Kansitás*, Vis.; *Pakayomkom-kastila*, Pam.

Uses.—This is one of the most popular Philippine remedies and its usefulness is vouched for by many physicians practicing in many different lands. Its antiherpetic properties are notable and the Tagalo name of the plant, "Gamut sa Buni," means literally "medicine for herpes." The natives use the juice of the leaf applied locally to the affected part. These properties have long been familiar to the Malays and to the Hindoos who in their medical works give the plant the Sanscrit name of "Dadrughna," meaning "to cure herpes." The Pharmacopœia of Bengal recommends cassia in the form of an ointment made by mixing the crushed tender leaves with simple ointment. This preparation is, in our opinion, undesirable on account of its liability to become rancid and vaseline should be the excipient used. Another application for herpetic eruptions is the juice of the leaves mixed with an equal quantity of lemon juice. The Malays use the leaves dried in the sun, adding to them a little water and rubbing them briskly on the affected parts, the vigorous treatment being an important part of the cure.

The decoction of the leaves is a laxative and according to Mr. J. Wood the tincture has an action similar to that of senna. Dr. Pulney Andy of India states that the extract prepared from the tender leaves is a good substitute for extract of colocynth.

Mr. A. Porte claims to have obtained the best results with an acetic extract of the fresh leaves. The following is his formula:

Fresh leaves of *C. alata*...............100 grams.
Acetic acid diluted in $\frac{2}{3}$ water............450 "

Macerate 10 or 12 days, filter and express, then filter again and evaporate to the consistency of an extract.

The seeds contain vermifuge principles.

The activity of this plant in herpes is due to the chrysophanic acid contained in it. The more recent the eruption the more certain is the effect.

The following species, all of which grow in the Philippines, contain principles analogous to those of the *C. alata*, viz.: *C. sophera*, L. and *C. tora*, L., called in Tagalo *manimanihan*.

BOTANICAL DESCRIPTION.—A shrub, 7–9° high, with a straight, ramose trunk 3–4′ in diameter. Leaves $1\frac{1}{2}$–2° long, opposite, abruptly pinnate, a thick stylet taking the place of the odd leaflet. Leaflets 10–13 pairs, the smaller ones 1–2′ long. Common petiole with 2 horizontal stipules at the base. Flowers in conspicuous, erect racemes. Calyx, 5 free concave, unequal sepals. Corolla, 5 petals of a beautiful yellow color. Stamens perigynous, 10 in number, 3 upper ones very small and frequently sterile, 3 lower very large. The bilocular anthers open by 2 pores. Ovary many-ovuled with filiform style. Pod long with 2 prominent wings on the sides and many seeds which slightly resemble a cross with blunt ends.

The *C. sophera*, L., is characterized by 10 stamens, all fertile and a smooth, linear, bivalved pod full of seeds separated by false partitions. The *C. tora*, L., bears a quadrangular pod about 15 centimeters long by 2 in diameter.

HABITAT.—Grows in all parts of the islands and is universally known by the natives. Blooms in May.

Tamarindus Indica, L.

NOM. VULG.—*Tamarindo*, Sp.; *Sampalok*, Tag., Pam., Bik.; *Sambak*, *Sumalagi*, *Kamalagi*, Vis.; *Tamarind*, Eng.

USES.—The pulp of the fruit is used to make a sort of sweet preserve and is very popular among the Filipinos. They prepare a refreshing drink from the pulp mixed with sweetened water and believing it to be beneficial to the liver, stomach and blood, they use too much of it. Its excessive use is rather prejudicial to the health, but given in moderation it is very efficient in allaying the thirst of fever patients. The pulp contains weak laxative properties and it is customary to administer it in solution with cream of tartar. Its chemical composition is as follows:

Citric acid	9.40
Tartaric acid	1.55
Malic acid	0.45
Potassium bitartrate	3.25
Sugar	12.50
Gum	4.70
Vegetable gelatin	6.25
Parenchyma	34.35
Water	27.55

(Vauquelin.)

At the end of any sickness, especially after labor, the first bath given to the convalescent is with a decoction of the leaves of the "sampaloc," to prevent convulsions, the native herb-doctors say.

BOTANICAL DESCRIPTION.—A large tree, somewhat resembling the elm in contour, with leaves opposite, abruptly pinnate. Leaflets 12 or more pairs, linear, with a notch at the apex, entire, glabrous. Flowers yellow-white, spattered dark red, racemose. Calyx, 4 sepals. Corolla, 5 lanceolate petals with crispate borders. Stamens monadelphous, dividing into 7 filaments above. The ripe pod is chocolate color, oblong, slightly compressed, straight or curved, 6–15 centimeters long, full of a light-brown pulp in which rest the seeds enveloped in a cellular membrane. These seeds are flattened, almost quadrangular; testa hard, of a chestnut color, shiny and without albumen.

HABITAT.—Very common everywhere in the islands. Blooms in May.

Bauhinia malabarica, Roxb. (*B. tomentosa*, Wall. and Blanco.)

NOM. VULG.—*Alibag̃bag̃*, Tag., Vis., Pam.

USES.—The leaves of this tree and of the species *B. tomentosa*, L., are quite acid and the Filipinos use them as an ingredient of many dishes. The fresh flowers possess anti-dysenteric virtues for which purpose they are given internally in infusion of 10–20 grams of the flowers to one-half liter of water. The decoction of the root bark is a common remedy for liver troubles along the coast of Malabar according to Rheede.

BOTANICAL DESCRIPTION.—A tree 20° high, with leaves alternate, peltate, slightly cordate, orbicular, the apex divided into two large lobules with a stylet between them, glabrous above, somewhat downy beneath; 2 large, flat glandules are situated at the base. Petioles short. Flowers cymose. Peduncle long. Calyx inferior, funnelform, with 4–5 sepals as long as the corolla. Corolla, 5 petals. Stamens 10, 5 alternate ones longer than the others. Stigma thick, peltate, 2 lobules. Pod 1° long, with linear stalk, containing many seeds separated by filamentous isthmuses.

HABITAT.—Common everywhere. Blooms in November.

LEGUMINOSÆ.

Mimosa Division.

Entada scandens, Benth. (*E. Pursætha*, DC. and Blanco.)

NOM. VULG.—*Gogo*, Tag.; *Bayogo*, *Balogo*, *Gohoĝ bakay*, Vis. and Pam.; *Gilla Nuts*, Indo-Eng.

USES.—The use made of the mashed bark of this tree is well known throughout the Philippines. Cut in strips and beaten thoroughly between stones it is sold under the name of "gogo"; it is macerated in water, to which it imparts a reddish color, and forms a substitute for soap. The Filipinos use this preparation for bathing, especially the hair, for which purpose there is no more useful or simple preparation. It cures pityriasis, and renders the hair very soft, without drying it too much as is usually the case with soap. The natives use it in treating the itch, washing the affected parts with the maceration and at the same time briskly rubbing them with the bark; in this way they remove the crusts that shield the acari. The treatment is successful in direct proportion to the energy of rubbing.

The seeds of "gogo" are very large, lenticular, flattened, 3–4 centimeters in diameter. Their chemical composition has been studied by Pettit. Alcohol dissolves the active principle, perhaps a glucoside, the study of which the author has not completed. Five centigrams of this substance administered to a guinea-pig causes paralysis of the hind quarters without any apparent inflammation. He also found saponin in the seeds, but it exists in much greater quantity in the trunk. In the Sunda Islands they eat the seeds roasted and also extract from them an illuminating oil.

The maceration of gogo is emetic and purgative; it is used in the treatment of asthma; it is exceedingly irritating, the slightest quantity that enters the eye causing severe smarting and a slight conjunctivitis for one or two days.

Botanical Description.—A high climbing shrub with stem as much as 7–8′ in diameter. Leaves opposite, twice abruptly pinnate, a stylet replacing the terminal leaflet; 5 pairs of elliptical leaflets, entire, glabrous and notched at the apex. Common petiole with 2 stipules at the base. Flowers in delicate spikes. Calyx obliquely truncate, 5-toothed. Corolla, 5 oval petals much larger than the calyx. Stamens 10–13. Filaments longer than the corolla. Anther with 1–2 white, globose glandules. Pod woody, 4–6° long by "4 fingers" broad, with large notches on the borders, many compartments containing many large, compressed, circular seeds with dark-colored testa, 3–4 centimeters in diameter.

Habitat.—Mountains of Luzon and Panay. Blooms in May.

Parkia Roxburghii, G. Don. (*P. brunonis*, Grah.; *P. biglobosa*, Benth.; *Mimosa peregrina*, Blanco.)

Nom. Vulg.—*Kopaĝ*, Tag.

Uses.—The fruit is edible. Its pulp is golden yellow with a sweetish taste and an odor like that of violets.

The roasted seeds are used in certain parts of Africa to make an infusion like coffee, for which reason they have been called "Soudan Coffee."

The pulp was analyzed by Heckel and Schlagdenhauffen in 1887; it contains 60 % of its weight of sugar (a mixture of dextrose and levulose), 0.98 % of free tartaric and citric acids, fats, albuminoids, etc.

Botanical Description.—A large tree of the first order. Leaves opposite, twice abruptly pinnate. Leaflets small, linear, more than 40 pairs. Principal petiole with one glandule at the base and often another higher up. Calyx long, tubular, with 5 unequal lobules. Corolla, 5 equal petals. Stamens 10, monadelphous. Ovary free, unilocular, multi-ovulate. Pod, 1° x 1′, woody, much compressed, brown, with many seeds embedded in a yellow pulp.

Habitat.—Abounds in the provinces of central Luzon. Blooms in December.

Acacia Farnesiana, Willd. (*A. Indica*, Desv.; *Mimosa Farnesiana*, L. and Blanco.)

Nom. Vulg.—*Aroma*, Sp.; *Cassie Flower*, Eng.

Uses.—The trunk bark is astringent and in decoction is of use in the treatment of prolapsed rectum and as an injection for leucorrhœa. A poultice of the tender leaves is applied to ulcers and sores previously washed with the decoction.

The tree exudes an abundant gum very similar to gum arabic which latter is the product of another species of acacia (*A. Arabica*, Willd.). The Manila pharmacist, D. Anacleto del Rosario, sent to the Paris Exposition of 1899 a specimen of this gum obtained on the plantation of D. P. P. Roxas, in Batangas. This specimen differed in no respect from gum arabic and it will surely sooner or later take the place of the latter in the Philippines, both for pharmaceutical and industrial purposes. It would be superfluous to describe here the properties of gum arabic.

BOTANICAL DESCRIPTION.—A small tree 9–12° high, very well known, trunk bristling with long thorns. Leaves twice abruptly pinnate. One or more pairs of leaflets, very small, linear. Common petiole with two thorns united at its base and a small glandule on the upper part. Flowers yellow, aromatic, axillary, joined in a globose head $\frac{1}{2}$–$\frac{3}{4}$′ in diameter, consisting of more than 50 minute flowerets. In each axil are 2 peduncles. In some heads all the flowerets are staminate, in others hermaphrodite. The hermaphrodite flowers have a calyx with 5 small teeth. Corolla, 5 petals. Stamens 40 or more. Pistil same length as the stamens. Staminate flowers: calyx, corolla, stamens and anthers as in the hermaphrodite flowers. Pistil none. Pod round, curved, with 8 or more elliptical, compressed seeds.

HABITAT.—Grows everywhere, but forms dense thickets in the provinces of La Laguna and Batangas. Blooms in January.

CRASSULACEÆ.

Orpine Family.

Kalanchoe laciniata, DC. (*Cotyledon laciniata*, Roxb.; *Bryophyllum serratum*, Blanco.)

NOM. VULG.—*Siempreviva* (*Live-for-ever*), Sp.-Fil.; *Katakatakā*, Tag.

USES.—The fleshy leaves are beaten up and applied to chronic ulcers and sores on which they exert a stimulant action. Applied to the temples they relieve headache. Ainslie testifies to the good effect of its local use in inflammations and as a wash for ulcers. The juice of the leaves is used in Concan in the treatment of bilious diarrhœa and gall stones.

BOTANICAL DESCRIPTION.—A well-known plant, about 2° high, with leaves sessile, opposite, oval, serrately toothed, fleshy. Flowers yellow, in umbels, the stalks reaching a height of 3°. Calyx very short, with 4 lanceolate, acuminate sepals, united at the base. Corolla salver-shaped, persistent, with border having 4 small lobules. Stamens 8, fertile. Ovaries 4, free, each with 1 many-ovuled cell. Styles same length as the stamens. Stigmas awl-shaped. Four seed vessels, each with 1 compartment containing many oblong seeds.

HABITAT.—Common in all parts of the islands.

COMBRETACEÆ.

Terminalia Catappa, L. (*T. molucana*, Lam.; *T. mauriciana*, Blanco.)

NOM. VULG.—*Talisay*, Tag.; *Almendro*, Sp.-Fil.; *Talisay*, *Banilak*, *Nato*, *Hitam*, Vis.; *Kalisay*, Pam.; *Lugo*, *Pandan*, Iloc.; *Indian Almond*, Indo-Eng.

USES.—The kernel is edible and has a very agreeable taste. It yields about 50 % of a fixed oil, sweet and savory. If left for some time, it deposits an abundance of stearin. It closely resembles oil of sweet almonds for which it, as well as the oil of Pili (*Canarium commune*, L.), which we have already described, makes a good substitute.

The trunk bark is astringent and in decoction is used for atonic diarrhœa and as a lotion for ulcers.

DECOCTION.—

Bark (ground and pounded)............12 grams.
Water..............................150 "
Simple syrup.......................40 "

To be given by the tablespoonful in 24 hours.

BOTANICAL DESCRIPTION.—A tree, 6–8 m. high. Branches horizontal and radiating from the trunk. Leaves purplish, bunched, cleft at the base, sometimes transversely ovate, sometimes oval, notched, glabrous. Petiole very short. Flowers axillary, racemose, with a scale at the base of the peduncle, some hermaphrodite and others lacking pistils. Staminate flowers: calyx downy within, with 5 lobes. Corolla wanting. Stamens

10, inserted on the calyx. Hermaphrodite flowers: pistil same length as stamens. Drupe, fleshy, inferior, oval with the borders turned upward containing a very hard and fibrous nut; seed long and sharp-pointed.

HABITAT.—Common in Luzon. In Manila it is cultivated extensively as an ornamental tree, especially along the Sabana Walk, General Solano Ave. and in Sampaloc and Malacañan.

Terminalia Chebula, Retz. (*T. reticulata*, Toth.; *Bucida cuminata*, Blanco.)

NOM. VULG.—*Diĝlas, Diglas*, Tag.; *Black Myrobalan Tree*, Indo-Eng.

USES.—The ripe fruit, called *myrobalans* in India, is purgative and six of them pounded up and given in decoction operate with certainty, producing 4 or 5 copious evacuations without nausea or other disagreeable symptoms. Dr. Waring has experimented with them and recommends them highly. The taste may be made more agreeable by adding a little cinnamon to the decoction. Dymock states that three fruits are sufficient, and Dr. Hove gives one as the effective dose. This lack of agreement may be explained by the fact that the fruits are of different sizes, and probably Waring refers to those of medium size. Contrary to what one would imagine, judging from its purgative action, the fruit contains astringent principles, and makes an effective injection for leucorrhœa as a substitute for nut galls. It is also of some merit in the treatment of piles.

The green fruit is highly esteemed by Radja Kalikesen as a carminative, tonic and purgative. Dr. Twining also mentions these same properties, recommends it as a tonic and aperient of great benefit in atony of the digestive organs and expresses surprise that the Europeans make no use of it. According to the same author a dose in the treatment of diarrhœa and dysentery is 4 grams twice a day. He quotes a case of hypertrophy of the spleen which he cured with this fruit.

Some of the leaves bear horn-shaped galls, flattened, narrow and hollow. They are caused by an insect which stings the leaves and deposits its eggs in them. These leaves with galls are astringent and very useful and effective in dysentery and diarrhœa, especially that of children. The dose for a child of more than one year is 0.40 to 0.50 gram a day, administered in fractional doses every two or three hours.

Fridolin has obtained from its fruit an acid, which he calls *chebulinic* ($C_{28}H_{25}O_{10}$) and presumes to be a mixture of tannic and gallic acids. As Stenhouse had formerly indicated, no principle has been discovered to which the purgative properties can be attributed, unless it be a green oleo-resin turned red by nitric acid, obtained from the fruit by Apery.

BOTANICAL DESCRIPTION.—A tree of the second order, with leaves 3′ long, alternate, lanceolate, entire and glabrous. Petioles short. Flowers terminal, in spiked panicles. Calyx superior, bell-shaped, colored, downy within, 5-toothed. Corolla wanting. Stamens 10, longer than the calyx. Anthers roundish. Ovary cylindrical. Style curved and longer than the stamens. Stigma simple. Fruit ovoid, 2–4 centimeters long, 5–10 acute angles, wrinkled, with blackish, hard, compact mesocarp; contains 1 seed.

HABITAT.—Batangas, San Mateo. Blooms in May.

Quisqualis Indica, L. (*Q. villosa*, Roxb.; *Q. spinosa*, Nares.)

NOM. VULG.—*Tagaraw*, *Niogniogan*, Tag.; *Tangolon*, Vis.; *Babebabe*, Pam.; *Tartaraw*, Iloc.

USES.—The fruit contains a kernel that tastes much like cacao, for which reason the Tagalogs call it "niogniogan" (like cacao). This kernel is a powerful anthelmintic, used also in India, the dose for a child of 4 years being 2–4, pulverized and mixed with a little molasses or sugar. A large dose produces hiccough, a fact well known to the natives. Dr. Bouton states that they may cause convulsions and other similar nervous disorders.

They yield a light green, fixed oil, probably the active principle of the plant.

Botanical Description.—A climbing shrub, 6–9° high, whose stem is thickly set with long, opposite thorns. Leaves in stars of 3, oblong, acute, entire, glabrous. Petioles very short. Flowers white, veined with red, in axillary spikes. Calyx very long, nearly cylindrical, 5-toothed. Corolla, 5 petals, inserted between the teeth of the calyx. Stamens 10, inserted on the calyx-tube, shorter than the corolla, arranged in 2 series, 5 higher than the rest. Style the same length as the stamens, united throughout nearly its entire length with the wall of the calyx-tube from which it separates near the stigma. Stigma rather bulky. Fruit 1′ long, ovoid, 5 sharp ridges in the woody, fragile, mahogany-colored pericarp, which contains a pointed kernel at one end.

Habitat.—San Mateo, and along the shores of Luzon. Blooms in May.

MYRTACEÆ.

Myrtle Family.

Psidium pomiferum, L. (*P. aromaticum* and *P. pyriferum*, Blanco.)

Nom. Vulg.—*Guayabas*, Sp.; *Bayabas, Guayabas, Tayabas*, Tag., and other dialects; *Guava*, Eng.

Uses.—The green fruit is acid and very astringent. The stage of development when it is best eaten raw, is just before it ripens, for then its acidity has lessened, it is not astringent and does not emit the strong odor, so disagreeable to many, that characterizes the ripe fruit. When fully ripe it is sweet, non-astringent and very bland, and this is the stage when it is best for making the jellies and preserves so popular in the Philippines.

The bark, especially that of the root, is highly astringent and a decoction of it is used for diarrhœa and as a wash for ulcers. Dr. Waitz has successfully used the following formula in treating the chronic diarrhœa of children:

Root bark of guava..................	15 grams.
Water............................	180 "

Boil till reduced one half. Dose, a tablespoonful every 2 or 3 hours according to age.

A decoction of the shoots is very useful in stomatitis, cutaneous eruptions and ulcers. Dr. Waitz advises his formula in prolapsus recti of children. It is also of value as an injection in diarrhœa and dysentery.

Botanical Description.—A tree, about 10° high, branches square and somewhat winged towards the ends. Leaves opposite, oblong, obtuse, downy, aromatic in odor. Petiole very short. Flowers axillary, solitary, white and fragrant. Calyx adherent, the border breaking in 3, 4 or more unequal parts when the flower expands. Corolla, 5–6 petals, inserted on the calyx, curved downward. Stamens numerous, inserted in the calyx, as long as the corolla. Style same length as stamens, awl-shaped. Fruit somewhat pear-shaped, with 4 or 5 ribs that disappear at maturity, 4 or more cells each with many small, hard, irregular seeds. In the Philippines the fruit grows to the size of a small pear.

Eugenia Jambolana, Lam. (*Calyptranthes Jambolana*, Willd. and Blanco; *Syzygium Jambolanum*, DC. and Blanco.)

Nom. Vulg.—*Lomboy, Duhat, Duat,* Tag., Pam., Vis.; *Jambul* or *Black Plum*, Indo-Eng.

Uses.—The ripe fruit, so dark a purple in color that it seems black, is edible and very popular in the Philippines, though not considered choice. Some suppose it to be harmful, but it is in reality very easy of digestion.

The syrup of the fruit juice, and the decoction of the trunk bark are both very efficacious in the treatment of diarrhœa and dysentery.

SYRUP OF JAMBUL.—

Juice of ripe fruit	500 grams.
White sugar	950 "

Dissolve in a covered water-bath, strain through woolen cloth and put aside.

DOSE.—60–200 grams a day.

The juice of the leaves is also used to treat diarrhœa. A Hindoo physician, Bhavaprakasa, advises the following receipt:

Juice of leaves of lomboy " " " " manga Pulp of *Terminalia chebula*	āā 4 grams.

Give in one dose in a little goat's milk and honey.

A sort of wine of very agreeable taste is made from the fruit juice. Lately the powdered seed has been recommended in the treatment of glycosuria or at least it has been stated that its internal use lessens and finally abolishes the glucose from the urine of the patient. It has even been affirmed that while under this treatment the patient may eat glucose-forming foods without fear of glycosuria supervening.

The chemical composition of the seeds are as follows:

Essential oil	Traces.
Chlorophyl and fatty matters	0.37
Resin soluble in alcohol and ether	0.30
Gallic acid	1.65
Albumin	1.25
Pigment soluble in water	2.70
Water	10.00
Insoluble residuum	83.73
	100.00

Dujardin-Beaumetz has tested the therapeutic value of these seeds in diabetes but with negative results. Scott has maintained that by adding the powdered seed to a mixture of malt and starch, fermentation is impeded; but Dr. Villy in the laboratory of Dujardin-Beaumetz has demonstrated that such is not the case. Contrary to the opinions of those physicians who stated that "jambul" was capable of causing the glucose to disappear from the urine of diabetic patients without concurrent diabetic regimen, Dujardin-Beaumetz observed in his trials of the drug that the slightest relaxation of the regimen was followed by an increase of glucose. Under the influence of the medicine in doses of 2–10 grams daily, at the same time maintaining a strict diabetic diet, the Parisian therapeutist noted that the glucose disappears from the third to the fifth day; but this occurred only in cases of medium intensity, whereas in severe cases the medication produced no effect. Upon stopping the treatment the sugar reappeared.

BOTANICAL DESCRIPTION.—A tree, 15–20° high, with leaves opposite, acute, entire, ovate, lustrous, very smooth. Flowers in racemose panicles with peduncles opposite. Calyx superior, with 5 small teeth and a deciduous cover composed of many orbicular pieces joined below. Corolla none. Stamens numerous, inserted on the edge of the calyx. Stigma pointed. Fruit black, oval, crowned with the calyx; one long cylindrical seed with membranaceous epidermis.

HABITAT.—Common all over the Archipelago. Blooms in February.

MELASTOMACEÆ.

Melastoma malabatrichum, L. (*M. obvolutum*, Jack.; *M. aspera* and *obvoluta*, Blanco.)

NOM. VULG.—*Granatis*, Tag.

USES.—A decoction of the leaves is of use as an astringent in diarrhœa and dysentery. A decoction of the bark is used as a gargle for aphthæ and catarrhal sore throat, and as a wash for ulcers and the itch.

The fruit is edible, resembling slightly the currant; it has doubtless received the name "granatis" on account of its many seeds.

BOTANICAL DESCRIPTION.—Small tree, with opposite branches, their ends covered with hairs. Leaves opposite, 3-nerved, 1′ long, very rough with short hairs. Flowers carmine, in terminal panicles. Stamens 10. Filaments alternating violet and straw-color.

HABITAT.—Mountains of Angat and San Mateo.

LYTHRACEÆ.

Loosestrife Family.

Ammannia vesicatoria, Roxb. (*A. baccifera*, L.; *A. Indica*, Lam.; *A. debilis* and *Celosia nana*, Blanco.)

NOM. VULG.—*Bias pogo*, Tag.; *Blistering Ammannia*, Indo-Eng.

USES.—The leaves contain an irritant and acrid principle that renders them vesicant when applied to the skin. The Pharmacopœia of India quotes Sir W. O'Shaughnessy to the effect that plasters made of the bruised leaves even when renewed every half hour require 24 hours to raise a blister and at the same time cause severe pain. He found it much more painful than cantharides and much less prompt to act. Dr. Dymock has prepared an ethereal tincture of the leaves and obtained with it results very different from those just mentioned; this is not surprising in view of the fact that the tincture holds in solution in a small quantity of ether, a considerable amount of the vesicant principle. This tincture has the same color as the "epispastic" of the English Pharmacopœia, causes less pain and rapidly raises a good blister, facts of which I have convinced myself by the use of a small quantity sent me from Bombay in 1891.

Dr. Bholanauth Bose recommends the internal use of the juice of the leaves as a remedy for chronic diseases of the spleen; this treatment, however, has caused severe pain and is absolutely uncertain in effect.

In Concan the juice of the leaves is given mixed with food to animals in heat, for its anaphrodisiac action. The fresh or dried plant is given in decoction mixed with ginger in intermittent fevers.

If the ethereal tincture be evaporated a resinous residue remains that has not been studied, but appears to be the vesicant principle. This tincture should be made from the dried leaves to avoid hydration of the ether.

BOTANICAL DESCRIPTION.—A small plant with stem red, straight, quadrate, ramose. Leaves opposite, lanceolate, and fringed with hairs. Flowers axillary, small, red, solitary. Peduncles short. Calyx inferior, bell-shaped, with 8-toothed border, the 4 alternate teeth larger. Corolla none. Nectary bell-shaped, surrounding the ovary, shorter than the calyx, with 4 toothlets which lengthening form the filaments of as many stamens. Anthers 4-celled. Ovary of 4 pluriovulate locules. Style almost wanting. Stigma fluted. Seed vessel glabrous, horizontally dehiscent, containing 15 or more angular seeds joined to a common axis.

HABITAT.—It grows in the marshes of Mandaloyon.

Lawsonia alba, Lam. (*L. spinosa*, L.; *L. inermis*, Roxb.)

NOM. VULG.—*Cinamomo del país (native cinnamon)*, Sp.-Fil.; *Henna, Camphire, Samphire*, Indo-Eng.

USES.—This is a very popular plant in the Orient, for many races use its leaves to impart a reddish-yellow stain to the nails, finger tips and palms of the hands. There is a tradition among the Mohammedans that the Prophet once called this plant "the best of all herbs." The leaf in form of a dry powder is sold in the bazars of India under the name of "henna"; mixed with water it gives it a yellow color, and when boiled the tone of the liquid becomes darker; the addition of an alkali turns it brown. In Persia they add indigo to this solution and use it as a hair dye.

The Hindoos apply the bruised leaves to the soles of the feet of small-pox patients, their purpose being to prevent the spread of the eruption to the eyes. They also use it locally in a disease known among them as "burning of the feet." Grierson and Waring obtained good results in this disease by making a paste of the bruised leaves and vinegar; cases that resisted such treatment yielded completely to a brisk rubbing of the feet with a simple paste of the leaf. The decoction and the bruised leaves are also used locally for contusions.

The bark has been given in jaundice, hypertrophy of the spleen, calculi of various sorts, leprosy and stubborn skin diseases, as an alterative. In decoction it is applied to burns.

An English physician, Dr. Newton, made an extract of the leaves and flowers with which he pretended to cure leprosy; it was but one more useless drug in the long list used to combat that terrible disease. The dose of the extract is a teaspoonful daily, given in 2 doses.

The juice of the leaves is given in sweetened water in some countries as a remedy for spermatorrhœa.

The flowers are given in decoction for headache and the fruit is emmenagogue.

Botanical Description.—A small tree, about 12° high. Leaves opposite, lanceolate, broad, entire, glabrous and tough, the edges turned downwards. Flowers yellowish-white, terminal in racemose panicles with opposite peduncles. Calyx inferior, bell-shaped, 4 acute sepals. Corolla, 4 petals, longer than the calyx. Stamens 8, inserted by pairs on the segments of the calyx, alternating with and longer than the petals. Anther kidney-shaped. Ovary at the bottom of the calyx. Styles of the same length as the stamens. Stigma obtuse. Seed vessel a little larger than a pea, globose, 4 chambers, many seeds.

HABITAT.—Common all over the Archipelago. Blooms in July.

Punica Granatum, L.

NOM. VULG.—*Granada*, Sp. and Fil. dialects; *Pomegranate*, Eng.

USES.—The decoction of the tender leaves is used as a gargle and wash in angina, aphthæ, and wounds within the buccal cavity.

The peel of the fruit is highly astringent and in decoction is a useful agent in treating chronic diarrhœa, and locally in injections of lotions for leucorrhœa and inflamed hæmorrhoids. It should not be given when rectal tenesmus exists. The Pharmacopœia of India contains the following formula for preparing the decoction of the peel:

Pulp of the fruit, mashed............. 60 grams.
Water............................600 "

Boil for 15 minutes in a covered vessel, cool, filter and add water enough to make a liter. Dose, 30–50 grams per diem.

This preparation is also used in astringent gargles and injections. For internal use the decoction is rendered more active by adding a small quantity of cloves or cinnamon. This mixture with the addition of opium gives excellent results in the treatment of diarrhœa among the natives of India and is highly recommended by Dr. Kirkpatrick.

The most important part of the pomegranate, however, is its root, the bark of which is a very efficient tænifuge and the most astringent portion of the plant. It should be used fresh, as drying destroys its activity and gives negative results. Many failures to expel the tænia are probably due to this fact. According to Béranger-Férand the root gives 25% to 40% of cures, whereas pumpkin seeds give but 5% to 10%.

Decoction.—(French Codex.)

Fresh bark of pomegranate root........	60 grams.
Water	750 "

Macerate 6 hours, boil over slow fire till reduced to 500 grams. Strain. Administer fasting, in 3 doses half an hour apart. The evening before the patient should eat a light meal and take a cathartic in order that the intestinal canal may contain the smallest possible quantity of fæcal matter. After taking the third dose of the decoction the patient should take a mild purgative such as 30 grams of castor oil to expel the tænia. This preparation has a most disagreeable taste. It is better to give the "tannate of pelletierine," a compound of tannin and one of the alkaloids that Tanret discovered in pomegranate root. A sufficient dose of tannate of pelletierine is 30–40 centigrams in wafer form, followed by a purge and with the other precautions and preparatory measures mentioned above. It causes toxic symptoms similar to those produced by curare, according to the experimental studies of Dujardin-Beaumetz and Rochenière. Its action is upon the ends of the motor nerves. A dose of 40 centigrams may cause in man such symptoms of intoxication as vertigo, inverted vision and muscular paralysis. Pelletierine should not be administered to children, but Béranger-Férand states that the tannate may be safely given them, as follows:

Tannate of pelletierine.............	0.30 grams.
Sweetened water....................	40.00 "

A coffee-spoonful of this solution contains 0.03 gram of the tannate, and this quantity may be given to a child, in a little milk. If no symptoms supervene within one-half hour give another similar dose and so on up to 3 or 4 doses or .12 gm. in all. After the last dose give the purgative as a routine. It is certainly imprudent to trust the administration of such a drug to any one incapable of recognizing the symptoms of intoxication, and as no one but a physician can judge the effects of the alkaloid he himself should remain with the patient until the efficient dose has been absorbed. This is manifestly impractical and we therefore maintain that the alkaloid is not suited for the treatment of children.

An analysis of the root bark made by the French chemist Tanret revealed the presence of four alkaloids: pelletierine, iso-pelletierine ($C_8H_{15}NO$), pseudo-pelletierine ($C_9H_{16}NO$), and methylpeletierine ($C_9H_{17}NO$).

BOTANICAL DESCRIPTION.—A shrub 6–9° high with branches terminating in thorns; some of the branches abort and form thorns. Leaves simple, oval, oblong, without stipules, with short petioles. Flowers axillary, solitary or in pauciflorous cymes. Calyx, 4–8 sepals, persistent, fleshy, yellow or red. Corolla, 4–8 petals, imbricated. Stamens numerous, free. Style 1. Stigma thick. Fruit with leathery rind, about size of small apple, packed with seeds, each imbedded in a small amount of crisp, juicy pulp.

ONAGRACEÆ.

Evening Primrose Family.

Jussiæa suffruticosa, L. (*J. villosa*, Lam.; *J. erecta*, Blanco.)

NOM. VULG.—*Malapoko*, Tag.

USES.—The entire plant reduced to a pulp and mixed with milk is used in India to treat dysentery. Ainslie states that the decoction is employed as a vermifuge and purgative.

BOTANICAL DESCRIPTION.—An herb with square stem, leaves alternate, lanceolate, nearly entire, glabrous. Flowers axillary, yellow, solitary. Calyx of 4–5 lobules. Corolla, 4 lanceolate petals inserted between the divisions of the calyx. Stamens 8, of these 4 alternate being shorter. Ovary very long, inferior, with 4 many-ovuled locules. Style the same length as the stamens. Stigma 4-lobuled. Seed vessels very long, with faint longitudinal ridges, crowned by the remains of the calyx, 4 pluriovulate locules.

HABITAT.—In the arable fields and along the banks of rivers. Blooms in January and March.

PASSIFLORACEÆ.

Passion Flower Family.

Carica Papaya, L.

NOM. VULG.—*Papaya,* in many Phil. dialects; *Papaya, Papaw,* Eng.

USES.—The decoction of the leaves is used locally in sores and atonic ulcers, followed by a poultice of the boiled and mashed leaves. The natives use the cold infusion of the leaves to wash clothes spotted with blood and the spots disappear rapidly by virtue of the ferment papain which digests the fibrin. The infusion is also very useful as a wash for sores and gangrenous ulcers, modifying their appearance very rapidly.

Before proceeding further it is desirable to give a description of papain, a digestive ferment which exists throughout the whole plant, fruit, trunk, leaves and petioles; it is contained in the milky juice which exudes from all these parts when cut. This juice was studied simultaneously by Wurtz in France and Peckolt in Brazil. The best method of collecting it is to make several superficial, longitudinal incisions in the green fruit without removing it from the tree; immediately an abundance of juice appears in the incisions and coagulates rapidly. The best time to do this is the early morning. The fruit does not suffer by this process but continues developing and ripens perhaps more rapidly, at the same time improving in flavor, becoming sweeter; the seeds, however, atrophy and lose their power of germination. Peckolt gives the following as the composition of the juice:

A substance analogous to caoutchouc........	4.525
Awa..................................	2.424

Soft resin	0.110
Brown resin	2.776
Albuminoids	0.006
Papayotin (Papain of Wurtz)	1.059
Extractive matter	5.303
Malic acid	0.443
Peptic material and salts	7.100
Water	74.971

The milky juice is neutral and coagulates rapidly, separating in two parts: a kind of insoluble pulp and a limpid colorless serum. If combined with fibrin, raw meat, white of egg or gluten it gradually softens them and completely dissolves them in 3 or 4 hours *in vitro* at 40° C. Combined with milk it coagulates it and soon precipitates the casein which is also dissolved a little later. It digests lumbricoids and tape-worms and the false membrane of croup, in a few hours. According to Wurtz and Bouchut papain is prepared as follows:

The fluid juice or the aqueous solution of the milky exudate is precipitated by the addition of ten times the volume of alcohol. The precipitate, after treating again with concentrated alcohol, is dissolved in water and the addition of subacetate of lead eliminates the albuminoids and peptones but does not precipitate the papain. The liquid is filtered and the lead salts separated by means of a current of hydrogen sulphide. It is filtered again and alcohol added gradually, which process first precipitates whatever sulphate of lead may have passed through the filter, and then the papain.

Papain is an amorphous substance, perfectly white, soluble in water, insipid, odorless. An aqueous solution, if shaken violently, foams like a solution of soap. Boiling makes it turbid and when concentrated it has a slightly astringent taste. It is precipitated by hydrochloric, nitric, picric and the metaphosphoric acids. Trommer's test gives it a beautiful blue violet color which, on boiling, changes to a red violet.

It is an extremely active digestive ferment, comparable with pepsin, but superior to the latter because it does not require an acid medium, as its digestive action takes place even in the presence of an alkaline medium and of antiseptic substances such as boric acid, phenol, etc. It is given in doses of 10–40 centigrams in different vehicles such as water, wine, etc. It should be given after meals carefully and properly diluted, in order that its action may not be exerted upon the gastric mucous membrane itself. Its use is contraindicated in gastric ulcer.

A watery solution prepared by macerating the green fruit has been used effectively to remove blemishes from the face, leaving the skin clean and smooth. The natives use little pieces of the green fruit to remove freckles (which they call *pecas*). The ripe fruit is edible and its taste quite agreeable; in some of the Malay Islands it is given for dysentery, but it must be remembered that the ripe fruit does not contain papain.

The pure exudate is given to children as an anthelmintic in doses of 2–6 grams with a little molasses, but it is not so harmless that it may be used with impunity in this form, Moncorvo and others having reported cases of peritonitis with symptoms suggestive of cholera following its use. It is drastic and digestive in addition to its anthelmintic action, but according to Rabuteau, boiling destroys the first property without affecting the others. Dr. Lemarchand of the island of Mauritius gives the following anthelmintic prescription:

Juice of papaya and molasses...... āā 1 tablespoon.
Add gradually while shaking the mixture.
Boiling water.....................4 tablespoons.

Cool and administer in one dose followed immediately by 30 grams of castor oil. For a child, one-half dose.

This treatment frequently causes colic, for the relief of which the author advises an injection of sweetened water. Sir O'Shaughnessy's prescription is preferable:

20–60 drops of the exudate in a little sweetened water. This dose cannot cause any untoward symptoms and is efficient in expelling both lumbricoids and tæniæ.

The triturated seeds may be given internally in doses of 1–2 grams with milk or molasses to expel lumbricoids. Analysis has revealed in the seeds the presence of a resinous oil, an oleaginous material of disagreeable odor and taste called by Peckolt *caricin*, a fatty acid, papayic acid and a resin. In India the seeds are considered emmenagogue. In some countries they wrap meat in papaya leaves for several hours before eating in order to soften it. For the same purpose they sometimes boil the meat in water containing a few leaves or pieces of the green fruit; some even go to the length of saying that it is only necessary to hang a piece of meat in a papaya tree for a time in order to soften it.

The decoction of the green fruit is given internally for indigestion, a treatment common in the provinces of Bulacan and Pampanga. The milky juice is used to remove corns and Dr. Daruty offers the following prescription for eczema and psoriasis:

Exudate of papaya	1.00	grams.
Borax (powdered)	0.60	"
Water	16.00	"

Mix.

Paint the affected part with feather or brush, 2–3 times a day. The same solution may be used for softening corns.

Botanical Description.—Trees 15° in height, trunk covered with large leaf scars, wood soft and brittle, the long-petioled, palmately-lobed leaves growing in a crown and giving the tree the general appearance of a palm. Flowers diœcious. Staminate tree: Flowers loosely clustered on long, hanging stems. Calyx, 5–6 teeth. Corolla tubular, 1′ long, limb divided into 5 oval parts. Stamens 10, inserted in the throat. Style short, awl-shaped. Pistillate tree: Flowers much larger, sessile, in axils of leaves. Calyx 5-toothed. Corolla large, 5 lanceolate petals curved outward, fleshy. Stigmas 5, fringed. Fruit about size of child's head or smaller, somewhat pear-shaped, juicy, pulp melon-like, 1 compartment with numerous seeds, each in a mucilaginous aril.

CUCURBITACEÆ.

Gourd Family.

Trichosanthes palmata, Roxb. (*T. tricuspis,* Mig.; *T. lucioniana,* Bares.)

NOM. VULG.—(?).

USES.—Roxburgh states that the fruit is toxic and sometimes used to kill crows. Dymock states that the leaf is smoked in Bombay as a remedy for asthma.

The extremely bitter taste of the fruit and rind induced Sir W. O'Shaughnessy to examine it for tonic and purgative properties; doses as high as 0.20 gram 3 times a day failed to exert a purgative effect. The root is used in veterinary medicine particularly for pneumonia. Mixed with equal parts of colocynth it is applied to carbuncles. In combination with equal parts of *Terminalia chebula* and ginger it is made into a sweetened infusion for internal use in gonorrhœa.

BOTANICAL DESCRIPTION.—A climber with broad, heart-shaped, serrate, 7-lobulate leaves. Flowers monœcious; staminate white and racemose; pistillate solitary, growing at the base of the staminate racemes. Staminate receptacle tubular, calyx inserted on the border of the receptacle, 5 sepals. Corolla, 5 petals. Stamens 5, of which 4 are in pairs. Pistillate: the receptacle dilates in its lower part in form of a globose vase and encloses the unilocular pluriovulate ovary. Fruit ovoid or pyriform, scarlet when fresh, orange-yellow when dry. Seeds of irregular form, somewhat triangular. Kernel oily.

HABITAT.—Luzon.

T. anguina, L. (*T. amara*, Blanco.)

NOM. VULG.—*Salagsalag*, *Pakupis*, *Salimpokot*, *Kukubitan*, *Halahala*, *Buyokbuyok*, Tag.; *Tabobog*, *Kukubitan*, *Pukopukot*, *Kuragda*, Vis., Pam.

T. cucumerina, L.

NOM. VULG.—Probably the same as *T. anguina*.

USES.—The fruit of *T. anguina* is purgative, emetic and anthelmintic. The natives use an infusion of the filamentous, reticulate portion surrounding the seeds, in doses of 0.50–0.60 gm., according to P. Blanco.

The second species, *T. cucumerina*, has a wider use. In India it is regarded as a febrifuge and laxative and is commonly given with some aromatic. Ainslie notes that the leaves, as well as the fruit, are bitter and purgative and that the Tamuls use them for their laxative and stomachic effect. Drury states that on the Malabar coast the seeds have a considerable reputation as a remedy for functional disorders of the stomach. Although the green fruit is very bitter the natives of that region use it as a condiment. The tender stems and the dry capsules, both bitter and purgative, are given in infusion and in a sweetened solution, as an aid to digestion. The seeds are febrifuge and anthelmintic. The juice of the leaves is emetic and that of the roots purgative. The decoction of the stem is expectorant.

In Bombay the plant is considered febrifuge, and is given in decoction with ginger, *Swertia chirata*, and sugar. The Mohammedan authors say that the *T. cucumerina* is effective in expelling lumbricoids and one of them mentions the following as a cure for stubborn fevers:

Seeds of *T. cucumerina*.... ....No. 180.
Seeds of coriander or cumin..........No. 180.
Boiling water ....200 grams.

Let stand over night, filter, add a little sugar, administer in 2 doses morning and evening.

In Concan they use the juice of the leaves as a liniment in remittent fevers, rubbing the hepatic region and in fact the entire body.

Botanical Description.—*T. anguina*, L., is a vine with 5-angled stem, bearing tendrils and spattered with white dots. Leaves heart-shaped, with 5 acute lobules, spiny-toothed. Petioles with a bifid swelling at their bases. Flowers white, monœcious. Staminate: calyx 5-toothed with dotted borders; corolla, 5 fringed petals; stamens 3; anthers 3, entirely united and forming a cylinder. Pistillate: 3 glandules in the corolla tube; style long; stigmas 3. Fruit ribbed, long, the compartments formed by reticular partitions; contains many irregular seeds, one border sharp, the other obtuse, covered by a very thin aril.

The *T. cucumerina*, L., is less common, bears a spindle-shaped or obovate fruit, is hairy and lacks ribs. Its seeds are ovoid, very smooth, encircled by a narrow wing. The reticulum within the fruit is similar to that of the foregoing species.

Habitat.—Common in all parts of the islands. Blooms in October.

Lagenaria vulgaris, Ser.

Nom. Vulg.—*Common Gourd, Bottle Gourd, Calabash*, Eng.

Var. **Lagenaria Gourda**, Ser. (*Cucurbita lagenaria oblonga*, Blanco.)

Nom. Vulg.—*Calabaza de peregrino*, Sp.; *Pilgrim's Gourd*, Eng.

Var. **L. courgourda**, Ser.

Nom. Vulg.—*Tabayag*, Tag.

Var. **L. clavata**, Ser. (*C. lagenaria villosa*, Blanco.)

Nom. Vulg.—*Calabaza blanca*, Sp.; *Opo*, Tag.; *White Gourd*, Eng.

Uses.—The three above-mentioned varieties of *L. vulgaris*, Ser., are commonly grouped under the name calabaza (gourd). All have the same action and hence the same therapeutic application. The green portion of the rind is bitter and possesses purgative and emetic properties. The decoction of the tender shoots is expectorant; in addition it appears to possess purgative properties and in India is used in jaundice.

The part of the plant most generally used is the seeds, the tænifuge properties of which are well known. Its action, however, is not always certain, which may be as truly said of all other known tænifuges. The seeds have the advantage of lacking the disgusting taste characteristic of other remedies of the same class; the taste is almost neutral and a little sugar conceals it completely. The dose is unlimited; some take 15 grams, others as high as 100, and no unpleasant symptoms of any kind have been reported. The only precaution to be observed is to give the patient a purgative 1–2 hours after his dose.

Heckel has analyzed the seeds and found a resin which he calls *pepo-resina;* it exists in the greenish pellicle that envelopes the embryo and appears to be the active principle of the seeds. Its dose is 0.80–1.00 gram (Dujardin-Beaumetz), the product of 250 grams of the seeds. The dose of 100 grams of the seeds mentioned above is very small, if the pepo-resin represents the entire active principle, for 100 grams of the seeds would only contain about 40 centigrams.

Botanical Description.—A very familiar vine, clammy, pubescent and musk-scented; large leaves, long-stalked flowers, white petals, greenish veiny fruit usually club-shaped or enlarged at the apex, the hard rind used for vessels, dippers, and so forth. It is noteworthy that none of the tænifuge varieties mentioned bears yellow fruit.

Luffa Ægyptiaca, Mill. (*L. pentandra*, Roxb.; *L. petola*, Ser.; *Momordica operculata*, Blanco.)

Nom. Vulg.—Probably bears the same names as the *Trichosanthes*.

Uses.—The root is a hydragogue cathartic even in minute doses. The fruit is emollient by virtue of the large quantity of mucilage it contains, but it is more interesting for other properties. When cut in two, deprived of epidermis and seeds, and washed until none of the mucilage remains, there is left a fibrous skeleton, a sort of skein of interwoven nets that constitutes the so-called vegetable sponge. It serves the same purpose as a sponge and has the advantages that its fibers do not rot and that they are easily kept clean. In view of its cheapness and plentifulness in the Philippines the above advantages should suffice to bring it into universal use for the toilet, for surgical purposes and for cleaning in general.

Botanical Description.—A vine with square, glabrous stem. Leaves alternate, cordate, 3–5-lobulate, dentate, rough, 5–7-nerved. Petioles short. Flowers monœcious. Staminate in axillary panicles; calyx bell-shaped; corolla yellow, 5 oval petals, borders entire; stamens 3; filaments short; two thick ones divide high up in 2 parts, thus giving the appearance of 5 stamens in all. Pistillate axillary, calyx adherent, 5 pointed sepals; corolla, 5 nearly triangular petals, finely dentate; style thick, short, the base encircled by 3 glandules; stigma cordate. Ovary, 3 pseudo-locules formed by the central union of the placentas; pluriovulate. Fruit oblong, terminating at the apex in a deciduous lid or cover, marked with 8 or 10 black longitudinal lines; the interior reticulate, 3 compartments with many seeds, oval, black, flat with thin borders. The natives do not distinguish between this specimen and the *Trichosanthes*, but it is to be noted that the corolla of the former is not ravelled or fringed.

Habitat. Common in Luzon and Panay. Blooms in January.

Momordica balsamina, L.

Nom. Vulg.—*Ampalaya*, *Ampalea*, Tag.; *Amargoso*, Sp.-Fil.; *Paria*, Iloc.; *Apalia*, Pam.; *Balsamina*, Sp.; *Balsam Apple*, Eng.

M. charanta, L. (*M. muricata*, Willd.; *M. cylindrica*, Blanco.)

Nom. Vulg.—The same as of *M. balsamina*.

Uses.—The fruit of both varieties is edible, though a bitter principle gives it such an intensely bitter taste that it is intolerable to the unaccustomed palate. It is eaten raw as a salad, or cooked with meat or fish. The juice of the leaves is prescribed internally as a purgative and anthelmintic. In Concan it is given alone or combined with aromatics, in bilious disorders as an emetic and purgative; externally they use it as an ointment for the itch and other skin diseases; in India it is mixed with cinnamon, pepper, rice and oil of *Hydnocarpus inebrians*, Vahl.

The fruit and leaves are used internally for worms and externally for leprosy. Some Hindoo writers state that the fruit is tonic and stomachic, and that it is useful in rheumatism, gout, diseases of the liver and spleen.

Botanical Description.—The first variety, *M. balsamina*, more common than the second, is a vine with angular stem and simple tendrils. Leaves, many serrate lobules with white dots on the ends. Flowers yellow, monœcious. Staminate solitary, peduncles very long, involucre cordate; calyx 5-lobed; corolla 5 petals; filaments simple, one separate, 2 approximated; anthers joined at their bases. Pistillate solitary; ovary, 3 locules and numerous ovules; stigma, 3 bifid divisions; fruit globose, narrowing at the ends, covered with tubercles; seeds numerous, lacking albumen, having red aril.

The second variety, *M. cylindrica*, has a downy stem, 5-angled with simple tendrils. The leaves are 5-lobuled, cordate, serrate, with short hairs on under surface. Melon hollow, glabrous, very long, cylindrical, tapering at the ends, covered with tubercles, some elevated in longitudinal lines, others depressed; seeds in 3 rows, enveloped in pulpy arils, white, long quadrangular, truncate above, encircled by 2 rows of obtuse toothlets.

HABITAT.—Both grow in all parts and are well known.

Citrullus Colocynthis, Schard. (*Cucumis Colocynthis*, L.)

NOM. VULG.—*Coloquíntida*, Sp.; *Colocynth*, *Bitter Apple*, Eng.

USES.—The part employed is the fruit pulp, official in all the pharmacopœias as a very energetic hydragogue cathartic. It is seldom given alone, but in combination with other drugs to modify its energy and its action.

In large doses it causes vomiting, bloody diarrhœa and a series of nervous phenomena that may end in death. Six to ten grams constitute a toxic dose. It operates with most force upon the large intestines and sympathetically upon the uterus.

DOSE.—Extract, 0.10–0.30 gram; powder, 0.30–1.00 gram.

The pulp contains a yellow, intensely bitter substance, quite soluble in water and in alcohol, discovered by Hubschmann and named by him *coloquintina*. The seeds contain 17% of an insipid oil.

BOTANICAL DESCRIPTION.—An herb with long, prostrate stems covered with stiff hairs. Leaves alternate, triangular, deeply cleft in 3 lobules that subdivide. Petioles long. The color of the leaves is pale green above, whitish or gray and covered with white hairs underneath. Flowers yellow, monœcious, solitary, axillary, with long peduncles. Staminate: receptacle cup-formed, 5 sepals and 5 free, yellow petals; 5 stamens in pairs, one free. Pistillate: the receptacle globose, covering the lower part of the ovary; 3 staminodes take the place of the stamens. Ovary unilocular, uniovulate, with a short style bearing 3 lobules at its apex. Fruit globose, 6–8 centimeters in diameter, smooth, greenish, later yellow with white spots; it is full of a whitish pulp that becomes dry and pithy and that contains the obovate seeds, smooth, flattened, brown, lacking albumen.

HABITAT.—Manila.

FICOIDEÆ.

Trianthema monogyna, L. (*T. obcordata*, Roxb.; *Portulaca toston* and *axiflora*, Blanco.)

NOM. VULG.—*Toston*, Tag.; *Alusiman*, *Ayam*, Vis.

USES.—This plant is edible, the natives eating it boiled, fried or in salad. The root is cathartic and is used powdered.

BOTANICAL DESCRIPTION.—A plant with prostrate stems, radiating branches. Leaves ensheathing the stem, opposite, oval, red-bordered, glabrous. Petioles with 2 stipules at the base and 2 small teeth near the middle. Flowers axillary, solitary, sessile. Calyx, 2 pointed sepals. Corolla, 5 oval petals. Stamens 15–20. Style simple. Seed vessels inversely pyramidal, dehiscence horizontal. Seeds numerous.

HABITAT.—Very common in the rice fields. Blooms in January.

UMBELLIFERÆ.

Parsley Family.

Hydrocotyle Asiatica, L.

NOM. VULG.—*Takip kohol*, *Takip suso*, Tag.; *Rabasa*, Sp.; *Indian Pennywort*, Indo-Eng.

USES.—Dr. Daruty, of Mauritius, has published a study of this plant, giving a résumé of its composition, therapeutic uses and physiological action. The writers of antiquity recognized the plant as a powerful alterative, tonic, diuretic, stimulant and vermifuge, especially effective in secondary syphilis and in ulcerative diseases of the skin.

Lépine and Boileau used it experimentally to treat leprosy and reported favorably; but later experience demonstrated that it did not exercise any specific effect, but benefited anæsthetic leprosy simply by improving the general condition of the patient.

The plant is official in the Pharmacopœia of India, as alterative, tonic and stimulant. It states that the drug has been found very useful in the treatment of secondary and constitutional syphilis, when the disease attacks the skin and subcutaneous tissue.

In Bombay it is a popular remedy for the mild dysentery of children, given as a decoction of 3 or 4 leaves with a little cumin seed and sugar; the bruised leaves are then applied to the umbilical region. In the Philippines the decoction of the leaves is given as a purge.

Dr. Dervegie reports good results in the treatment of eczema, administering the powdered leaf in dozes of 0.10 gram and applying locally the powder or an ointment of the same. The most marked and constant effects of the drug are a considerable increase of the urinary secretion, elevation of the temperature of the skin and profuse diaphoresis.

Dr. Boileau, quoted above, himself contracted leprosy of which he died; he experimented on himself with "hydrocotyle" and on one occasion a dose of 3 grams nearly proved fatal; tetanic symptoms supervened with suffocation, palpitation, epistaxis and rectal hemorrhage, abating finally with profuse sweating and diuresis.

Dr. Lépine, a pharmacist of Pondicherry, has analyzed the plant and isolated a substance that seems to be the active principle; he has named it *vallarin*, from "vallarai," the Tamul name of the plant. "Vallarin" is a thick, pale yellow oil of a piquant and persistent taste and an odor peculiar to the plant. It changes under the influence of air, moisture or heat and volatilizes at 120°. It is soluble in alcohol. The plant contains $\frac{8}{10}$ to 1 % of this oil, a dark resin and a green resin.

The Pharmacopœia of India gives 2 official formulæ, a powder and a cataplasm. The powdered leaf is given internally in doses of 0.30 to 1.50 grams and is applied locally to superficial ulcers.

Botanical Description.—Plant herbaceous with reniform or heart-shaped leaves, forming a sort of funnel, dotted with little hairs, dentate with white tips. Petioles very long, ensheathing each other by 2 wings at their bases. Flowers 3–4, sessile, springing directly from the root, greenish-white, growing in horizontal rows on either side of a short, common peduncle. Common involucre of 2–3 leaflets. Calyx adherent, flattened, faintly toothed. Corolla, 5 small petals, ovate. Stamens 5, equal in height, inserted on the receptacle, alternating with the petals. Filaments short. Anthers globose, cleft at the base in 2 diverging parts. Ovary inferior, cordate, much flattened. Styles 2, short. Stigmas simple. Fruit truncate, oval, downy, indehiscent, marked with furrows, with 2 compartments each containing a seed inserted on the wall.

Habitat.—Grows in shady and moist places. Blooms in July.

Carum copticum, Benth. (*C. ajowan*, DC.; *Ammi copticum*, L.; *A. glaucifolium*, Blanco; *Daucus opticus*, Pers.; *D. anisodorus*, Blanco.)

Nom. Vulg.—*Lamudio, Damoro,* Tag.; *Lamudio,* Vis.; *Caraway,* Eng.

Uses.—The fruit, of which both form and taste remind one of anise, is official in the Pharmacopœia of India as a carminative, stimulant and antispasmodic. It is indicated in flatulent colic, atonic dyspepsia and diarrhœa and gives very good results. It has been used in cholera, but is of little value in that disease. In moderate doses it increases salivary and gastric secretion.

The P. of India contains the 2 following official formulæ: *Oleum*—obtained from the fruit by distillation; is colorless when fresh but soon turns yellow; possesses the odor of the fruit and an acrid, burning taste. *Aqua*—600 grams of the fruit ground and mixed with 9 liters of water; this is distilled till 4½ liters have gone over, these constituting the "aqua cari."

DOSE.—1–2 drops of the essential oil in emulsion or on a piece of sugar. Of the "aqua," 30–60 grams as a carminative or to disguise the taste of other drugs (such as castor oil), thus frequently preventing nausea or vomiting.

BOTANICAL DESCRIPTION.—Leaves finely pinnately compound. Common petiole clasps the stem at the base. Flowers white, in flat compound umbels. The secondary peduncles 12. Flowerets of each partial umbel about 16. Calyx of flowerets superior, 5 globose sepals. Corolla, 5 equal petals, with rounded lobules. Stamens 5. Ovary tuberculate. Styles 2, very short. Seeds 2, united, furrowed and nearly glabrous at maturity.

HABITAT.—Cultivated in gardens. Blooms in October.

Fœniculum vulgare, Gaertn. (*F. officinale*, Allion; *F. panmorium*, DC.; *Anethum fœniculum*, Blanco.)

NOM. VULG.—*Anis*, Sp.; *Fennel*, Eng.

Coriandrum sativum, L. (*Cuminum cynimum*, Wall.)

NOM. VULG.—*Cominos*, *Culantro*, Sp.; *Coriander*, Eng.

USES.—The fruit of both species has the same therapeutical application being stomachic and carminative par excellence. It yields an aromatic essential oil with stimulant properties, popular because of its agreeable odor and taste.

As a rule the infusion is given in doses of one liter a day (15–30 grams of the seeds to one liter of water). The essence and the alcoholate are also employed, the former obtained by distillation, the latter by macerating the fresh seeds in alcohol. The dose of the essence, 4–8 drops on a piece of sugar or in potion; the alcoholate, 2–10 grams in sweetened water or infusion of aromatic herbs.

Both plants are official in the Spanish Pharmacopœia and they and their preparations are common in all drug stores.

HABITAT.—Common, cultivated in the gardens and well known.

BOTANICAL DESCRIPTION.—*F. vulgare:* Aromatic, stout, smooth herb, 4–6° high. Leaves with many slender thread-like divisions. Large umbel of yellow flowers, no involucre and no involucels. *C. sativum:* Low aromatic herb, leaves pinnately compound, small umbels with few rays, flowers white.

CORNACEÆ.

Dogwood Family.

Alangium Lamarkii, Thwaites. (*A. decapetalum, hexapetalum* and *tomentosum*, Lam.)

NOM. VULG.—(?)

USES.—According to Mooden Sheriff, the root bark is an efficient emetic in doses of 3 grams. In smaller doses it is febrifuge and produces nausea. The bark is extremely bitter; its reputation in the treatment of skin diseases is undeserved. It is a good substitute for ipecac, having given good results in all conditions in which the latter is indicated, with the exception of dysentery.

The febrifuge dose is 0.35–0.60 gram; alterative, 0.15–0.30 gram.

It is furthermore prescribed in India for syphilis and leprosy and is one of the many remedies used for the bites of rabid animals. The bruised leaves are applied to the joints of rheumatic patients.

BOTANICAL DESCRIPTION.—A tree 20–30 meters high, leaves alternate, persistent, petiolate, no stipules, oblong, dentate, acuminate, pinnately nerved. Flowers whitish, regular, hermaphrodite, in terminal cymes. Receptacle concave. Calyx short, 10-toothed. Corolla, 10 narrow, elongated ribbon-like petals. Stamens 30–40, filaments free and glabrous. Ovary inferior, held in the concavity of the receptacle, one-celled, with 1 seed, crowned by an epigynous disc, above which rises a simple style with dilated stigma. Fruit a globose drupe, crowned by the calyx, with 10 inconspicuous ribs. The putamen encloses an albuminous kernel.

HABITAT.—The mountains of San Mateo.

DICOTYLEDONOUS, GAMOPETALOUS.

RUBIACEÆ.

Madder Family.

Hymenodictyon excelsum, Wall. (*H. Horsfieldii*, Miq.; *Chinchona excelsa*, Roxb.; *Exostema Philippicum*, Blanco.)

Nom. Vulg.—*Huligaga*, Tag.

Uses.—The bark of this tree has a wide reputation in India as a tonic and febrifuge. The inner layer of the bark possesses astringent and bitter properties much like quinine. Ainslie states that it is used in India to tan hides and therapeutically where an astringent is required. O'Shaughnessy experimented with it in the hospital of the Medical College of Calcutta and reported good tonic and antipyretic effects.

In 1870, according to Dymock, Broughton analyzed the fresh bark and reported that the bitter taste was due to *esculin*, which after drying and coming in contact with decomposing organic matter is transformed into the almost tasteless *esculetin*. Naylor studied the bark at a later period, and attributed the bitterness to an alkaloid that he named *hymenodictyonine*. This substance exists in the form of a gelatinous mass, cream-colored, very hygroscopic. An ethereal solution, carefully evaporated, deposits it in the form of crystals. Its empirical form is $C_{23}H_{40}N_2$; it is probably volatile and is notable for its lack of oxygen. It differs from *quinoidine* in that it is inactive (?) and that in combination with platinum it retains less of this metal than does quinoidine. It differs from *paricine* in its proportion of hydrogen, and from *berberine* in containing more carbon. In the presence of sulphuric acid its solution assumes a yellow color, changing to wine-red and then to dark red.

Naylor extracted another principle which he found combined with the alkaloid in a soda precipitate of the latter; it is a product of the decomposition of a glucose, the formula of which is $C_{25}H_{49}O_7$. This compound remains insoluble when the alkaloid is treated with ether. Repeated boiling in alcohol renders it colorless. It is bitter, soluble in alcohol and dilute acids; insoluble in ether and chloroform. Reaction, neutral.

Botanical Description.—A large tree, with leaves opposite, oval, entire, acute, downy. Petioles long, flat above, with 2 stipules. Flowers axillary, in compound verticillate racemes. Calyx adherent, with 5 promptly deciduous teeth which leave a scar that also disappears. Corolla much longer than the calyx, funnel-form, the limb 5-cleft. Stamens 5, inserted near the middle of the tube. Filaments rudimentary. Anthers 2-celled. Style longer than the corolla. Stigma globose. Seed-vessel rather rough, ovoid, flattened, of 2 compartments, where are inserted numerous seeds, imbricated, circular, encircled by an entire wing.

Habitat.—Angat and the woods of San Mateo. Blooms in August. (P. Blanco states further that this tree grows to a height of about 3 yards in Angat and that it exhales a strong odor resembling that of vinegar at times, and again like that of tobacco.)

Oldenlandia corymbosa, L. (*O. biflora*, Lam.; *O. ramosa*, Roxb.; *O. herbacea* and *scrabrida*, DC.; *O. burmaniana*, Mig.)

Nom. Vulg.—Doubtful.

Uses.—The Sanscrit writers often mention this plant as an important remedy for the fevers due, according to their theories, to disordered bile, *i. e.*, remittent fevers, accompanied by gastric irritability and nervous depression. The entire plant is used to make a decoction, often combined with aromatics. Dymock observed in Goa that this plant could be gotten in all the shops of the herb-venders, and that it was widely used as an alterative in mild fevers in combination with "*Hydrocotyle Asiatica* and *Adiantum lunulatum.*"

In Concan they apply the juice to the hands and feet in fevers, giving at the same time a dose of one "tola" (6.80 grams) in sweetened water or milk. This juice is obtained by soaking the bruised plant in water. In remittent fever the decoction is also used as a liniment for the whole body. It is given internally for skin eruptions due to excessive heat, especially "lichen tropicus."

BOTANICAL DESCRIPTION.—A small herb, stem straight, about 30 centimeters high, glabrous, dichotomous. Leaves opposite, linear, green, lanceolate, stipulate. Flowers small, hermaphrodite, axillary, solitary, or in pairs, alternate or opposite. Calyx gamosepalous with 5 short teeth. Corolla gamopetalous, funnel-shaped. Stamens 5, free, inserted in the tube of the corolla. Ovary inserted in the hollow of the receptacle, 2 many-ovuled locules. Style simple, ending in a bifid stigma. Capsule rounded-oval, membranous. Seeds numerous, polyhedrous, albuminous, surface granular.

HABITAT.—In the rice fields.

Randia dumetorum, Lam. (*R. longispina*, DC.; *R. aculata*, Blanco; *R. stipulosa*, Miq.; *Gardenia spinosa*, Blanco.)

NOM. VULG.—*Sinampaga*, Tag.

USES.—The fruit is used in some parts of India to kill the fish in ponds and sluggish rivers, the same use to which they sometimes put the "Cocculus Indicus." It is prescribed as an emetic by the Sanscrit and Arabic medical authors of India. Mooden Sheriff ascribes its emetic properties to the pulp alone, the epicarp and seeds being inactive according to his authority. It is a substitute for ipecac even in the treatment of dysentery in which case the decoction of the trunk bark is also used.

The dried and powdered pulp is given in dose of 2.50 grams as an emetic and 1–2 grams as an antidysenteric. To prepare the fresh fruit for administration as an emetic, mash 2–3, macerate 15 minutes in 150–200 grams of water and filter. It acts in a few minutes and its effect may be hastened by giving tepid water or tickling the fauces.

BOTANICAL DESCRIPTION.—A shrub with straight, thorny stem, leaves sessile, springing from the buds, occurring in threes, obtusely lanceolate, entire, glabrous. Flowers solitary or in pairs, very fragrant. Calyx gamosepalous with 10 toothlets. Corolla twisted, arched, cleft in the middle, throat nude, limb slashed in 5 large glabrous parts. Stamens 5. Filaments short, inserted on corolla. Style 1. Stigma bifid. Fruit inferior, about the size of a crab apple, crowned by the remains of the calyx, smooth, yellow, fleshy, 1-celled with many seeds.

HABITAT.—On the coast of Luzon. Blooms in May.

Ixora coccinea, L. (*I. bandhuca*, Roxb.)

NOM. VULG.—*Santan*, Tag.

USES.—The handsome red flowers are used in decoction for hæmoptysis and catarrhal bronchitis. Both root and flower are astringent and are given for dysentery. In Concan they cook 2 "tolas" (13.60 grams) of the flowers in lard, together with coriander and "mesua ferrea," add a little candied sugar and divide the mass into large pills to be given twice a day.

The fresh root in the form of an alcoholic tincture has been recommended by Deb for dysentery, the dose 2–4 grams in an appropriate potion. The tincture of the fresh plant is prepared by macerating 126 grams of the fresh root 15 days in 473 grams alcohol. The plant has been used in intermittent fevers and various skin diseases.

BOTANICAL DESCRIPTION.—A shrub cultivated in all gardens, 6–8° high. Leaves oval, entire, glabrous. Flowers in terminal umbels, white, pink or red. Corolla tubular with limb cleft in 4 rounded lobes. The plant is so well known that further description would be superfluous.

Coffea Arabica, L.

Nom. Vulg.—*Cafe*, Sp.; *Coffee*, Eng.

Uses.—The infusion of roasted and ground coffee seeds constitutes a beverage of Arabic origin, but now common all over the world. In the Philippines, where a few years ago the coffee plant was only cultivated in gardens, the harvest has assumed such proportions that it now constitutes one of the greatest sources of agricultural wealth. Its use is becoming more general every day and the discovery of its alkaloid "caffeine" the therapeutical use of which is also steadily increasing, has given new importance to the seed on account of its increasing demand in the drug trade. When newly harvested its taste is not very agreeable, for it needs considerable time—2 or 3 years—in which to dry completely, before it acquires the aromatic properties and the savor of which it is susceptible. General Morin relates an incident of having drunk a delicious infusion of coffee made from authentic Moka that had been kept for fifty years, of course under ideal conditions of preservation.

In civilized countries coffee is an article of prime necessity as a food; here we shall consider it therapeutically under two heads, as a tonic-stimulant and as an antiseptic. As caffeine is the principle that acts upon the heart we shall consider the cardiac properties of coffee under the head of that alkaloid, so important that it may best be studied separately.

There are two preparations of coffee, the decoction used by the Arabs and the infusion, used in Europe and adopted in the Philippines. The decoction forms a tonic and aromatic drink devoid of any excitant properties, but the infusion is highly excitant and should not be taken in such large amounts as the decoction, for its action may be powerful enough to cause headache, nausea, trembling of the extremities and disorders of vision and hearing. These phenomena however are not dangerous and rapidly subside as soon as the urine eliminates the substances that cause them.

Infusion of coffee stimulates especially the cerebral functions and the circulation; as to its digestive properties, opinion is divided but it is more probable that it lacks them and that coffee taken after meals owes its reputation as a digestive aid to two distinct factors—the temperature and the sugar. Without doubt it exerts an anaphrodisiac action, on account of which the illustrious Linneus called it the "drink of eunuchs." This action seems incompatible with the fact that the Arabs, who are so much given to the abuse of the pleasures forbidden to eunuchs are most addicted to the use and abuse of coffee. The explanation rests in the form in which they consume their coffee, namely the decoction, which is free from the sedative principle of the seed, that undoubtedly resides in the aromatic ingredient "cafeol."

Coffee is contraindicated in hysterical and nervous persons, in children and in those who suffer with insomnia or palpitation. It counteracts sleep and coma, being very useful in poisoning by opium or its alkaloids. Its stimulant action is as rapid as that of alcohol. On several occasions it has yielded me marked results when given by stomach or by enema in cases of nervous and cardiac depression. Indeed it is a remedy that I cannot recommend too highly and each day leaves me more convinced of its therapeutic activity and certainty.

Attention has only lately been directed to the antiseptic property of coffee though we have long been availing ourselves of that property without knowing it; this is true of many other medicinal agents, indeed of all that the modern studies of bacteriology have presented to us as antifermentives and microbicides. Roasted coffee in powder form gives good results if dusted over ulcers and gangrenous sores, rapidly improving their appearance and destroying the fœtid odor. It corrects the unhygienic properties of non-potable water and therefore enters into the army and navy ration of nearly all the nations of Europe. In epidemics of disease every physician should advise its use in mild infusion as a regular beverage.

Dr. Luderitz, experimenting in the Hygienic Institute of Berlin, reported that no bacteria could resist the action of coffee in infusion. He attributed this action not only to the tannin, which is present in high percentage, but principally to the empyreumatic substances formed by the roasting. The caffeine takes no part in this action. Dr. Luderitz exposed the coffee to the open air for six days and found it free from bacteria at the end of that time. Whatever may be the explanation of its activity the fact remains that coffee is highly antiseptic, and this should be kept in mind by physicians not only because it is everywhere easily obtained and an infusion easily prepared, but because it in addition possesses the great advantage of being nontoxic.

The chemical analysis of the seed is as follows:

Cellulose	34.000
Water	12.000
Fatty matters	10 to 13.000
Glucose, dextrin, undetermined acid	15.500
Legumin, caffeine	10.000
Chlorogenate of caffeine and potassa	3.500 to 5.000
Albuminoids	3.000
Caffeine, free	.800
Essential oil, solid	.001
" " liquid	.002
Mineral substances	6.697

Caffeine, the only one of the ingredients that interests us, was discovered by Hunge in 1821 and recognized as an alkaloid by Herzog. It also exists in tea, formerly known as "theine" which is now known to be identical with caffeine; both are expressed by the formula $C_8H_{10}N_2O_2+H_2O$. It crystallizes in fine, silky needles, is colorless, odorless and slightly bitter.

It is considered a substitute for digitalis, especially valuable as a diuretic and where cerebral anemia exists. Germain See values it as a preventive medicine, acting principally upon the heart and thus preventing fatigue; with this end in view he advises its use before long marches, violent exercise and all conditions where the heart will be called upon to do a greatly increased amount of work. Dose 0.25 gram to 1 or 2 grams a day given by stomach or hypodermic injection.

Caffeine is also useful in headache, neuralgia, and asthma and as a general tonic. For the latter action it is best given in pill form, 0.02–0.04 gram a day, with the extract of cinchona or other bitter tonic.

"Etoxy-caffeine," which is caffeine in which an atom of H has been replaced by the C_2H_5O, exists as white, needle-like crystals, slightly soluble in water; it is narcotic and sedative to the cerebro-spinal system. In doses of 0.24 gram it is useful in headache.

Botanical Description.—"A small tree that reaches a height of 8–9°. It grows readily in the province of Batangas without cultivation," Blanco.

A small tree or shrub with leaves opposite, smooth, glossy, rich green, oval, edges fluted. Flowers fragrant, white, growing in small clusters in the axils of the leaves. Calyx 4–5-toothed. Corolla short-tubed with 4–5 spreading lobes of about the same length. Berry red, containing two plano-convex seeds enveloped in arils.

The plant is widely cultivated in gardens. It finds ideal conditions for growth in some of the hilly and mountainous regions of Luzon, notably in Benguet and Batangas.

Morinda citrifolia, L.; variety: **bracteata**, Hoock, Jr. (*M. ligulata*, Blanco.)

NOM. VULG.—*Bankundo, Pankundo, Bag̃kuro, Nino, Kulit, Tumbog̃aso, Lino, Mamboy, Takpus*, Tag. and Vis.; *Taliantar*, Pam.; *Apalot*, Iloc.; *Indian Mulberry*, Indo-Eng.

USES.—In the Philippines, as well as in India, the root of the plant is widely used as a red dye. As a medicine the Tamul physicians use it in decoction to treat diarrhœa and dysentery. The fruit is emmenagogue and perhaps aperient. In Bombay the mashed leaves are applied to wounds and ulcers to hasten cicatrization; they also use the decoction internally as a febrifuge and tonic, 10 grams to 500 of water, a wineglassful twice a day.

The root bark contains a crystalline substance called by Anderson *morindin*, $C_{28}H_{30}O_{15}$. It is a glucoside and exists in the form of yellow needles, soluble in alcohol and in cold water, insoluble in ether; dissolves in alkalies producing an orange-red color.

There is another species, *M. tinctoria*, Roxb.; *M. Royoc*, Blanco, called in Tagalog *Tumboug̃ aso kapay*, the roots of which are used by the Filipinos for the same purposes as the leaves of the former species; the dose, 8 grams a day. The powder is also applied to ulcers and sores, especially those of gangrenous aspect.

BOTANICAL DESCRIPTION.—A small tree 11 or more feet high, branches opposite, quadrate at the extremities. Leaves opposite, oval, oblong, smooth, entire, glabrous. Petioles very short, with 2 broad, lanceolate stipules curved outward. Flowers white, opposite the leaves, fixed on globose, solitary receptacles from which spring the flowerets. Calyx proper, very short, monophyllous, a lanceolate leaflet springing from the border. Corolla tubular, woolly inside about the middle, with 5 lobules. Stamens 5, inserted on the walls of the corolla. Anthers thin, incumbent. Pistil somewhat longer than the corolla. Stigma cleft in 2 laminæ. Fruit: the receptacle of the flowerets ripens to a globe bristling with the remains of the calyces, like a berry covered with many smaller ones, each containing 2 monospermous, quadrangular seeds.

M. tinctoria, Roxb., is a climbing shrub with leaves opposite, ovate, keeled; petioles very short; flower and fruit like the foregoing species.

HABITAT.—In Luzon and, especially the *M. tinctoria*, in Malinta, Calauan and Tanauan.

Pæderia fœtida, L. (*P. sessiflora*, DC.)

NOM. VULG.—*Kantutan*, *Kantutæ*, Tag.; *Lilitan*, *Tæ-tæ*, Vis.

USES.—The fœtid odor of this plant has suggested both the technical and common names for it. The natives regard it as a cure for rheumatism. The root is emetic. The leaves, boiled and mashed, are applied to the abdomen in retention of urine; the decoction of the leaves is used for the same purpose and also has some reputation as a solvent for vesical calculus. For fever, cloths soaked in the decoction are applied to the head, the same preparation being given internally at the same time.

BOTANICAL DESCRIPTION.—A slender, twining plant with leaves 3′ by 1′, opposite, oval, acute, entire, long petioles and caducous stipules. Flowers dark rose color, in compound axillary and terminal cymes. Calyx of 5 persistent lobules. Corolla tubular, pubescent, 5 lobules. Stamens 5, free. Ovary inferior, flattened, 2 uniovulate locules. Style with 2 stigma-bearing branches.

HABITAT.—Luzon, Mindanao, Cebu, Panay.

COMPOSITÆ.

Eupatorium Ayapana, Vent.

NOM. VULG.—*Aya-pana*, Sp.; *Ayapana*, *Apana*, Tag.; *Ayapan*, Indo-Eng.

USES.—A native plant of Brazil now naturalized and well known in the Philippines and many other tropical countries;

it is called by its Brazilian name, Aya-pana, more or less modified. The entire plant is aromatic and its infusion has an agreeable, bitter taste. Its virtues have been much exaggerated, but it is certainly a good stimulant, diaphoretic and tonic. An infusion, 30 grams of the leaves to 1 liter of water, is given in dyspepsia, a small cup after each meal. In the island of Mauritius this infusion was widely used as a stimulant and aromatic in the cholera epidemics of 1854 and 1856.

It is used internally and locally for the bites of venomous snakes and insects. The leaf-juice is a good application for foul ulcers, as is also the decoction of the entire plant. "It appears probable that this plant has fallen into unmerited neglect."—Pharm. of India.

Botanical Description.—An aromatic plant 3° high, leaves opposite, sessile, coherent at the base, lanceolate, entire, glabrous. Flowers in racemose panicles. Common calyx cylindrical, of many imbricated, awl-shaped scales, the lower ones smaller; within are 20 or more hermaphrodite disk-flowers. Corollas are funnel-form, 5-lobed. Style a little longer than the stamens. Stigmas 2, long. Seed 1, quadrangular, with simple, downy, sessile pappus. Receptacle nude.

Habitat.—Common in fields and gardens. Blooms in January.

Blumea balsamifera, DC. (*Conyza balsamifera*, L.)

Nom. Vulg.—*Sambon*, Tag.; *Lakbandulan*, *Hamlibon*, *Lalakdan*, *Lakadbulan*, *Gintingintin*, *Gabuen*, *Ayoban*, *Alibun*, Vis.; *Sobsob*, Iloc.

Uses.—Sambon is a panacea among the Filipinos; its virtues are prodigious according to the ignorant natives who wear the leaves in the hat or the "salakod" (rain hat), to prevent "tabardillo" ("burning fever"; tabardillo pintado = spotted fever). They use the decoction to bathe convalescents, and for rheumatism they vaporize it in an improvised bath-cabinet consisting of a chair in which the patient sits enveloped in blankets that reach to the floor and retain the steam.

The hot infusion of the leaves is a good diaphoretic taken by the mouth, especially useful in catarrhal bronchitis, and prized as an expectorant by the Chinese and Javanese. Furthermore it is stomachic, antispasmodic and emmenagogue.

The camphorous odor of the plant suggested to me its application as an antiseptic lotion for varicose ulcers and my results have been very satisfactory. The infusion for internal use is 30 grams to the liter of water.

Botanical Description.—A woody plant 6–9° high. Leaves 1° long, 3′ wide, oblong, lanceolate, acutely serrate, rugose, soft, downy, whitish. Flowers yellow in panicles. Involucre conical, of many linear scales, enclosing 15 or more hermaphrodite disk-flowers and several pistillate ray-flowers. Hermaphrodite: corolla infundibuliform, 5-toothed. Pistillate: corolla very minute, infundibuliform, obscurely 4-toothed. One seed crowned with a simple hairy pappus.

Habitat.—Grows universally in the islands and is well known. Blooms in January.

Sphœranthus Indicus, L. (*S. hirtus*, Willd.; *S. mollis*, Roxb.)

Nom. Vulg.—*Sambog̃-gala*, Tag.

Uses.—This plant seems to possess anthelmintic properties and for this purpose it is administered in powder, 2–4 grams with a little molasses or syrup. It is bitter and aromatic and is given in diseases of the stomach and intestines for its tonic and stimulant effect. The odor of the drug is transmitted to both urine and sweat. In India it is used in "bilious diseases" and to dissipate all sorts of tumors. The Hindoos cook it with flour, lard and sugar and eat the mixture as a tonic and to prevent gray hair and baldness. They also give the seed, fried in oil, as an aphrodisiac. The aqueous distillate is a good preparation as it contains the active principle of the plant, a yellow, viscid, essential oil.

BOTANICAL DESCRIPTION.—A plant about 1° high, stem and branches bearing 3 serrate wings. Leaves premorse, lanceolate, decurrent, downy. Flowers white, in a globose head, divided into 50 or more groups each with its own calyx of 9 or 10 leaflets surrounding 2 or 3 hermaphrodite, 5-toothed, campanulate flowers. Anthers 5, united. Style 1, thick at extremity. Stigma none. Corolla of pistillate flowers very minute, with 3 obscure teeth. Stigma of 2 down-curved divisions. One seed, 4-angled, imbricated.

HABITAT.—The rice fields. Blooms in January.

Spilanthes Acmella, L.

NOM. VULG.—*Hagonog*, Tag.; *Agonoy*, Sp.-Fil., Vis. (?); *Palunay*, Pam.

USES.—Some native herb-doctors use the root as a purgative, giving a decoction of 4–8 grams to a cup of water. The infusion is used locally for itch and psoriasis. Internally it has a diuretic effect and is reputed to be a solvent of vesical calculi. The leaf juice and the bruised leaves are applied to wounds and atonic ulcers. These leaves with those of "sambon" and "sampaloc" (tamarind) are used to prepare aromatic baths for convalescents, rheumatics and pregnant women.

BOTANICAL DESCRIPTION.—A plant with stem drooping, square, grooved, covered with drops of gum resin. Leaves opposite, cordate, oval, lanceolate, serrate, 3 prominent nerves covered with short down. Petioles short, grooved. Flowers yellow, in a sort of umbel, with 3 or more flowerets on long peduncles. Common calyx, 9–11 narrow sepals, concave, fleshy, in 2 rows. Hermaphrodite disk-flowers 40 or more. Corolla tubular, 5-toothed. Anthers longer than corolla. Pistil longer than stamens. Style bifid. Pistillate flowers, 15 or more, forming the rays. Corolla monopetalous, 3-toothed. Style and stigma as in hermaphrodite flowers. Seeds of hermaphrodite flowers quadrangular, crowned by one long awn, and the rudiment of another. Seeds of ray flowers small and sometimes flattened, 2 awns, of which one alone lengthens and becomes conspicuous. Receptacle covered with concave scales.

HABITAT.—Grows along the shores of the sea and of rivers. It is very well known.

Artemisia vulgaris, L. (*A. Indica*, Willd.)

NOM. VULG.—*Ka-María, Santa María, Tinisas*, Tag.; *Indian Wormwood*, Indo-Eng.

USES.—The native women use the infusion of its aromatic leaves to induce menstruation. It is also used as an abortifacient, but is too mild a uterine stimulant to be reliable for that purpose. Its stomachic and tonic properties are common knowledge in the Philippines. The Hindoos use it for those effects and as an antispasmodic in amenorrhœa and hysteria. Dr. Wight states that the leaves and tops are useful in nervous troubles resulting from debility and that a decoction of them makes a good fomentation for phagedenic ulcers.

The infusion is prepared in the proportion of 10–30 grams of leaves to 1 liter of water and the powdered leaves are given in doses of 4–8 grams; the aqueous extract 30–40 grams a day. For amenorrhœa the drug is given daily for a week preceding the menstrual date.

BOTANICAL DESCRIPTION.—A plant 3° high, stem straight, woody, square toward ends of branches. Leaves alternate, tomentose, decurrent, divided in several places, medium lanceolate. Flowers straw-colored, in axillary and terminal, 1-ranked spikes. Common calyx cylindrical, 2 circles of oval, scarious leaflets around its border, 11 hermaphrodite disk-flowers and about 5 pistillate ray-flowers. Hermaphrodite: Corolla bell-shaped, 5 obtuse teeth; stigmas 2, bent to the sides. Pistillate: Corolla diminutive, 5 toothlets; anther none; stigmas 2.

Seeds of both small and quadrate, smaller in the latter. Receptacle nude.

HABITAT.—Grows throughout the islands and is well known.

Carthamus tinctorius, L.

NOM. VULG.—*Azafrán de la tierra*, Sp.; *Biri*, *Kasubha*, *Katsumba*, *Lago*, Tag.; *Kasabba*, Vis.; *Kasubha*, *Kastumba*, Pam.; *Bastard Saffron*, *Dyer's Safflower*, Eng.

USES.—This plant must not be confounded with *Curcuma longa*, L., whose tuber is also frequently called saffron (azafrán), and is used to color food.

The flower is the part employed as a condiment coloring the food yellow. Some use them internally in doses of 4 grams to cure icterus. The leaves coagulate milk. The seeds are purgative in dose of 8–16 grams, bruised and taken in emulsion, or 15–30 grams in decoction.

The following is the chemical analysis of the plant:

Yellow coloring matter, soluble	26.1–36.0
Carthamic acid	0.3– 0.6
Extractive matter	3.6– 6.5
Albumin	1.5– 8.0
Wax	0.6– 1.5
Cellulose, pectin	38.4–56.0
Silica	1.0– 8.4
Oxide of iron, aluminum, oxide of manganese	0.4– 4.6

(Salvetat.)

BOTANICAL DESCRIPTION.—A plant 3° high, root gray and spindle-shaped. Stem straight, few branches. Leaves scattered, sessile, partially embracing the stem, lanceolate, serrate with hooked teeth. Flowers yellow, terminal in a sort of corymb. Common calyx semiglobose, with imbricated scales, the border often bearing thorns; numerous hermaphrodite disk flowers, with corolla very long, funnel-form, 5-toothed. Style longer than the stamens. Stigma bifid. Seed large, lacking pappus.

HABITAT.—Cultivated in the gardens.

PLUMBAGINEÆ.

Leadwort Family.

Plumbago Zeylanica, L. (*P. viscosa*, Blanco.)

NOM. VULG.—*Sagdikit*, Tag.; *Bagbag*, *Talankaw*, Iloc.; *White-flowered Leadwort*, Eng.

USES.—The root is vesicant and is used by the natives for this purpose. (*P. rosea*, L., common in India, is more powerful. The Pharmacopœia of India states that both species are worthy of further investigation.) According to the Sanscrit authors it increases the appetite and is useful in dyspepsia, piles, dropsy, diarrhœa and skin diseases. The Filipinos use the infusion locally for itch with good results. A favorite medicine of the Hindoos for flatulence is the old recipe of Susrutas, composed of equal parts of the following substances in powder:

Leadwort root, root of *Cissampelos Pareira*, *Picrorrhiza kurroa*,[1] *Aconitum heterophyllum*,[1] and *Terminalia Chebula* in dose of 4 grams a day.

Dr. Oswald has employed the alcoholic tincture of leadwort in the intermittents, with satisfactory results, and claims that it is a powerful diaphoretic.[2] The mashed root is mixed with rice flour and made into a caustic paste to apply to buboes, destroy warts, etc. Women also use the scraped root to induce abortion, introducing it through the vagina into the *os uteri*. This practice should be strongly condemned on account of its dangerous consequences—metritis, peritonitis and often death.

[1] Do not grow in the Philippines.

[2] Waring, loc. cit., p. 170.

The chemical composition of the root has been studied by Dulong.[1] It includes a non-nitrogenous principle, plumbagin, existing in the form of orange-yellow needles, bitter, acrid, volatile, neutral, slightly soluble in cold water, more soluble in ether, alcohol and hot water. The aqueous solution becomes cherry-red on the addition of an alkali, which color is changed to yellow by acids. Basic acetate of lead causes the same color change.

BOTANICAL DESCRIPTION.—Plant with stem declined, angular. Leaves lanceolate, entire, rather downy. Petioles at their base embrace the stem. Flowers white, in axillary spikes. Individual involucres, 3 oval leaflets, the lower larger. Calyx long, cleft almost to the base in 5 lineal parts thickly set with small glands, exuding a sticky gum. Corolla salver-shaped, the tube long, square, throat bare, limb divided into 5 obovate parts, ending in stylets. Stamens 5, inserted near the base of the corolla, almost as long as the tube. Style a little shorter than the stamens. Stigma, 5 parts. One long seed enclosed within the calyx, pentangular, covered with a membranaceous skin.

HABITAT.—In Tanauan (Batangas).

SAPOTACEÆ.

Sapodilla Family.

Achras Sapota, L.

NOM. VULG.—*Chico*, Sp.-Fil.; *Tsiku*, Tag.

USES.—The *chico* is one of the popular fruits of the Philippines, much appreciated by Europeans as well as the natives. When not entirely ripe it yields a resinous juice that sticks to the lips and affords a disagreeable taste; but when once thoroughly ripe it has a slightly vinous, sweetish taste and is easily digested. Therapeutically its seeds are used as a diuretic, but

[1] Journal de Pharmacie, Vol. XIV., p. 441.

large doses should be avoided as they contain a small proportion of hydrocyanic acid. The proper dose is 5–6 mashed seeds in sweetened water. They contain, in addition to the above, a fatty substance of the consistency of butter.

The trunk bark is tonic and febrifuge; Mr. Bernon[1] has isolated from it a crystalline alkaloid, *sapotine*, soluble in ether, chloroform or alcohol, but not in water; a large per cent. of *sapotanic acid* and two resins.

The trunk exudes, when incised, a milky resin, closely resembling guttapercha and possibly susceptible of the same uses.

Botanical Description.—Trees, about 11° high, with leaves lanceolate, keeled, entire, glabrous. Flowers pure white, solitary or by twos, terminal, very long peduncles. Calyx, 6 sepals, 3 within the others, inferior persistent. Corolla jug-shaped, the border divided into 12 parts, the 6 smaller ones alternating and within the others. Stamens 6, inserted near the border of the inner petals and opposite the outer circle. Filaments very short. Style long. Stigma obtuse, fruit globose, resembling a small pear, russet brown, crowned with the hardened style, more than 10 compartments, each containing a seed. Seed oval, flattened, joined to a central fleshy axis.

Habitat.—Common all over the Archipelago. Blooms in April.

Mimusops Elengi, L.

Nom. Vulg.—*Kabiki*, Tag.

Uses.—Its flowers are fragrant and generally well known. The trunk bark is astringent, and in decoction is given by mouth for fevers and diarrhœa. Locally is used as an injection for blenorrhœa, as a gargle for sore throat or relaxed uvula, and a mouth wash to harden the gums. Horsfield states that the Javanese use it as a tonic and antiperiodic. In India an aqueous distillate is employed as a perfume and therapeutically as a stimulant. In Concan they chew the green fruit for tooth-

[1] L'Union Pharm., Vol. XXIII., p. 291.

ache and to harden relaxed gums. The decoction of the green fruit serves the same purpose and besides is used to wash wounds and ulcers.

BOTANICAL DESCRIPTION.—A large ornamental tree with leaves alternate, oblong, coriaceous, green. Flowers small, straw-colored, star-shaped, very fragrant. Calyx, 8 sepals. Corolla gamopetalous, 16 oblong, lanceolate divisions. Stamens 8, free, short, alternating with 8 petaloid, conical, pubescent staminodia. Ovary free, many ovules. Fruit fleshy, oval, smooth, yellow when ripe, with one or several locules according to the number of matured seeds. Seeds solitary, oblong, flattened.

HABITAT.—Cultivated in the gardens.

OLEACEÆ.

Olive Family.

Jasminum Sambac, Aiton. (*Nyctanthes Sambac*, Blanco.)

NOM. VULG.—*Sampaga*, Tag.; *Sampaguitas*, Sp.-Fil.; *Arabian Jasmin*, Eng.

USES.—The flower is the most popular and beloved of any in the Philippines (and is commonly referred to as the national flower). In decoction it is used as an eye-wash in catarrhal conjunctivitis. In India the flowers and the leaves have a merited reputation as a lactifuge; 2 handfuls of flowers bruised and applied without moistening, once or twice a day, sometimes checks the secretion of the milk within 24 hours, but generally 2 or 3 days are required for a complete effect.

BOTANICAL DESCRIPTION.—Stems scarcely climbing, flattened, pubescent. Leaves opposite, cordate base, lanceolate-ovate, entire, glabrous. Flowers in small, close clusters, white, fragrant. Calyx-teeth 8–9, long and awl-shaped. Corolla, long tube, 7–8 rounded lobes. Stamens 2. Style 1. Stigma cleft in 2 laminæ.

APOCYNACEÆ.

Dogbane Family.

Allamanda cathartica, L.

NOM. VULG.—Not known.

USES.—As this plant has no common name in the Philippines it is most probable that the natives do not use it. The Portuguese introduced it into India from Brazil. A decoction of the leaves is purgative and is used in lead colic. The milky juice of the plant is emetic and cathartic in large doses, but simply laxative when given in doses of 8 or 10 drops. On account of its possible violent cathartic action great prudence should be exercised in prescribing it.

BOTANICAL DESCRIPTION.—A twining shrub with leaves in fours, bright green, oblong, covered with rough hairs. Flowers in compound spikes, yellow. Calyx 5-toothed. Corolla 5-lobed, funnel-form. Stamens 5, inserted in throat of corolla, which above them is closed by a crown of hairs. Ovary 1-celled with 2 many-ovuled placentæ. Style cylindrical, terminating in a bilobulate cone. Capsule globular, about the size of a pea, black, coriaceous, thorny, bivalvate. Seeds numerous, each encircled by a broad membranous wing.

HABITAT.—In Calauang and other parts of Luzon and Panay.

Thevetia nerifolia, Suss. (*Cerbera Thevetia*, L. and Blanco.)

NOM. VULG.—*Campanelo*, Sp.-Fil.; *Exile or Yellow Oleander*, Eng.

USES.—This shrub is very common in gardens, well known by its pretty yellow, bell-shaped flowers. The trunk bark possesses antiperiodic properties first described by Descourtilz and confirmed later by Dr. G. Bidie and Dr. J. Short. Both the latter used the tincture in 10–15-drop doses 3 times a day. This tincture was prepared by macerating for one week in 150 grams of alcohol 30 grams of fresh bark finely divided. This preparation operates as an emetic and purgative in doses of 30–60 drops. It is evident that the plant possesses very active, even poisonous properties and should be employed with great caution. The decoction of the bark is given as an emetic and cathartic, but very imprudently because there is no means of determining the quantity of active principle, shown by chemical analysis to be a dangerous product.

The fruit is very bitter and acrid. The seeds yield by expression 35 to 41% oil (De Vry) and 57% when treated with benzol. It has an agreeable odor resembling that of sweet almonds, its density is 0.9148 at 25° and it is perfectly clear and transparent at that temperature. At 15° it thickens and at 13° solidifies. According to Oudemans it consists of 63% triolein and 37% tripalmin and tristearin; it is not poisonous. After expression De Vry obtained from the caked residue 4% of a crystalline glucoside called by him *thevetin*. Blas, of the Academy of Medicine of Belgium, studied it later and described it as a white powder of small colorless scales, odorless, very bitter, soluble at 14° in 122 parts of water, in alcohol, in crystallizable acetic acid, insoluble in ether; formula $C_{54}H_{34}O_{24}$. Concentrated sulphuric acid dissolves it, producing a dark red color that changes to cherry red and then after several hours to violet. The color disappears if water be added. Boiled in acid solution the glucoside changes to a new substance, *theveresin* ($C_{48}H_{70}O_{17}$), white, amorphous, slightly soluble in boiling water and in alcohol, insoluble in benzine or chloroform, soluble in alkalies, very bitter. Both substances are energetic narcotic poisons; but the plant contains another even more powerful poison isolated by Warden, of Calcutta; it does not form crystals, it is very bitter, freely soluble in water, and is turned yellow by sulphuric and nitric acids.

Thevetin and theveresin exercise a marked toxic effect on the heart. The former induces emetic and cathartic phenomena, trembling and progressive weakness. The latter does not cause vomiting or diarrhœa, but anæsthesia and rigidity of the limbs. Both poisons arrest the heart in systole. Injected hypodermically they are irritant, are eliminated by the liver, but are not found in the urine.

Botanical Description.—A shrub, about 10° high, with leaves nearly sessile, somewhat bunched at the ends of the branches and overlapping, lanceolate, entire, glabrous. Flowers about 2′ long. Calyx 5-toothed. Corolla straw-colored, cylindrical, very narrow below, but the limb very large, spreading into 5 lobes with greenish, superimposed borders. Stamens 5, inserted in the throat, anthers lanceolate. Ovaries 2, united at base, free above, unilocular. Style simple, enlarging at the base in a bilobed stigma. Fruit a fleshy drupe resembling somewhat a small apple, the pit very hard, semilunar, flattened, with 4 compartments and as many solitary seeds.

Habitat.—Common in all gardens and on the seashore.

Cerbera Odallam, Gaertn. (*C. manghas*, Bl. & Blanco.)

Nom. Vulg.—*Toktok-kaló*, Tag.

Uses.—The milky juice of the plant is emetic and purgative. The chemist De Vry has isolated from it a poisonous alkaloid analogous to "thevetin," which has just been considered. The seeds are likewise emetic and toxic. The Javanese call the fruit "bimaro" and affirm that it possesses the same properties as "datura." The bruised leaves are used locally for hepatic eruptions; the bark is used for the same purpose and is purgative.

The use of the plant is dangerous and is condemned by the Pharmacopœia of India.

Botanical Description.—A small shrub with forked branches. Leaves (overlapping) at ends of branches, lanceolate, entire, glabrous. Flowers in umbellate spikes. Calyx, 5 caducous lobules. Corolla white, twisted, cylindrical, with salver-shaped limb divided in 5 rhomboid lobes, throat stellate and woolly. Stamens 5. Filaments joined to the corolla, their ends thickened. Anthers arrow-shaped. Ovary, 2 uniovulate locules. Style, same length as stamens. Stigma thick, conical, lobulate. Two drupes joined at the base (one usually aborted), brown, large, oval, fleshy, with woody fibrous nut of a single flattened seed.

HABITAT.—Luzon. Blooms in July.

Plumeria acutifolia, Poir. (*P. alba*, Blanco.)

NOM. VULG.—*Calachuche*, Sp.-Fil.; *Kalatsutsi*, *Kalasusi*, Tag.

USES.—This tree, beloved for its fragrant flowers, has a wide therapeutic use in India and the Philippines. The bark is a bitter hydragogue cathartic and is given in decoction (5–10 grams to 200 water) principally for dropsy; however the milky juice of the trunk is preferable for this purpose, given in emulsion in doses of 0.50–0.80 grams. The bark and the tips of the branches are given as an emmenagogue.

The bark of the root and of the trunk is an excellent remedy for blenorrhagia. The fresh bark is thoroughly comminuted and mixed with sweetened water in the proportion of 60 grams to 4 liters; this mixture is put in the sun for 4 days, and shaken from time to time. It is then strained and given in doses of 4–5 glassfuls a day, at the same time with refreshing and emollient drinks, and prolonged tepid baths. At first this preparation exerts a purgative action, but later acts upon the urinary organs, rapidly lessening the suppurative process in urethritis. The bark may also be associated with wine or beer, in the proportion of 30 grams to the liter, the dose being 2–4 small cupfuls a day and Dr. Grosourdy employs the extract of the bark in doses aggregating 0.20–0.25 gram a day, gradually increased till at the end of a week 6 grams are taken daily (Dr. J. Amadeo).

The bruised leaves are applied locally to contusions to reduce the swelling. The juice is used externally as a rubefacient in rheumatic affections of the joints. In Concan they use a decoction of the root for diarrhœa. The flower buds are chewed with *buyo*, for intermittent fever and the juice is applied locally for itch.

Peckolt and Geuther isolated from the bark the glucoside, *agoniadin* ($C_{10}H_{14}O_6$), which crystallizes in silky crystals fusible at 155°, slightly soluble in water, alcohol, bisulphuret of carbon, ether and benzine; soluble in nitric or sulphuric acids. In solution it is a golden yellow soon changing to green. Boiled in a dilute acid it splits into glucose and an undetermined substance. Oudeman obtained *plumieric* acid ($C_{10}H_{10}O_5$) from the milky juice deprived of its resin; the acid exists as microscopic, needle-like crystals, soluble in boiling water, alcohol and ether. It melts and decomposes at 130°.

Botanical Description.—A tree, 12–18° high, commonly cultivated for ornament, well known in the islands, almost constantly bearing fragrant flowers, but rarely bearing fruit. Branches forked and peculiarly stumpy at the ends. Leaves alternate, broad lanceolate, entire, glabrous, the apices curved downward. Petioles short. Flowers creamy white, light yellow in the throat. Calyx 5-toothed. Corolla twisted, funnelform, 5-lobed. Stamens 5, hidden in depths of the tube. Anthers dart- or arrow-formed. Style very short, thickened above. Stigma 2-parted. Two horizontal, cylindrical and long follicles joined at their bases, with numerous seeds in hollow receptacles, each seed encircled by a wing.

Alstonia scholaris, Br. (*Echites scholaris*, L. and Blanco.)

Nom. Vulg.—*Dita*, Tag.; *Dallopawen*, Iloc.; *Dita* or *Alstonia Tree*, Eng.

Uses.—The trunk bark is a febrifuge of great importance; it is official in the Pharmacopœia of India and is widely used in the Philippines. Personally I have had occasion to use it in several cases of malarial fever in the town of San Mateo near Manila. It is astringent, anthelmintic and antiperiodic, highly useful in chronic diarrhœa and dysentery, not only for its astringent effects but for its tonic and restorative action. As a tonic it gives as good results as quinine. The dry powdered bark is given internally in wafers of 20–30 centigrams. The infusion is prepared from 15 grams of the dry comminuted bark to 300 of water. The dose is 30–60 grams 2 or 3 times a day.

Another convenient preparation is the tincture, 75 grams of the powdered bark macerated 7 days in 500 grams of alcohol, shaking from time to time. It is then filtered and enough alcohol added to make up the 500 cc. The dose is 4–8 grams a day.

I have often used the following wine as a tonic for convalescents and patients suffering from general debility: Finely powdered bark, 25 grams, muscatel or dry sherry one bottle; macerate a week, shaking every day, and filter; dose ½ wineglass with equal parts water a few minutes before each meal; children or very weak patients should take it after eating; it should always be diluted.

G. Grupe, a Manila pharmacist, treating the bark in 1883 by the same process as that used in the preparation of quinine, obtained a bitter substance which he named *Ditaine*. According to Grupe Dr. Pina used this substance with great success in the treatment of malarial fevers, but neither Grupe's report nor Pina's experiment are of any scientific value, inasmuch as they have neglected to mention the doses in which the so-called alkaloid was employed. Later analyses by Hesse and Jobst revealed several principles: two alkaloids *ditamine* ($C_{16}H_{19}NO_2$), soluble in ether; *Ditaine* or *Echitamine* ($C_{22}H_{28}NO_4 + H_2O$) insoluble in ether, soluble in water; acetic acid and two amorphous substances dextrogyrous in ethereal solution, one of them a resin, *Echicauchina* ($C_{25}H_{40}O_2$), the other neutral, *Echiretin* ($C_{35}H_{56}O_2$); two crystallizable principles, dextrogyrous: *Echicerin* ($C_{30}H_{48}O_2$), *Echitein* ($C_{42}H_{70}O_2$) and *Echitin* ($C_{32}H_{52}O_2$).

Ditaine is employed under the same circumstances and in the same dose as quinine. (The Hindoo writer, K. L. Dey, states that the plant yields an inferior quality of gutta-percha.)

BOTANICAL DESCRIPTION.—A tree, 50 or more feet high, the trunk covered with small eminences resembling the scars of thorns. Branches radiating. Leaves radiating, 5, 6 or more, somewhat elliptical in form, pointed at the apex. Petioles very short, with a pointed glandule on the inner surface of the base. Flowers white, terminal, in umbellate racemes. Calyx very short, 5-toothed. Corolla twisted, tubular, the limb 5-lobuled; throat open, encircled with down. Stamens 5, hidden within the throat and inserted on the tube. Filaments almost wanting. Anthers arrow-shaped. Style as long as the stamens, somewhat flattened, a scarcely visible line throughout its length. Stigma bifid, placed above a cylindrical zone, two follicles, 1° long and 1″ thick, twisted like a string, containing the seeds in a row. Seeds cylindrical with a hairy awn at both ends.

HABITAT.—In the forests of Luzon, especially in Batangas. Blooms in April.

Nerium odorum, Aiton. (*N. oleander*, L. and Blanco.)

NOM. VULG.—*Adelfa*, Sp.; *Baladri*, Tag.; *Sweet-scented Oleander*, Eng.

USES.—In the Philippines and in Spain this plant is well known to be poisonous. The bark and the leaves of both the red-flowered and white-flowered varieties are boiled in cocoanut oil and the product is used for inunction in itch and other skin diseases. The bruised root is a useful application for chancroids.

We have stated that the plant is poisonous, and indeed it is actively so in the tropics. It is now recognized as an energetic cardiac poison, comparable with strophanthus, destined to play an important part in therapeutics. Dr. Pouloux has made a study of the hydro-alcoholic extract of oleander and reports that it exerts a marked effect on the heart of frogs and rabbits, arresting them in systole. Where there is asystolia, such as we encounter in Bright's disease, without compensation, it stimulates the heart and increases the urine in the same manner as digitalis. No contraindications to its use are as yet known. It occasions no disagreeable symptoms and may be used many days consecutively provided that the daily dose does not exceed 10–15 centigrams.

The poisonous properties of the plant reside in two alkaloids isolated by Lukowsky from the leaves : *oleandrine*, extremely toxic and *pseudo-curarine*, as its name indicates, resembling curare in its action. Oleandrin is yellow, semicrystalline, soluble in water, alcohol, ether, chloroform and olive oil ; fusible at 70–75° and changing to a greenish oil. With HCl it forms a crystalline salt. It is a violent irritant of the mucous membranes and given internally it causes emesis, diarrhœa, tetanic convulsions and death. It arrests the cardiac movements in doses of 25 milligrams.

Loiseleur-Deslongchamps experimented with the drug on his own person, using a solution of 30 grams of the extract in 120 grams of wine. He began by taking three drops of this preparation four times a day, adding a drop to each dose every day, so that at the end of 12 days he was taking 48 drops between 6 a. m. and 9 p. m. He reached a maximum of 64 drops a day but was forced to abandon his experiment at that point on account of the unpleasant symptoms induced—loss of appetite, great weakness and muscular pains. His deduction was that the plant contained a "destructive and irritant principle." The experiment is of interest as demonstrating the maximum dose of the drug.

The active principles of the plant reside principally in the leaves and bark, but that they are abundantly present in other parts is proved by the death of several soldiers in Corsica from having eaten meat roasted on a spit of oleander wood.

Botanical Description.—A small tree, about 6° high. Leaves coriaceous, lanceolate, entire, glabrous. Flowers in terminal cymes, rose-color or white, single or double. Calyx 5-parted. Corolla 15 petals, the inner ones larger, disposed in 3 groups of 5. Stamens 10, fixed on receptacle; filaments short. Style shorter than stamens. Two follicles, sharp-pointed, channeled, containing many imbricated seeds each with an awn.

ASCLEPIADACEÆ.

Milkweed Family.

Calotrops gigantea, R. Br. (*Asclepias gigantea*, Willd. and Blanco.)

Nom. Vulg.—*Kapal-kapal*, Tag.; *Swallow-Wort*, Eng.; *Mudar*, Indo-Eng.

Uses.—This plant is official in the Pharmacopœia of India as an alterative, tonic, diaphoretic and emetic. J. J. Durant, having observed that the natives used it for dysentery, experimented with it quite successfully in that disease. For adults he gradually raised the dose from 1.10 to 4 grams, preferring smaller doses, however, for mild cases. To children he prescribed 5–10 centigrams for each year of age, 3 or 4 times a day. He remarked that the effects produced were identical with those of ipecac administered in Brazilian fashion.

The part of the plant used is the dry root powdered. The usual dose is 15–50 centigrams 3 times a day, gradually increased; as an emetic 2–4 grams.

The milky juice that escapes from the stem on the slightest abrasion is a drastic purgative, given commonly in dropsy, lumbricoids, etc. Pledgets of cotton impregnated with the juice and packed in the cavities of carious teeth, relieve toothache.

It is applied locally for various skin diseases, including syphilitic ulcers, and as a depilatory.

Some races of India, such as the Rajputs of the districts of Allahab and of Khangor, use this milk-juice to poison their female infants whom they are accustomed to regard as a vexatious burden. Therapeutically they use it with honey, locally for sore throat.

The dry and powdered juice has been used in small doses as an alterative in the treatment of tuberculous leprosy, but it has not given results any better than many other drugs. In syphilis and mercurial cachexia its results are less doubtful.

In 1881 Dr. Riddell obtained a sort of gutta-percha from the juice, previously observed by Professor Redwood.

Mooden Sheriff states that the most active parts of the plant are the root bark and the dried juice. He adds that the action of the juice is irregular and even dangerous, and that the bark is active in direct proportion to its age. He recommends that the inert tuberous layer of the bark be removed; prepared thus and powdered it is emetic in doses of 2.50–3 grams.

Duncan claims to have isolated from the bark an active principle which he called *mudarin* from "mudar," the Indian name of the plant. Following the same process Flückiger was unable to obtain the substance, but did isolate $1\frac{1}{2}$ % of an acrid resin, soluble in ether and in alcohol; a mucilage and a bitter principle decolorized by chloroform and ether. It is probable that this is the active principle of the "Calotropis gigantea."

Warden and Waddell in 1881 isolated a substance crystallizable in nodular masses, with the formula $C_{17}H_{28}O$, analogous to the *albana* of gutta-percha.

Botanical Description.—A small tree, 7–8° high, with straight stem, branched and woody. Leaves sessile, opposite, cleft at the base, oval, fleshy and woolly. Flowers lateral in simple umbels of 3 or more flowerets. Calyx 5-cleft. Corolla monopetalous, 5 acute lobes, white, of rare and beautiful form. Nectaries 5, united throughout their length with the receptacle, their bases curved like the sides of the fleur de lis.

Above the nectaries is a 5-angled crown, the extremity of the receptacle; in each angle a black anther. Two large follicles narrowed at the ends, woolly, the apex somewhat curved to one side, containing many imbricated seeds, each with a tuft of long hairs.

HABITAT.—Bauang, Taal and the volcanic island of Taal. Blossoms in April.

Tylophora asthmatica, Wight. (*Asclepias asthmatica*, Roxb.)

NOM. VULG.—(?)

USES.—We are ignorant of the uses the Filipinos make of this plant. It is official in the Pharmacopœia of India, the dry powdered leaf being the part employed, and its emetic, diaphoretic and expectorant properties are well known in that country. Roxburgh has used the root as an emetic and Anderson has employed it in the same manner as ipecac in dysentery. Later the experience of Anderson was confirmed by O'Shaughnessy; though in place of the root he used the leaf, the properties of which he regards as more certain and uniform.

Dr. J. Kirkpatrick has noted that the juice of the root and its powder are used by the natives of Mysore as an emetic, and adds that he himself has used it for that purpose in a thousand cases with good results. In its effect on dysentery as well as in its emetic effect it resembles ipecacuanha. He used the powder in doses of 1.20–1.80 gr., to which he added 3–6 centigrams of tartar emetic when he desired to obtain an energetic emetic action. Like O'Shaughnessy he prefers the powdered leaves. He considers it a good substitute for ipecac, not only as an emetic, but as a remedy in asthma, dysentery and catarrhal affections; Drs. Oswald and Mooden Sheriff have made the same observations. The latter advises the administration of the juice of the plant for snake bites till vomiting is produced; then follow with diffusible stimulants.

The emetic dose of the powdered leaves is 1.20–1.80 grams, the expectorant and diaphoretic dose 10–30 centigrams. The concentrated infusion of the leaves has an acrid taste. Tannic acid, the neutral acetate of lead and caustic potash produce with it an abundant precipitate; the perchloride of iron colors it a dark green. Broughton, of Ootacmund (India), informed Hanbury and Flückiger, from whom we quote, that in 1872 he obtained a very small quantity of crystals from a large quantity of leaves. He had not enough to make an analysis, but injected a solution of the crystals into a dog with resulting vomiting and diarrhœa.

Botanical Description.—A vigorous plant with scandent stem 2–4 meters long, the more recent growth woolly. Leaves opposite, entire, 5–12 centimeters long and 2–6 broad, oval or rounded. Petiole striated and short. Flowers in umbelliferous cymes, compound, axillary, solitary and alternate, with woolly peduncles; hermaphrodite, regular, small, of a pale green color inside and a light purple outside. Calyx gamosepalous, with 5 lobules. Corolla gamopetalous, 5 oval, twisted lobules. Staminal crown composed of 5 fleshy scales, joined to the staminal tube. Stamens 5, inserted on the throat of the corolla, filaments joined to form a very short tube with anthers straight, short and crowned by a membranous bilocular appendix. The gynœcium consists of 2 unilocular ovaries each containing an indefinite number of ovules. Style with a pentagonal stigma which bears in each angle a glandular body. Fruits compound with two separate follicles, large, lanceolate, smooth, 8–10 centimeters long and 5 in circumference. Each encloses a seed, hairy, albuminous with straight embryo and flattened cotyledons.

Habitat.—Mountains of San Mateo.

LOGANIACEÆ.

Logania Family.

Strychnos Ignatii, Berg. (*S. Philippensis*, Blanco; *Ignatia amara*, L.; *Ignatia Philippinea*, Lour.)

Nom. Vulg.—*Pepita Fruta*, Sp.-Fil.; *Pepita sa katbaloĝan*, *Kabaloĝan*, Tag., Pam.; *Pangaguason*, *Aguason*, *Kanlara*, *Mananaog*, *Dankagi*, *Kataloĝa*, *Igasud*, Vis.; *St. Ignatius Bean*, Eng.

Uses.—The part of the plant employed is the seed, known in addition to the above common names as Pepita de San Ignacio and Pepita de Cabalonga (for *katboloĝan*). The natives handle it with the greatest imprudence, selling everywhere in the markets and in the Chinese shops, called *tindaĝ-bayaĝ*. It is not only a remedy among them, but a sort of panacea, to which they attribute, among other virtues, that of expelling evil spirits, simply worn about the neck. They grate it with a piece of earthen pot, mix with a little "tuba" vinegar and apply it to the temples for headache. In bites of poisonous animals they advise the application of the powdered seed over the wound, a treatment which instead of being beneficent might easily be harmful to the patient. Before proceeding further, let us give the chemical composition of the seeds in order that their uses may be the better understood.

Strychnine is found in them in the proportion of ½–1½% and *brucine* ½%–1.4%. Flückiger and Hanbury by drying it over sulphuric acid and burning it with "cal sòdica" obtained 1.78% of nitrogen which represents 10% of albuminoid material. Strychnine and brucine exist in combination with igasuric acid discovered by Ludwig in 1873. The proportion of both the alkaloids is greater than in the seeds of nux vomica which contain only .25–.50% strychnine and .12–.05% brucin, although some authors give it as high as 1.01%. Strychnine can be obtained more readily and in larger proportions from St.

Ignatius bean, but it is generally obtained from nux vomica seeds on account of the cheapness of the latter.

It is more energetic than nux vomica and its use in medicine should be condemned, preference, however, being given to the official preparations among which the best known is that commonly called "Bitter Drops of Beaumé," of which the following is the composition:

Grated St. Ignatius' beans...........	500 grams.
Potassium carbonate.................	5 "
Soot (?)......................... ..	1 "
60% alcohol	1,000 "

Macerate for 10 days, strain, express and filter. Dose, 1–16 drops in a little water or wine before each meal, for dyspepsia, anæmia, convalescence from fevers, and other conditions in which a tonic is indicated. The indications for the use of this drug are the same as those for nux vomica, keeping in mind the difference in dose.

Botanical Description.—This plant grows in the deep forests of Samar and Masbate. That industrious and distinguished botanist, D. Regino García, found it growing abundantly in Paranas, Island of Samar. It is a robust vine, the trunk sometimes as thick as a man's thigh, climbing to the tops of the highest trees, apparently without preference as to its host, inasmuch as he saw it growing indifferently on *Ficus*, *Dipterocarpus*, *Litsaea*, etc. The seed which most interests us and is very common, is about the size of an olive, round and convex on one side, angulose and flattened on the other by being compressed with many others within the fruit which contains 50 of them. Its surface is blackish with a gray-blue tinge. It is hard and corneous. Its taste is extremely bitter.

Branches opposite, smooth, the ends square. Leaves opposite, oval, much pointed at the apex, entire, glabrous, with 3 prominent nerves. Petioles very short. Flowers in panicles of many flowerets. Calyx inferior, 5-cleft, very short. Corolla 6–7 times longer than the calyx, funnel-form, 5-lobed. Anthers 5, sessile, fixed in the throat of the corolla. Ovary very small. Style filiform, same length as the stamens. Stigma truncate and thick. Drupe globose, often oval, large, smooth, with thick, woody shell of a single compartment containing seeds as described above.

BORAGINACEÆ.

Borage Family.

Ehretia buxifolia, Roxb. (*Carmonea heterophylla*, Blanco.)

NOM. VULG.—*Mağit, Alağitğit*, Tag., Vis.

USES.—The leaves dried in the shade are used in some Visayan towns, in infusion to take the place of tea. The root is used by the Hindoo physicians as an alterative. Dr. R. Ross has employed it for that purpose in a decoction of 60 grams to 500 cc. of water; 60 cc. a day of this preparation gave him good results in secondary and constitutional syphilis. The Mohammedans of India consider the root an antidote for vegetable poisons.

BOTANICAL DESCRIPTION.—Small tree, 5–6° high, trunk straight. Leaves alternate or bunched in 3's or 4's at the nodes, lanceolate or spatulate, 3-toothed at apex, sometimes serrate toward the apex, set with short, stiff hairs. Petioles very short. Flowers axillary, in racemose panicles of a few flowers each. Common peduncle long, pedicel short. Calyx free, bell-shaped, persistent, divided almost to base into 5 narrow, downy parts. Corolla bell-shaped, 5 oval lobules. Stamens 5. Ovary oval, within the flower. Style bifid. Stigmas simple, truncate. Drupe globose, with hard, slightly furrowed putamen of 6 locules and solitary seeds.

HABITAT.—Malinta and many other parts of the Visayas. Blooms in January.

CONVOLVULACEÆ.

Convolvulus Family.

Ipomœa hederacea, Jacq. (*I. nil*, Roth.; *Convolvulus nil*, L. and Blanco.)

NOM. VULG.—*Bulakan*, Tag.; *Kala-Danah*, Indo-Eng.

USES.—This plant is not used as a medicine by the Filipinos, but is official in the Pharmacopœia of India from which we copy its indications and official preparations.

The seed is the part employed, its cathartic properties being much like those of jalap, though less energetic. An excellent substitute for the latter is 2 or 3 grams of *kala-danah* seeds in powder form, and no unpleasant effects attend its operation.

The official preparations are:

EXTRACT OF KALADANA.—Dose, 30–60 centigrams in pill.

Powdered seeds	500 grams.
Alcohol	2 liters.
Water	4½ "

TINCTURE OF KALADANA.—Dose, 8–12 grams.

Seeds	75 grams.
Alcohol	500 "

COMPOUND POWDER OF KALADANA.—Dose, 3–3½ grams.

Powdered seeds	150 grams.
Acid tartrate of potassium	270 "
Powdered ginger	30 "

The last is an excellent substitute for the corresponding preparation of jalap.

RESIN OF KALADANA.—Dose, 30–50 centigrams. It is prepared like resin of jalap and is a safe and sure purgative. In mass it has a dark color, but is gray when powdered. The odor is rather unpleasant, the taste sweetish and then acrid, nauseous, persistent, exciting the saliva and irritating the fauces. It was introduced into practice by Dr. G. Vidie.

BOTANICAL DESCRIPTION.—A twiner with round, downy stem. Leaves heart-shaped, 3-lobed, the middle one broad-lanceolate, the lateral ones rather rectangular with petioles of equal length with the leaves. Flowers large, rose color or pale blue, in axillary cymes of 2 or 3 flowers each. Calyx, 5 long, downy parts. Corolla bell-shaped, 5 faint lobes. Stamens 5, free, inserted in the corolla. Ovary free, 3 biovulate locules. Style simple. Stigma trilobed. Seed vessels globose with 3 locules each containing 2 seeds. Seeds convex on dorsum, ½ cm. broad by 1 cm. long, testa black.

HABITAT.—Manila. Blooms in August.

Ipomœa pes-capræ, Roth. (*Convolvulus pes-capræ* L. and Blanco.)

NOM. VULG.—*Katagkatag, Lagayray, Lampayog, Bagasoa, Kamigag, Daripay, Tagaray, Arodayday, Lambayog,* Tag., Vis.; *Lambayog,* Iloc.

USES.—The dry, powdered leaves are dusted over bruises and ulcers. The entire plant is very mucilaginous and the bruised fresh leaves are applied like poultices to cancers and ulcerating tumors. In India the boiled leaves are applied locally in colic and in rheumatism; the juice is given internally in dropsy as a diuretic, the pounded leaves at the same time serving as a poultice to the œdematous parts.

BOTANICAL DESCRIPTION.—A plant that creeps extensively, the stem taking root. Leaves with 2 well-marked lobules. Flowers rose-lilac color, in axillary panicles with long pedicels. Corolla very large, bell-shaped, the limb 5-angled and 5-nerved. Stamens 5, unequal in height. Stigma globose, marked by a line; later it divides in two. Seed vessel ovate, 2-celled, in each cell 2 downy seeds convex on one side, angular on the other.

HABITAT.—Very common on the seashore. Blooms in January.

Ipomœa Turpethum, R. Br. (*Convolvulus Turpethum*, L.; *C. maximus*, Blanco.)

Nom. Vulg.—*Albohol*, Sp.; *Turpeth Root, Indian Jalap*, Eng.

Uses.—The root, known in the Philippines as "turbita," is a purgative and is a component part of the tincture of jalap, one of the most positive and active of known cathartics. But turpeth root is seldom used alone, for its action is so uncertain that Sir W. O'Shaughnessy pronounced the plant unworthy of a place in the Pharmacopœia of India. The dose of the powder is 1–4 grams, the resin 40–50 cgms., the decoction of the root 4–12 grams. The active principle is a resin soluble in ether and a glucoside, *turpethin*, $C_{34}H_{56}O_{16}$.

In the east of India they make offerings of the flowers to the god Shiva, and also put them to more practical use by applying them to the head for neuralgic headache.

Botanical Description.—A vine with quadrangular stem. Leaves heart-shaped. Flowers axillary, numerous, in umbels. Calyx deeply cleft in 5 imbricated, ovate, fleshy parts. Corolla bell-shaped, folded. Stamens 5, unequal in height. Ovary inserted on an hypogynous disk, with 2 biovulate compartments. Style same length as stamens. Stigma bilobulate, globose. Seed vessel square, encircled by calyx, 2 locules each with 2 seeds.

Habitat.—Common in Bauang and Pasig. Blooms in November.

SOLANACEÆ.

Nightshade Family.

Solanum nigrum, L.

Nom. Vulg.—*Hierba mora*, Sp.; *Konty, Onty, Gamagamatisan*, Tag.; *Lagpakon, Bolagtob, Lubilubi*, Vis.; *Kuty, Lubilubi*, Bic.; *Black* or *Common Nightshade*, Eng.

Uses.—In the Philippines the entire plant is boiled and used for food, with the precaution of pouring off the first 2 or

3 waters in which it is cooked, which contain an active principle capable of causing such disagreeable symptoms as vertigo and nausea. A decoction of the leaves serves to cleanse chronic sores and in fact improves their condition; it is also used as a lotion for various forms of dermatitis, for erysipelas and old burns.

The plant is narcotic, antispasmodic and like belladonna it dilates the pupil.

In India the decoction is given internally, 200–250 grams, for hypertrophy of the liver, and it is considered a good diuretic and alterative. For such uses they heat the above dose in a clay vessel till the color changes from green to brown, when it is cooled and given next day. Its action is diuretic and hydragogue-cathartic. Mooden Sheriff recommends this treatment highly, and for dropsy further advises the aqueous extract, 12 grams during the day divided into 3 or 4 doses. Small doses of 30–60 grams of the decoction prepared as above described, are of use in some chronic skin diseases such as psoriasis.

In 1821 Defosses, of Besançon, obtained *solanine* from the fruit, previously isolated from the *S. Dulcamara*.

Botanical Description.—A plant about 2° high, stem straight, 3–4-angled, with white dots. Leaves lanceolate. Flowers white, in 2-ranked racemes. Calyx inferior, 5 persistent teeth. Corolla, 5 petals somewhat down-curved. Berry small, black when ripe.

Habitat.—Universally common. Blooms in January.

Capsicum fastigiatum, Bl. (*C. minimum*, Roxb.)

Nom. Vulg.—*Chili picante*, Sp.-Fil.; *Sili*, Tag.; *Capsicum*, *Red Pepper*, etc., Eng.

Uses.—The fruit of this species of pepper plant is called *agí* in Cuba and Porto Rico; it is in common use as a condiment in the Philippines. As a tonic and stimulant it is a useful article of food in hot countries where the digestive functions become sluggish. Used in moderation it prevents dyspepsia and consequent diarrhœa. It is used as a gargle for hoarseness, decreasing the congestion of the larynx and vocal cords.

GARGLE.—

Tincture of capsicum..................	8 grams.
Water..............................	160 "

Mix.

Recently capsicum in powder, extract, or tincture, has been recommended internally in the treatment of incipient hemorrhoids. The dose is .50 to 3 grams of the powder in pills or capsules; watery extract, 0.30–0.60; tincture, 10–30 drops.

The *C. annuum*, L., and other varieties of red pepper serve the same uses as the above.

BOTANICAL DESCRIPTION.—Stem 4-angled. Leaves opposite, ovate-lanceolate, entire. Petioles short. Flowers greenish-white in little clusters, drooping. Corolla wheel-shaped. Fruit straight, conical, slender, scarcely 1′ long.

HABITAT.—Universally common in the islands. Blooms at all times.

Datura alba, Nees. (*D. Metel*, Roxb. and Blanco.)

NOM. VULG.—*Talamponay*, Tag., Pam.; *Takbibuĝ*, Vis.; *Dhatura*, Indo-Eng.

USES.—The applications of this species are identical with those of *D. Stramonium* and it is official in the Pharmacopœia of India. It is antispasmodic, narcotic and toxic, and is used quite commonly with criminal intent in India and Indo-China. The cooked and bruised leaves make an efficient poultice in articular rheumatism.

The symptoms of poisoning by "dhatura" are: dilatation of the pupil, general malaise, dryness of the fauces and skin, hallucinations, rapid pulse, coma and death or permanent mania.

The dry leaf is smoked to abort asthma, and though its action is uncertain, it is one of the many remedies that should be tried, which though ineffective in one case may in another afford positive relief in this distressing disease. Not more than 1.50 grams should be smoked in one day and their use should be discontinued if any symptom of intoxication supervenes. The Pharmacopœia of India contains a tincture made from 75 grams of the ground seeds and 500 grams of alcohol. Dr. Waring states that 20 drops of this tincture are equivalent to 6 centigrams of opium and that in some cases it has given him better narcotic results than the opium. The extract is made from 500 grams of the powdered seeds, 500 cc. ether, 500 cc. alcohol and 500 cc. water. Dose, 5–20 centigrams a day in 4 doses.

The *D. fastuosa*, L., known in Manila by the common name of *Talamponay na itim*, Tag., possesses the same properties as the above. The Filipino physician, Sr. Zamora, successfully employed a poultice of bruised leaves cooked in vinegar and applied to the forehead and backs of the hands to reduce the fever of tuberculous patients.

Neither the leaves nor seeds of these two varieties of *Datura* have been studied from a chemical standpoint, but there is little doubt that the active principle is the *daturine* (atropine and hyoscyamine) that exists so abundantly in *D. Stramonium*.

Botanical Description.—Plant 5–6° high, with nodose branches, forked. Leaves ovate, angled, somewhat downy. Flowers large, white, axillary, solitary. Calyx tubular, 5-toothed. Corolla funnel-shaped, the limb 5-angled and 5-folded. Stamens 5, same length as calyx. Anthers long, flattened. Stigma thick, oblong, divisible in 2 leaves. Seed vessel globose, thorny, 4-valved over the base of the calyx. Seeds numerous, flattened, kidney-shaped. (Resembles closely the common Jamestown Weed of America, though much taller with much larger flowers.)

HABITAT.—Common on the shores of the sea. The *D. fastuosa* is differentiated by its violet flowers and double corolla.

Nicotiana Tabacum, L.

NOM. VULG.—*Tabaco*, Sp.; *Tobacco*, Eng.

USES.—Tobacco is a powerful sedative and antispasmodic, but owing to the accidents it may give rise to, its use in therapeutics is very limited. Like all the active Solanaceæ it is effective against neuralgia and spasm of the muscular tissues and is therefore indicated in strangulated hernia and in intestinal obstruction. In these conditions the infusion of 1–5 grams of the dried leaf to 250 grams of water is given by enema. Trousseau advises non-smokers who suffer from chronic constipation to smoke a cigarette fasting, a practice which, according to him, stimulates defecation. For the same condition the people of southern India are accustomed to apply a poultice of the bruised leaves to the anal region.

Tobacco has been used by enema to combat tetanus; Dr. Lesth, of the General Hospital for Europeans, Bombay, claims to have obtained excellent results by applying a poultice over the entire length of the spinal column. Dr. Dymock has confirmed this practice.

A decoction of the leaves is used as a lotion to destroy "pediculi capitis and pubis," and to wash gangrenous ulcers.

The daily increasing practice of smoking, like all other subjects, divides mankind into two camps, one for and one against the habit. Both parties exaggerate their arguments. The abuse of the plant without doubt sets up disturbances of the digestion, the heart and the nervous system. It is furthermore positive that persons of a certain disposition and with certain ailments are injured by even a moderate use of tobacco. The above facts serve as arms for the opponents of the habit; the robust who smoke and drink to excess and meet with an accidental death on a railroad or from an acute disease that overtakes them in the midst of perfect health, serve as arguments for the defenders, to prove the innocence of the custom. The antiseptic qualities of the smoke and of the entire plant also lend the smoker a defensive argument, as he may uphold the habit as hygienic and highly useful in preventing microbic infection. The antiseptic power of tobacco smoke is undoubted, but it is intolerable that a physician under the pretext of avoiding self infection should enter the house of his patient and continue smoking at the bedside.

Chronic nicotine poisoning is the result of a gradual intoxication by the absorption of the active principle of tobacco, the alkaloid nicotine. Excessive smoking conduces to nicotism, more common in Europe than in the tropics, because the natives of Europe smoke the pipe and being confined in closed dwellings, breathe continuously an atmosphere of smoke; in the Philippines, on the contrary, the pipe is almost unknown and owing to the nature of the dwellings the smoking is carried on practically in the open air. An injurious practice of the Filipino smokers is that of "swallowing the smoke," and this is a fitting point to call attention to an error of Dujardin-Beaumetz, who states that "in those who habitually swallow the smoke the nicotine acts directly upon the stomach." The expression "swallow smoke" (tragar el humo) does not mean to force it into the stomach by an act of deglutition, and I am sure no one attempts to dispose of it in that way; but to inspire or breath it into the air passages. It is evident that this latter habit does not involve the stomach, but those who practice it expose themselves more to nicotism than those who keep the smoke in the mouth or expel it through the nose.

The first cigar causes symptoms familiar to nearly everybody; dizziness, malaise, cold sweat, vomiting, diarrhœa, dilatation of the pupils and rapid heart action—an acute intoxication. Chronic intoxication or nicotism manifests itself by disturbances of digestion, vision and especially circulation. It has been assigned as one of the causes of early atheroma and of angina pectoris. It should therefore be proscribed in persons who present symptoms of gastro-intestinal or of heart disease, and in every patient who complains of slight precordial pains, commonly attributed to flatus, but in reality cardiac neuralgia, a fugitive symptom announcing the possibility of that grave accident, angina pectoris, capable of ending the life of the patient with one stroke.

Nicotine ($C_{10}H_{14}N_2$) is an oleaginous liquid heavier than water, colorless, changing to dark yellow on contact with the air. *Nicotianin* or "camphor of tobacco" is another substance found in the leaves, crystalline, tasteless, with an odor resembling tobacco. Nicotinic acid is a product of the combustion of nicotine.

BOTANICAL DESCRIPTION.—The tobacco plant is so familiar to all Americans that its description here would be superfluous. It grows in all parts of the islands, the best qualities being cultivated in the northern provinces of Luzon, especially Cagayan and La Isabela.

SCROPHULARIACEÆ.

Figwort Family.

Limnophila menthastrum, Benth. (*Tala odorata,* Blanco.)

NOM. VULG.—*Tala, Taramhampam,* Tag.; *Talatala,* Pam.; *Taratara,* Iloc.

USES.—An infusion of the leaves is given as a diuretic and digestive tonic. The plant is aromatic. It is seldom used, but is given for the same troubles and in the same doses as chamomile and *Eupatorium Ayapana.*

BOTANICAL DESCRIPTION.—A plant 1° high, with leaves opposite, lanceolate, ovate, serrate, hairy, many small pits on the lower face. Flowers rose color, solitary, sessile. Calyx, 5 sharp teeth. Corolla tubular, curved, compressed, downy within, limb cleft in 4 unequal lobes. Stamens didynamous. Ovary conical. Style shorter than the stamens. Stigma 3-lobuled. Seed vessel, 2 multiovulate chambers.

HABITAT.—Known universally. Blooms in June.

BIGNONIACEÆ.

Bignonia Family.

Oroxylum Indicum, Vent. (*Bignonia Indica*, L.; *B. quadripinnata*, Blanco; *Colosanthes Indica*, Bl.)

NOM. VULG.—*Pinkapinkahan, Pinkapinka, Taghilaw, Abaĝabaĝ*, Tag.; *Abaĝabaĝ*, Vis.

USES.—The Hindoos consider the trunk bark an astringent and tonic and use it commonly in diarrhœa and dysentery. In Bombay it has a wide use in veterinary practice as an application for the sore backs of the domestic cattle. Sarangadhara recommends for diarrhœa and dysentery the infusion of the roasted bark mixed with infusion of *Bombax malabaricum.*

Dr. Evers experimented with the powder and an infusion of the bark obtaining a strong diaphoretic action. He obtained the same effect with baths containing the bark and reported successful results in thus treating 24 cases of rheumatism. The dose of the powder was 0.30–1 gram a day in 3 doses; the infusion (30 grams bark to 300 boiling water), 90 grams a day in 3 doses. Combined with opium it had more pronounced diaphoretic effects than the compounds of opium and ipecac. The plant possesses no febrifuge properties.

BOTANICAL DESCRIPTION.—A tree, 5–6 meters high, trunk straight, hollow, the hollow space containing many thin partitions covered with small points; branches opposite. Leaves 4 times odd pinnate. Leaflets obliquely ovate, acute, entire, glabrous. Flowers in racemes with long, primary peduncles, large, fleshy, lurid, violet color, odor mawkish. Calyx inferior, cylindrical, monophyllous, entire. Corolla much longer than calyx, fleshy, bell-shaped, 5-lobed. Stamens 5, all fertile, fixed on the corolla, nearly equal in height. Style longer than stamens, flattened. Stigma cleft in 2 flat leaves. Silique or pod about 3° long and 2′ wide, flattened, borders grooved and curved downward, containing a great number of seeds encircled by a broad, flat, imbricated wing.

HABITAT.—Common in many parts of Luzon, in Mindanao, Cebú and Paragua.

PEDALIACEÆ.

Pedalium Family.

Sesamum Indicum, L.

NOM. VULG.—*Ajonjoli*, Sp.; *Lig̃á*, Tag.; *Log̃á*, Vis.; *Lag̃is*, Pam.; *Sesamé*, Indo-Eng. (*Benné Oil, Til Oil, Jinjili Oil.*)

USES.—The leaves are emollient and in the Philippines, India and the Southern States of North America they are commonly used to make poultices, as a substitute for linseed.

The decoction is prescribed internally as an emmenagogue and demulcent and externally as a lotion. It has the reputation of stimulating the growth of the hair and is used for this purpose quite commonly by the women of India.

The seeds are emollient, laxative, diuretic and emmenagogue; they contain an oil to which we shall refer presently. In some countries they form an article of diet; in the Philippines they are much used as a condiment. Waring reports good results in amenorrhœa, adding a handful of the bruised seeds to a hot sitz-bath. Two or 3 dessert-spoonfuls of the seeds eaten fasting and washed down with a glass of water, are very efficient in chronic constipation, both by their mechanical effect and the oil they contain; being non-irritant they are especially indicated in cases of constipation with hemorrhoids.

The seeds contain up to 45% of oil known in the Philippines under the name of *lana*, an Ilocano word meaning "oil." It is bright yellow, viscid, does not easily become rancid and is used for illuminating purposes in some Philippine provinces. In Japan and among the poor of India it serves as a food; in the latter country it is also very commonly used as a cosmetic, perfumed with various essences and used to anoint the hair and the body after the bath. In America it is given in place of castor oil in doses of 30–60 grams. In pharmacy it may be properly substituted for olive oil, especially in Linimentum Calcis prepared for burns.

BOTANICAL DESCRIPTION.—A plant 2–4° high, stem straight, square, grooved. Leaves trifoliate. Leaflets lanceolate, serrate, slightly downy. Common petiole long; secondary petiole very short. Flowers pinkish white, in spikes, each flower bearing 2 small glands. Calyx with 2 bracts at the base, top-shaped, monophyllous, 5 lanceolate teeth. Corolla large, 5-lobed, bell-shaped, expanded in the middle where it is spattered with small spots. Stamens didynamous. Anthers long. Ovary downy, quadrangular. Style same length as stamens. Stigma bifid. Seed vessel quadrangular, elongated, 4 opposite grooves, 4 chambers each containing many small ovoid seeds.

HABITAT.—Universal. Blooms in October.

ACANTHACEÆ.

Acanthus Family.

Acanthus ilicifolius, L.

NOM. VULG.—*Diliwariw*, *Dolo-ariw*, *Tiĝlog*, *Lagiwlagiw*, Tag.; *Titiw*, Vis.; *Dulawari*, Pam.

USES.—We are not familiar with the medicinal uses of this plant in the Philippines, but believe that its sole use is in the soap-making industry; the ash of the plant is rich in soda and potash salts and lye is prepared from it.

In Goa the leaves, rich in mucilage, are used locally in fomentations for rheumatism and neuralgia. Rheede mentions

16

as useful the application of the bruised sprouts to snake bites. Bontius attributes expectorant properties to the plant. The natives of Siam and Cochin China use it as a cordial and as a medicine for paralysis and asthma.

In Concan the sweetened decoction of the plant with a little cumin seed is given for dyspepsia with pyrosis.

Botanical Description.—A plant about 3° high, stem straight, beset with sharp eminences. Leaves opposite, membranaceous, lanceolate, pinnatifid, large teeth ending in prickles. Petioles very short, 2 thorns at the base. Flowers purplish white in spikes. Calyx double; the outer one of 2 parts, the inner 4. Corolla bell-shaped, lower lip broad, keeled, fleshy, notched above. Upper lip wanting, a notch in its place. Stamens 4, didynamous. Ovary superior, conical. Style of equal length with stamens. Stigma bifid. Seed vessels 2-celled, each cell with 2 heart-shaped, flattened, rough seeds.

Habitat.—Very common in regions inundated by salt water.

Barleria Prionitis, L. (*Barreliera Prionitis*, Blanco.)

Nom. Vulg.—*Kokoĝmanok, Kulanta*, Tag.

Uses.—This plant is not used medicinally in the Philippines. The natives of Bombay are accustomed to use its juice to anoint the soles of their feet during the rainy season in order to toughen the skin and prevent fissures due to prolonged maceration.

The leaf juice is bitter and acid; it is a favorite with the natives of India in the treatment of the catarrhal fevers common among their children, administered in doses of 2 tablespoonfuls a day mixed with sweetened water.

In Concan the dry bark is given for whooping-cough and the juice of the fresh bark in doses of 2 "tolas" (7.60 grams) for anasarca. Dr. Bidie states that the action is diaphoretic and expectorant.

Botanical Description.—A plant 2–3° high, stem creeping, the ends rising; enlarged at the joints, glabrous. Leaves smooth, opposite, lanceolate, finely serrate, fringed, somewhat downy below, glabrous above. Petioles short, 4 axillary spines. Flowers straw-color, axillary, sessile, solitary. Calyx deeply cleft in 4 parts, ovate, ending in spines. Corolla funnel-shaped. tube short, throat nude, limb 5-lobed. Stamens 4, didynamous, Ovary 2-celled. Style same length as stamens. Seed-vessel ovate, flattened and sharp-pointed, 2-celled, each cell with a flat, heart-shaped seed.

Habitat.—In Guadalupe, Mandaloyon and San Juan del Monte. Blooms in April.

Justicia Gendarussa, L. (*Gandarussa vulgaris*, Nees.; *Dianthera subserrata*, Blanco.)

Nom. Vulg.—*Kapanitulot*, Tag.; *Bunlaw*, Vis.

Uses.—In the Philippines this plant has the same applications as the *Lagundi* or *Vitex*, soon to be described. In India they give a decoction of the leaves for chronic rheumatism, the action probably being diaphoretic. The juice is employed for the coughs of childhood and externally as a resolvent for enlarged cervical glands. The bark of the young branches has a purplish color; in Java it is considered a good emetic.

Botanical Description.—A shrub 5–6° high, stem straight, branches smooth, obscurely 4-angled. Stems and leaves violet color, emitting a disagreeable odor (Blanco). Leaves opposite, lanceolate, acute, glabrous, obtusely serrate. Flowers terminal, white-green, in racemes of 3 sessile flowers with lanceolate bracts. Calyx, 5 long teeth. Corolla, short tube, 2-lipped, upper lip notched, lower lip broad with palate, ending in 3 lobules. Seed vessel with 4 seeds in its lower part.

Habitat.—Luzon, Mindanao, Panay.

Adhatoda vasica, Nees. (*Justicia Adhatoda*, L.)

NOM. VULG.—(?)

USES.—The Filipinos are but slightly familiar with this plant and it has no place in their therapeutical armamentarium. In India, however, it is very common and enjoys much reputation in the treatment of catarrhs, the grip, asthma and non-febrile, especially chronic, bronchial affections. The flowers, leaves and roots, but especially the flowers, possess antispasmodic properties and are prescribed in certain forms of asthma; they are bitter and slightly aromatic, and are given in infusion or electuary.

Drs. Jackson and Dott have testified from their own experience to the usefulness of the drug in chronic bronchitis, asthma and afebrile catarrh. Dr. Watt states that the natives of Bengal find relief for asthma in smoking the leaves. In Bombay its expectorant action is commonly known and its juice is used, mixed with borax and honey.

The dose of the aqueous extract made by evaporating the juice of the leaves, is .25–1 gram. The tincture is preferable, made by dissolving this extract in alcohol; dose 2–4 grams. Its efficiency is increased by the addition of pepper seeds (Waring). The Sanscrit writers recommend for cough, 3.80 grams of the leaf juice with honey. "It is very desirable that further trials be made to test the value of this remedy."—Pharmacopœia of India.

BOTANICAL DESCRIPTION.—A shrub with straight, smooth, ashy-gray trunk. Branches of same color but smoother. Leaves opposite, lanceolate, acute, smooth on both faces, 12–15 cm. long by 3–4 broad, petioles short. Flowers irregular and hermaphrodite in axillary spikes with long peduncles, opposite, large, white, covered with rusty spots, the lower part of the 2 lips purple. Calyx gamosepalous, regular, five deep clefts. Corolla gamopetalous, irregular, short tube, limb 2-lipped, the lower lip ending in a spur. Ovary free, 2-celled, each cell containing 2 ovules. Style filiform, long, inserted in a sort of canal formed by the upper lip of the corolla. Stigma bilobulate. Seed vessel depressed, 4 flattened, lenticular seeds.

HABITAT.—Luzon and Panay.

Rhinacanthus communis, Nees. (*Justicia nasuta*, L.)

NOM. VULG.—*Tagaktagak*, Tag.; *Nagamulli*, Indo-Eng.

USES.—The plant has much reputation in India in the treatment of skin diseases, and indeed its efficiency is great in the stubborn *Tinea circinata tropica*, known throughout the Orient as "dhobie-itch." In this disease it is applied for several days to the affected part in the form of a paste composed of the bruised leaves, the juice of the leaves and lemon juice. The fresh root also may be employed. The Hindoo physicians state that the root decoction in milk is aphrodisiac; the root is also regarded as an antidote for the bite of the "cobra da cabelho," but its virtue is purely imaginary. Of late years the plant has been used in Europe under the name of "tong-pang-chong," to treat chronic eczema.

Liborius made an analysis of the root in the laboratory of Dorpat, separating 13.51% ash and 1.87% *rhinocanthin*, as well as other ingredients. Rhinocanthin ($C_{14}H_{18}O_4$) is supposed to be the active principle of the root. It is analogous to quinon and resembles in many particulars chrysophanic and frangulic acids. It forms a resinous, amorphous mass, cherry red, odorless and tasteless, slightly soluble in water, forming a mildly alkaline solution in alcohol. It does not yield glucose when boiled with dilute hydrochloric acid. Liborius believes that it exists only in the intercellular spaces of the "root bark."

BOTANICAL DESCRIPTION.—A shrub, about 4° high, stem ash-colored, no spines. Leaves lanceolate, undulate, downy. Flowers white in spikes. Calyx gamosepalous, 5-toothed. Corolla long, filiform, limb 4-lobed, the 3 lower lobes ovate, the upper pointed. Stamens 2. Ovary free, 2 biovulate locules. Style simple. Stigma bifid. Seed vessel club-shaped, 4 seeds in the upper part.

HABITAT.—Common in the gardens of Manila.

VERBENACEÆ.

Vervain Family.

Lippia nodiflora, Rich. (*Verbena nodiflora*, L.; *V. capitata*, Blanco.)

NOM. VULG.—*Tsatsatsatsahan*, *Chachachachahan*, Tag.

USES.—The Filipinos drink an infusion of the leaves in place of tea, the long Tagalog name meaning "resembling tea." In India they drink the hot infusion to aid digestion. In some places the decoction of the leaves is given internally as an emollient and diuretic for gonorrhœa.

BOTANICAL DESCRIPTION.—A small plant with creeping stem taking root where it touches the ground, obscurely angular, covered with short down. Leaves opposite, smooth, clasping the stem, inversely ovate, serrate only above, slightly downy. Flowers white, slightly purplish, axillary on a common peduncle, in a rough conical head. Corolla somewhat bowed, funnel-form, gaping, throat narrow, limb 4-lobed, one lobe shorter than the rest. Stamens 4, 2 longer. Filament almost wanting. Anthers 4, fertile. Ovary superior, style very short. Stigma semi-globose. Fruit, 2 seeds covered by the pellicle of the ovary.

HABITAT.—Very common in the rice fields.

Tectona grandis, L.

NOM. VULG.—*Teca*, Sp.; *Tikla*, Tag.; *Dalondón*, *Yate*, *Kalayati*, Vis.; *Teak Tree*, Eng.

USES.—The powdered wood made into a paste with water is undoubtedly a useful application in acute dermatitis, especially that due to contact with the caustic oleo-resin of the cashew nut (*Anacardium*). A decoction of the powder gives good results as a gargle for aphthæ, gingivitis, and other inflammations within the buccal cavity. In India they give internally 6–12 grams as a vermifuge, and for dyspepsia with "heartburn."

The flowers are diuretic according to Endlicher; the bark is astringent; the leaves and the seeds are purgative, the latter yielding an oil which they use in India to stimulate the growth of the hair. Gibson considers the seeds diuretic and quotes two cases where abundant diuresis immediately followed by the application of a poultice of the bruised seeds over the pubis. In Concan they make a sort of extract from the wood and apply it to the yoke sores of the cattle to prevent the growth of maggots. This disinfectant action marks the plant as worthy of further experiment.

Rumphius is authority for the statement that the infusion of the leaves is used in cholera. The Chinese make vessels of the wood to preserve their drinking water at sea; the first and second waters are bitter and are thrown away, but after that the water has no disagreeable taste and is said to aid digestion.

It has been said that the wood was poisonous because at one time several workmen died from the effects of wounds caused by splinters of the wood, but the statement has not been confirmed by later cases and the deaths were most probably due to a septic infection independent of the chemical composition of the splinters.

R. Romanis has extracted a resin from the wood by alcohol; it is soft, and on distillation yields a crystalline body called by the author *tectoquinon* ($C_{18}H_{10}O_2$), on account of its resemblance to the quinons. It melts at 171° and volatilizes slightly at ordinary temperature.

Botanical Description.—A tree with leaves almost round, oval, entire, 30–60 centimeters by 20–40, the under surface covered with hoary down. Petioles very short, flattened.

Flowers in panicles. Primary peduncle square. Calyx inferior, bell-shaped, very large when ripe, 5-cleft. Corolla white, longer than calyx, covered with a mealy substance, bell-shaped, 5-lobed. Stamens 5 or 6, inserted in the corolla. Filaments flattened, somewhat longer than the corolla. Anthers semi-globose, a yellow zone below and a black circle above. Ovary free, rounded, 4 locules each with 1 seed. Style same length as stamens. Stigma bilobulate. Drupe globose, woolly, spongy, depressed, covered by the membranous inflated calyx; contains one nut, very hard, 4 apartments each containing one seed.

HABITAT.—The mountains of Morong and Tanay (of La Laguna Province) bear some specimens. Very common in the island of Negros and in Mindanao. It also grows in the Visayas, Mindora and Paragua. Blooms in September.

Vitex trifolia, L. (*V. repens*, Blanco.)

NOM. VULG.—*Lagundi*, Tag.; *Gapasgapas*, Vis.; *Dangla*, Iloc.

Vitex Negundo, L. (*V. Leucoxylon*, Blanco.)

NOM. VULG.—*Lagundi, Malawin*, Tag.

USES.—Both species are used medicinally in the Philippines and both enjoy high repute. A variety of the first that seems to possess the same virtues is the *V. repens*, Blanco, called *lagundiĝ gapaĝ* by the Tagalos.

V. trifolia is regarded in India as the most powerful species and Bontius has extolled it highly, calling attention to the anodyne, diuretic and emmenagogue properties of the leaves. These are very effective applied in fomentation to rheumatic joints and their use is extensive both in India and the Malay Archipelago. A decoction of the leaves is used locally and as a vapor-bath in the treatment of beriberi. A large earthen pot is filled with leaves and water and brought to a boil; the pot is then placed under a chair in which the patient sits enveloped in a sheet or blanket. If necessary the pot may be removed 2 or 3 times, heated and replaced until abundant sweating is induced. An apparatus to conduct the steam under the chair would be much handier, but it is unsafe to place a small stove or lamp under the chair for fear of setting fire to the cloth.

In India and the Philippines there is a peculiar inflammation localized in the soles of the feet and characterized by an intense burning rather than pain, not described in the textbooks, but called by the natives "burning of the feet" ("quemadura del pié" or "ignipedites"); in our own experience and according to the consensus of the physicians of India, the application of these leaves 3 or 4 times a day to the soles of the feet has afforded marked relief. The leaves are heated in an earthen pot without the addition of water, and when sufficiently hot are applied and held in place by a bandage.

Dr. W. Ingledew states that the natives of Mysore (south of India) treat rheumatism and febrile catarrhs by steam baths of the decoction of vitex. A decoction of the leaves is in common use in the Philippines, Malay Islands and India as a bath for women in the puerperal state.

The dry leaves are smoked for headache and catarrh. According to creditable authority the application of the heated leaves in orchitis produces good results. The root is tonic, febrifuge and expectorant and the fruit nervine and emmenagogue according to the Sanscrit writer.

Botanical Descriptión.—*V. trifolia* is a small tree, 3–4 meters high. The fruit and leaves are said to emit the odor of rosemary. Leaves ternate. Leaflets oval, entire, hoary below, no secondary petioles. Flowers purplish in forked panicle. Corolla bell-shaped with palate. The lower lip 3-lobed, the middle lobe larger; upper lip smaller, 2-lobed. Stamens 4, free, didynamous. Ovary free. Style simple, with stigma-bearing lobules. Berry-like drupe, with 4-celled nut, one seed in each cell.

HABITAT.—Common on the seashore. Blooms in June.

The *V. Negundo* is a small tree like the preceding, but when it grows in the forest it develops to a tree of the first order, yielding a valuable building wood called *molave* (Sp.) or more properly *molawin*. Leaves compound with 5 leaflets. Secondary petioles short. Flowers in dichotomous panicle. Fruit like that of the foregoing species.

Clerodendron infortunatum, L. (*C. fortunatum,* Blanco.)

NOM. VULG.—*Kasupaĝit, Gubat,* Tag.; *Saliĝ-wak,* Vis.

USES.—The fresh juice of the leaves is used in India as a vermifuge, according to K. L. Dey; it is also used as a bitter tonic in malarial fever, especially of children. As a tonic and antipyretic it is certainly worthy of recommendation.

Dr. Bholanauth Bose calls attention to this plant as a good substitute for *Ophelia chirata,* DC. as a tonic and antipyretic.

The infusion of the bruised leaves (10 grams to water 300 cc.) is given up to 200 cc. a day in 3 or 4 doses; the tincture (leaves 60 grams, alcohol 90 %, 500 cc.) is given up to 10 grams a day in 5 or 6 doses.

BOTANICAL DESCRIPTION.—A shrub with nearly round stem; leaves opposite, ovate, oblong; acute, entire, slightly downy. Flowers terminal in umbellate panicles, the umbellets opposite and each bearing 3 flowerets. Calyx bluish, long, tubular, somewhat expanded in the middle, divided in 5 parts. Corolla twice as long as the calyx, tube filiform, limb 5-lobed. Stamens didynamous, their lower parts grown to the tube of the corolla. Filaments longer than the corolla. Ovary conical. Style of same length as the stamens. Stigma bifid. Berry dry, quadrate, depressed, the shell hard, 4 grooves, 4 cells, each containing a seed.

HABITAT.—Very common in Manila and in the forests.

LABIATÆ.

Mint Family.

Ocimum basilicum, L. (*O. Americanum*, Blanco.)

NOM. VULG.—*Solasi*, Tag., Pam.; *Bonak*, Vis.; *Sweet Basil*, Eng.

Ocimum gratissimum, L. (*O. virgatum* Blanco.)

NOM. VULG.—*Lokoloko*, Tag., Pam.; *Kolonkogon*, Vis.

Ocimum sanctum, L. (*O. flexuosum*, Blanco.)

NOM. VULG.—*Balanoy*, Tag.; *Sacred Basil*, Eng.

USES.—All three species possess a characteristic camphoraceous odor and are commonly grouped under the one name, *albahacas* (sweet basil). Some natives call them *solasi* and others *balanay*, but many are able to distinguish the various species correctly. All three have analogous properties, but the most widely used is the *O. basilicum*. These properties are stimulant, diaphoretic, and expectorant, and the infusion is used commonly for flatulent colic and painful dyspepsia. The dry powdered leaves of the *O. sanctum* are taken as snuff by the natives of India in the treatment of a curious endemic disease characterized by the presence of small maggots in the nasal secretion; this disease is called peenash, and possibly exists in the Philippines though I have never encountered it.

Martins states that in Brazil they use a decoction of the mucilaginous leaves of the *O. gratissimum* in the treatment of gonorrhœa and Dr. Waitz highly recommends a strong decoction of these leaves for the aphthæ of children, which he claims to have cured by this means after all European drugs had failed. This fact and the action of the snuff above mentioned, demonstrate the antiseptic properties of the plant, due doubtless to its abundant aromatic principles.

O. basilicum contains a green essential oil, very aromatic, becoming solid; it is a sort of camphor ($C_{20}H_{16}6HO$, Raybaud) and crystallizes in 4-faced prisms.

All the plants are used to prepare aromatic baths for cases of atrophy and debility in children (Waitz) and for the treatment of rheumatism and paralysis.

BOTANICAL DESCRIPTION.—*O. gratissimum* is a plant 2–3° high, stem straight, downy. Leaves medium lanceolate, finely serrate from the middle upwards, with short hairs and transparent dots. Flowers in long terminal racemes. Calyx, upper lip horizontal, round; lower lip 3 pointed parts, the middle one subdivided in two. Corolla yellowish, inverted, one lip cleft in 4 obtuse lobes; the other longer, narrow, serrate. Stamens didynamous, 2 shorter. Anthers semilunar. Stigma bifid. Seeds 4.

The *O. Americanum* has leaves lanceolate, ovate, acute, full of pores, somewhat downy. It is more fragrant than the other species and its flowers are bluish-white in racemes.

The *O. sanctum* is the most sacred plant of the Hindoos, dedicated to Vishnu; its branches are wavy or cauliflexuous, leaves obliquely ovate, obtuse, serrate, nearly glabrous.

HABITAT.—All species are very common and universally known.

Coleus aromaticus, Benth. (*C. suganda*, Blanco.)

NOM. VULG.—*Orégano*, Sp.-Fil.; *Suganda*, Tag.; *Marjoram*, Eng. (The Sp. and Eng. names are incorrect.)

USES.—The fleshy, aromatic leaves of this plant are bruised and applied locally for the bites of centipedes and scorpions. They are also applied to the temples and forehead for headache, held in place by a bandage. In Cochin China they are used in asthma, chronic bronchitis, epilepsy and other convulsive diseases. The juice of the leaves is a carminative and is given to children suffering with wind colic. Dr. Wight claims to have observed occasional intoxicating effects following its use, but Dymock states that he has never observed such effects. The plant contains a coloring matter, *colein* ($C_{10}H_{10}O_3$), red, insoluble in ether, soluble in alcohol, slightly soluble in water. On the addition of ammonia the solution changes to purple, then violet, indigo, green, and, finally, greenish-yellow.

Another species, the *C. atropurpureus*, Benth. (*C. grandifolius*, Blanco), well known in the Philippines by its common name *mayana*, is used in the treatment of bruises, the bruised fleshy leaves being the part employed ; these leaves are downy and dark violet in color.

BOTANICAL DESCRIPTION.—Leaves opposite, nearly sessile, cordate, obtuse, downy and very fleshy. Flowers in a quadrangular raceme, each group of these flowerets having a concave scale at the base. Calyx bell-shaped, 2-lipped; the upper lip longer and entire; the lower with 4 narrow teeth. Corolla a pale violet, 5 times longer than the calyx. Stamens didynamous, straight, longer than the corolla. Style bifid. Seeds 4.

HABITAT.—Universally abundant.

Rosmarinus officinalis, L.

NOM. VULG.—*Romero*, Sp. ; *Rosemary*, Eng.

USES.—This is one of the plants most valued by the Filipinos. Its infusion is used as an eye-wash for slight catarrhal conjunctivitis, applied 3 or 4 times a day. It is one of the aromatic plants used so commonly to bathe women in the puerperal state, and in vapor baths for rheumatism, paralysis and incipient catarrhs. The entire plant is a stimulant and carminative but little used internally ; in atonic dyspepsia it has given good results taken in the same form as the infusion of manżanilla.

It contains a large per cent. of an essential oil which gives the plant its agreeable odor. This oil enters into the composition of "Cologne Water"; it is said to arrest falling of the hair and is a diffusible stimulant which may be given internally in doses of 3–5 drops. It is colorless and liquid when fresh, but in time becomes dark and viscid. It combines freely with alcohol and its density is 0.885.

BOTANICAL DESCRIPTION.—A plant from 2 to 3° high. Leaves sessile, linear, obtuse, margins revolute, white-hoary beneath. Calyx tubular, 2-lipped. Corolla rose-violet color, gaping; the upper lip concave, 2-lobed; the lower lip longer, 3-lobed. Stamens, 2 fertile and 2 sterile. Style, same length as the stamens. Stigma simple. Fruit, 4 seeds in the depths of the calyx.

HABITAT.—It is carefully cultivated throughout the Philippines.

Anisomeles ovata, R. Br. (*Phlomis alba*, Blanco.)

NOM. VULG.—*Taligharap*, Tag.; *Jerusalem Sage*, Eng.

USES.—The infusion of the leaves is bitter and aromatic and is used in catarrhal inflammations of the stomach and intestines and in intermittent fevers. Used as a vapor-bath it produces abundant diaphoresis, and the infusion given internally has a like effect. The leaves, when distilled, yield an oil which is used as an external application in rheumatism.

BOTANICAL DESCRIPTION.—A plant 6° or more high. Root fibrous, trunk and branches enlarged at the joints. Leaves opposite, ovate, obtusely serrate, soft and downy. Flowers pink, verticillate, in opposite clusters around the stem, with several linear and hairy involucres at the base of each cluster. Calyx, 5 sharp teeth. Corolla, 2-lipped; the lower much larger, downy within, 3-lobed, the middle lobe larger and broader, notched at the extremity, and its borders turned downward; the other 2 lateral lobes very small, narrow; the upper lip much shorter and smaller, entire, enveloping the stamens. Stamens didynamous. Style about the same length as the stamens. Stigma bifid. Fruit, 4 small seeds.

HABITAT.—Very common on the fields of Manila Province.

Leucas aspera, Spreng. (*Phlomis Zeylanica*, Blanco.)

NOM. VULG.—*Pansipansi, Solasolasian, Karukansoli,* Tag.; *Pansipansi, Paypaysi,* Vis.

USES.—The bruised leaves are applied to the bites of serpents or poisonous insects. In India they are similarly used. The juice of the leaves is very useful in the treatment of certain skin diseases, especially psoriasis.

BOTANICAL DESCRIPTION.—A plant about 2° high, very well known to the natives. Leaves sessile, lanceolate, finely serrate and covered with short hairs. Flowers terminal, white, verticillate, with the characteristics of the mint family.

PLANTAGINACEÆ.

Plantain Family.

Plantago erosa, Wall. (*P. crenata* and *media*, Blanco.)

NOM. VULG.—*Llantén,* Sp.-Fil.; *Lantín,* Tag.; *Plantain,* Eng.

USES.—The leaves of this popular plant are the commonest remedy in the Philippines for abscess of the gums. They are bruised and applied with a little lard over the swollen cheek. It is emollient and, in decoction, is used as a substitute for flaxseed.

BOTANICAL DESCRIPTION.—This plant is so universally known that there is no fear of confusing it with others. It flourishes as a common weed in the U. S. as well as the Philippines.

NYCTAGINACEÆ.

Four-O'Clock Family.

Mirabilis Jalapa, L. (*M. longiflora*, Blanco.)

NOM. VULG.—*Maravillas, Suspiros,* Sp.-Fil.; *Gilalas,* Tag.; *Four O'Clock, Marvel of Peru,* Eng.

USES.—The root is purgative and possesses the same active

principles, the same properties and is given in the same dose as jalap. According to the experience of Shoolbred, Hunter, W. O'Shaughnessy and Ainslie, its purgative action is weak and uncertain and therefore unworthy of use as a substitute for jalap. The bruised leaves are used as poultices to hasten suppuration, but according to Waring they are capable of causing dermatitis.

BOTANICAL DESCRIPTION.—The flowers open toward the end of the day and close again at sunrise. The root is blackish and spindle-shaped. The stem smooth, branches forked. Leaves opposite, lanceolate-cordate, acute, somewhat downy along the borders and the upper surface. Petioles short. Flowers fragrant, almost constantly blooming, of different colors even in the same plant, terminal, in umbels. Pedicels very short. Calyx persistent, 5-toothed. Corolla superior, very long, its tube downy, funnel-form, limb 5-lobed. Stamens 5, longer than the corolla. Style longer than the stamens. Stigma globose. Nut small, black, globose, many-ribbed, full of a mealy substance.

HABITAT.—Common in gardens.

AMARANTHACEÆ.

Amaranth Family.

Amaranthus spinosus, L.

NOM. VULG.—*Kilitis, Orayi*, Tag.; *Ayantoto*, Pam.; *Kalitis, Tilites, Bayaĝ-bayaĝ*, Vis.; *Kuanton*, Iloc.; *Thorny Amaranth*, Eng.

USES.—The entire plant is emollient and its principal use is as a poultice for inflammations, bruises, etc. The decoction of the root is diuretic and antiphlogistic and is used in Mauritius (30 grams root to 750 cc. water) as an internal remedy for gonorrhœa ; indeed it is there regarded as a specific for that disease, checking the discharge and the "ardor urinæ." It should be continued till the cure is complete.

The bruised leaves are used locally for eczema.

Botanical Description.—A plant 2–3° high of a reddish color. Leaves alternate, lanceolate, broad, notched at the apex, wavy, glabrous. Petioles with a pair of spines in their axils. Flowers small, yellow-green, in round axillary clusters and in long terminal spikes. The pistillate flowers are sometimes separated from the staminate, sometimes mixed with them in the lower part of the spike. Staminate: No corolla, calyx 2–5 parts, stamens 4–5. Pistillate: Style and stigma 2 or 3, otherwise the same as the staminate. Seed vessel with 1 seed.

Habitat.—Common in all parts. Blooms in October.

Achyranthes obtusifolia, Lam. (*A. aspera*, Blanco.)

Nom. Vulg.—*Hangor, Hangot, Dokotdekot, Libay*, Tag.; *Angod*, Pam.

Uses.—The plant has astringent and diuretic properties; the latter were observed by Dr. Cornish, who communicated the facts to Waring, calling special attention to the good service the drug had afforded him in dropsy. Other physicians in India have confirmed these observations of Cornish. The decoction is made of 60 grams of the entire plant to 750 cc. water, boiled till reduced one-half and strained under pressure. Dose, 60 cc. every 2 hours till diuresis is induced.

The ashes of this plant, like those of the *Amaranthus spinosus*, L., contain a large quantity of potassa, and are used for washing clothes; on this account it has received its Sanscrit name *Apamarga* (the washer). The ashes are also mixed in an infusion of ginger and given internally in dropsy.

The flowers are bruised and applied to the bites of snakes and other poisonous animals. In India there is a superstition that carrying these flowers about the person will keep off scorpions.

Botanical Description.—A plant about 3° high, the stem angular and downy. Leaves opposite, downy, clasping the stem, lanceolate, very obtuse and wavy. Flowers bent

17

downward in a long spike bearing many flowerets. Calyx, 5 tough scales. Corolla wanting. Nectary much smaller than the calyx, monophyllous, 5-lobed. Stamens 5. Ovary top-shaped, upper part somewhat concave. Style same length as stamens. Stigma coarse, bifid. Fruit, a seed covered with 2 membranes, one enveloping it completely, the outer one adherent in only one part.

HABITAT.—Common in Luzon. Blooms in November.

CHENOPODIACEÆ.

Goosefoot Family.

Chenopodium ambrosioides, L.

NOM. VULG.—*Alpasotes*, Sp.-Fil.; *Pasotis, Apasotis*, Tag.; *American Worm-seed, Mexican Tea*; Eng.

USES.—This plant is a native of Mexico. It has a peculiar, somewhat offensive odor and an acrid, aromatic taste due to an essential oil resembling peppermint (?). According to Padre Mercado, "When the seeds are taken with wine, sensation is so dulled that the drinker may be whipped without feeling the lashes, and even if put to the torment, does not feel it." These properties, if true, make this plant one of the most useful in the Philippines. The entire plant is stimulant. The infusion, given internally, causes sweating, excites the circulation, is diuretic, tonic, stomachic, and useful as well as an antispasmodic in nervous troubles. The leaves are employed in making the infusion, 8 grams to 200 of boiling water. It is widely used in bronchial catarrhs and in asthma on account of its sudorific and expectorant action. It seems also to possess emmenagogue properties. The seeds yield on distillation a yellow essential oil with a strong and disagreeable odor, density 0.908. Both seeds and flowers are vermifuge, and are used as such in Brazil in doses of 8 grams in infusion or with an equal dose of castor oil. The anthelmintic dose of the essential oil is 5–15 drops with powdered sugar.

Rilliet and Barthez recommend the following potion for infantile chorea:

Leaves of chenopodium	4 grams.
Water	500 "

Make an infusion and add syrup of orange flowers 50 grams. Dose, several tablespoonfuls a day.

Botanical Description.—A plant 2° high; stem beset with hairs, many-angled. Leaves lanceolate, varying from entire to cut-pinnatifid. Flowers green, sessile, axillary, in small clusters. Calyx 5-parted. Corolla wanting. Stamens 5. Filaments flattened, inserted near the center of the flowers opposite the parts of the calyx. Anthers in 2 globose parts. Ovary superior, globose, depressed, unilocular, uniovulate. Style none. Stigmas, 2, 3 or 4, short, divergent. Fruit a lenticular seed covered by the membrane of the ovary.

Habitat.—Common in gardens and fields. Blooms in May.

ARISTOLOCHIACEÆ.

Birthwort Family.

Aristolochia Indica, L.

Nom. Vulg.—*Timbagan, Malaubi,* Tag.; *Indian Birthwort,* Eng.

Uses.—The root has a wide use in medicine in the Philippines; it is bitter, of a nauseating odor and has the reputation of being a powerful antidote for the bites of poisonous serpents and insects. It has further use in the treatment of malarial fever, in dyspepsia, and in the flatulent colic of teething children. It is regarded as tonic and emmenagogue. In various forms of diarrhœa it appears to be effective and Dr. Gibson states that it is useful in intestinal disorders. In the Philippines it is not only given internally but also externally applied over the abdomen, mixed with hot cocoanut oil (10 grams of the powdered root to 100 oil).

The first Portuguese settlers in India called the drug "Cobra Root," because the natives regarded it as an antidote for the bite of the terrible "Cobra da Capello." This reputation, however, seems not to have been deserved, judging from the fearful mortality in India and Ceylon due to the bite of the cobra.

Dr. Imlach, a surgeon of Singapore, states that in one season in one collectorate, Shikapore, no less than 306 cases of snake bites were officially reported, the mortality being 63, or about 20.58 per cent. Other reports make it safe to conclude that in the entire province during the year no less than 300 deaths were due to this cause alone. Dr. Waring believes that if an antidote for snake bite exist in the vegetable kingdom it will most probably be found in the natural order Aristolochiaceæ.

In North India this drug is used as emmenagogue and anti-arthritic, and in Banda for intermittent fevers and intestinal disorders. The juice of the leaves is emetic. The dose of the powdered root is 3–5 grams daily.

Botanical Description.—A twining shrub, with leaves heart-shaped, ovate, acute, glabrous. Petioles short. Flowers dark reddish-gray, in panicles. Calyx wanting. Corolla globose below, the tube cylindrical, expanding at the top. Anthers 6, in pairs. Filaments, none. Styles 6, very coarse, a membrane at the base including all. Stigmas simple. Seed vessel inferior, 6-ribbed, 6 cells and many winged seeds. The seed vessel after casting the seeds resembles a pair of balance scales with its little plates or pans. Hence the Tagalo name *Timbaĝan* meaning "balance."

Habitat.—In Luzon and Panay. Blooms in November.

PIPERACEÆ.

Pepper Family.

Piper Betle, L. (*Chavica Betle* and *C. auriculata*, Miq.; *Piper Betel*, Blanco.)

Nom. Vulg.—*Hojas de buyo*, Sp.-Fil.; *Itmó*, Tag.; *Mamin*, Bic.; *Buyo*, *Mamón*, Vis.; *Samat*, Pam.; *Betel Pepper*, Eng.

Uses.—A masticatory, used all over the extreme Orient, is composed of the leaves of this plant, a little slaked oyster-shell lime and a rounded slice of the bonga or areca nut; the Filipinos call this combination *bayo*, though the name is not of native origin; the Tagalos call it *hitsú*. The use of buyo by careless persons is decidedly repugnant, for the mixture of the lime and the pigment of the bonga imparts a blood-red or rather brick-red color to the saliva which they spit in mouthfuls into the streets and other public places with no thought of the feelings of others. Unless the mouth is carefully cleaned the teeth become encrusted with a sort of black enamel and the breath assumes a detestable odor. When used in small quantities and with proper toilet of the mouth, and this is the common practice among the Filipinos, buyo seems to be a very useful preservative of the teeth and a gingival and stomachic tonic. These properties are readily understood when we consider that the lime is antacid, the bonga astringent and tonic and the betel aromatic and stimulant.

The buyo leaf plays a very important part in the therapeutics of the infant of the Philippines: in its indigestions, colics and diarrhœas the heated leaves are applied to the abdomen previously anointed with hot cocoanut oil. In bronchitis and laryngitis the heated leaves are applied over the chest or neck after rubbing the parts with oil. It undoubtedly produces good effects and the physicians of India recommend it in the same cases and in the same form as in the Philippines. Applied to the breasts of parturient women it dries up the milk and in the same way tends to reduce any glandular enlargement.

Dr. Kleinstück of Java recommends the essence of the leaves in all sorts of catarrhs and as an antiseptic in doses of one drop to 140 of the vehicle. This essence is obtained by distillation; it is dark in color, has an acrid taste and an odor resembling that of tea. Its density is 1.020. The dried leaves contain one-half per cent. of the essence and it is probable that the fresh ones contain a greater proportion.

BOTANICAL DESCRIPTION.—A plant with yellow flowers and scandent stem, climbing straight up trees or artificial supports. Leaves cleft at the base, acute, entire, glabrous, dark green. According to Blanco it is cultivated best in somewhat sandy soil. Pasay, near Manila, and Bauang, in Batangas, furnish a leaf most highly appreciated.

Piper nigrum, L.

NOM. VULG.—*Pimienta*, Sp.; *Paminta*, *Malisa*, Tag.; *Black Pepper*, Eng.

USES.—The berry-like fruit of the pepper is more extensively used as a condiment in cooking than in the treatment of disease. Used in moderation, however, it is of considerable value as a convenient stomachic and aid to digestion in tropical countries where the digestive functions readily become sluggish. Its abuse may lead to serious consequences, such as inflammation of the gastro-intestinal mucous membrane, of the portal system and the liver itself.

Pepper is used as a febrifuge in the various forms of malarial fevers, in the form of granules of 8 or 10 berries in a cup of brandy and anise (Spanish); this is taken by the patient in one dose at the beginning of the cold stage and followed by large quantities of water to relieve the thirst caused by the pepper. This treatment causes the cold stage to rapidly subside and more rapidly induces and intensifies the sweating stage. It is said that no further attack of fever follows.

Piperin ($C_{17}H_{19}NO_3$) is febrifuge and is given in pill form internally in doses of 30–60 centigrams; the action of the crude drug is evidently due to this neutral principle.

BOTANICAL DESCRIPTION.—The plant is a perennial, climbing shrub. Leaves oval, tapering at both extremities, 7-nerved. Flowers yellow, in a spike. Stigmas 2, bifid. Fruit globose, with one seed.

Habitat.—The dried fruit of the pepper is universally familiar. It was at one time cultivated in the Philippines, especially in Batangas, and Gen. Basco promulgated a series of orders to encourage its cultivation. Padre Gainza, afterward Bishop of Nueva Cáceres, wrote a report about its cultivation, but since then the subject has entirely disappeared from notice.

CHLORANTHACEÆ.

Chloranth Family.

Chloranthus officinalis, Bl. (*C. Indicus*, Wight.; *C. inconspicuus*, Blanco.)

Nom. Vulg.—Unknown.

Uses.—All parts of the plant are aromatic. The leaves and stems lose this property after drying, but the roots, if properly dried, preserve it for a long time. They have a camphoraceous odor and bitter, aromatic taste, reminding one of that of *Aristolochia Serpentaria*. The mountaineers of Java use an infusion of the powdered root and the bark of the *Cinnamomum Culilowan* to treat puerperal eclampsia. Combined with carminatives like anise and onion, they use it with some success in virulent small-pox of children. The infusion seems to be efficacious in fevers accompanied by debility and suppression of the function of the skin. It has also been prescribed in the intermittent fevers of Java, mixed with an infusion of the leaves of the *Cedrela Toona*. Blume states that it is one of the most powerful stimulants known.

Botanical Description.—A plant 3–4° high. Stem quadrangular. Leaves opposite, broad, lanceolate, serrate, with stiff-pointed teeth and somewhat scaly beneath. Petioles very short, clasping the stem at their base, with 2 intermediate stipules ending in two awl-shaped points. Flowers compound in axillary spikes, which bear the flowerets in 2 ranks, each flower with a keeled bract. The corolla (if it may be so called) a fleshy, 3-lobed lamina. Perianth wanting. Receptacle dome-shaped. Anthers 4, inserted on the surface of the lamina, 2-valved. Ovary 1-celled, with 1 ovule. Style short. Berry-like fruit, globose, with 1 seed covered by a somewhat brittle membrane.

HABITAT.—La Laguna and other provinces of Luzon. Blooms in September.

LAURACEÆ.

Laurel Family.

Cinnamomum pauciflorum, Nees. (*Laurus culilaban*, Var., Blanco.)

C. tamala, Nees. (*L. culilaban*, Blanco.)

NOM. VULG. (of both).—*Kaliĝag, Makaliĝag*, Tag., Vis.; *Kandaroma*, Iloc; *Cassia Lignea* or *Cassia*, Eng.

USES.—The bark of both species is known in pharmacy as Chinese cassia or Chinese cinnamon (cassia cinnamon). Indeed it is very like the cinnamon of Ceylon, comes in curled quills, has the same odor and taste though not so delicate; but it is darker in color, with a surface less clean and smooth. Its chemical composition is identical with that of the latter and nowadays it forms an important article of commerce.

Cinnamon renders good service in therapeutics as a stimulant of the digestive tract and a heart tonic. In the atonic diarrhœas so common in the Philippines a tincture of cinnamon in doses of 8–10 grams a day, or the powder in cases where alcohol was contraindicated, have given me unhoped-for results.

In Spain and the Philippines it is very popular as a condiment in the kitchen of the confectionery and as a flavor for chocolate; in fact in those countries it takes the place of vanilla in France. It enters into the composition of several elixirs and compound tinctures, such as "Botot's Water" (dentifrice), "Elixir of Garus" (tonic stimulant), "Balsam of Fioraventi" (external stimulant), laudanum and the elixir of the Grande Chartreuse (diffusible stimulant).

Lately it has been demonstrated that the essence is a powerful antiseptic, in the presence of which typhoid fever bacilli cannot develop.

BOTANICAL DESCRIPTION.—A tree, 15–20° high. Leaves opposite, lanceolate, 3-nerved, entire, glabrous. Flowers yellow, paniculate, umbellate. Common peduncles very long, those of the flowerets long. Calyx none. Corolla, 6 ovate, hairy petals. Stamens 9; 6 external to the rest and bearing the anthers, 4 on each filament, 2 below the others; the 3 inner stamens bear 2 anthers each.

Inc th second species the flowers form loose, terminal panicles. Stamens 9; 6 filaments inserted on the receptacle, spatulate, each bearing 4 anthers on the inferior face; the other 3 filaments thick, each bearing 4 anthers. Between the last filaments are 8 nearly globose glandules.

HABITAT.—Both species are common in the forests of Luzon. The first species blooms in May, the second in January.

Cassytha filiformis, L.

NOM. VULG.—*Malabohok.*

USES.—This plant has no therapeutical uses in the Philippines. In Senegal it is employed, according to Dujardin-Beaumetz, mixed with lard to treat urethritis; its action is to decrease the ardor urinæ. It is not stated whether this mixture is used internally or externally.

In Cochin China the same writer states that it is used as an antisyphilitic. In India it is used for the piles and as an alterative for bilious disorders. It possibly acts as a circulatory stimulant.

BOTANICAL DESCRIPTION.—A slender, thread-like, cylindrical vine, without leaves, that covers the trees like a mantle, so luxuriant is its growth. Flowers yellow, in axillary spikes. Calyx small, 3 sepals. Corolla, 3 fleshy concave petals. Stamens 12 in 4 verticils, 9 fertile and 3 inner sterile. Ovary 1-celled, 1-ovuled. Style cylindrical. Drupe globose, 1–2″ in diameter, covered by a fleshy envelope, formed by the receptacle. Seeds without albumen.

HABITAT.—Luzon, Mindanao, Cebú, on the seashore.

EUPHORBIACEÆ.

Spurge Family.

Euphorbia pilulifera, L. (*E. capitata*, Lam.; *E. hirta*, Blanco.)

NOM. VULG.—*Golondrina*, Sp.-Fil.; *Gatasgatas*, *Batobatonis*, *Sayikan*, Tag.; *Buyayawa*, *Tawawa*, *Bowi*, Vis.; *Malismalis*, *Sisiwhan*, *Bolobotones*, *Magatas*, Pam.

USES.—This plant has a reputation in the Philippines as a hæmostatic of great efficiency, for which purpose the whole plant is crushed and applied as a poultice over the wound. Like all members of this family it abounds in milky juice. We have had no occasion to employ it as a hæmostatic, but do not doubt its action in view of the effect that it exercises on the circulation and the heart when given internally. In toxic doses experiment has demonstrated that it kills animals by suspension of the respiratory movements and those of the heart, which at first beats faster but gradually more slowly. It has no effect upon any other organ and is eliminated by the liver.

Matheson recommends it as an antispasmodic and has employed it also in dyspnœa of cardiac origin. I have used it in both these conditions in Manila with highly satisfactory results. I have found the most convenient form of administration to be the tincture in doses of 15–40 drops a day given in an infusion of althæa every 3 or 4 hours; the vehicle should be used liberally as it diminishes the irritant action of the euphorbia on the stomach. A decoction of 15 grams of the plant to 2 liters of water may be given in doses of from 6 to 12 tablespoonfuls daily. A proper dose of the alcoholic extract is 10 centigrams in 24 hours. Dr. Daruty, of Mauritius, gives the following formula:

Euphorbia pilulifera dried in the shade....30 grams.
Water..............................$1\frac{1}{2}$ liters.

Boil till reduced to 1 liter, cool and add:

Rum or cognac.......................30 grams.

DOSE.—1 wineglassful 3 times a day.

This decoction relieves the most obstinate asthma, as well as cough and bronchial irritation. It is necessary to use the entire plant. The decoction is usually given in the morning, fasting, in the middle of the afternoon and at bedtime. In very stubborn cases another dose may be given in the middle of the night. Frequently the relief is immediate and in some cases a liter of the decoction is enough to effect a cure. If the symptoms return, it is easy to abort them; they are less distressing and, according to the statements of patients, the medicine "gives them air."

Dr. Hicks Bunting found, in an analysis of the drug, 60 per cent. of insoluble residue, wax, "caucho," resin, tannin, sugar, albuminoids, oxalate of calcium and other salts.

Dr. Marsset states that the active principle is soluble in water, in dilute alcohol; insoluble in ether, chloroform, bisulphide of carbon, and turpentine, but does not give the reaction.

The toxic dose is 1 gram of dried plant for each kilogram of weight of the animal.

BOTANICAL DESCRIPTION.—A small creeping plant with milky juice. Stem 1–2° high, cylindrical, hairy and reddish in color. Leaves opposite, obliquely ovate, rhomboid, serrate, hairy. Petioles very short. Two pointed stipules at the base. Flowers yellowish in hemispherical umbels of 5 divisions, each subdivided in 2. · Involucre universal. Calyx bell-shaped, laciniate, in 5 parts. Corolla, 5 petals, inserted on the divisions of the calyx, fleshy, orbicular, with an orbicular appendix at the base, concave and differing from the corolla in color. Stamens 8, inserted on the base of the calyx; filaments unequal in length, each bearing 2 anthers. Four filaments lacking anthers. Ovary with stalk longer than the flower, curved downward. Styles 3, bifid. Stigmas simple. Seed vessels 3, united, hairy, 3-angled, each bearing 1 red globose seed with a wrinkled surface.

HABITAT.—Common in all parts of the islands and well known to the natives. The name by which it is best known in Manila is "golondrina."

Euphorbia neriifolia, L. (*E. ligularia,* Roxb.; *E. pentagona,* Blanco.)

NOM. VULG.—*Sorosoro, Sorog-sorog, Bait,* Tag., Pam.; *Karambauaya,* Iloc.; *Lengua de perro,* Sp.-Fil.

USES.—The principal medicinal use of this plant in the Philippines is the introduction of the hot juice of its fleshy leaves into the external auditory canal in cases of otorrhœa or of simple earache, whatever its cause.

The root is regarded in India as an antidote for snake bite and, indeed, the plant is sacred to Munsa, the snake divinity. During the months of July and August in some parts of India the natives make offerings of rice, milk and sugar to this sacred tree every Tuesday and Thursday, praying for protection from the bites of serpents.

The leaves contain an abundance of milky juice, acrid and very active, used in the treatment of several skin diseases. Like the species *E. pilulifera* it possesses antiasthmatic properties; Dr. S. C. Amcobury reports 6 cases treated with satisfactory results. Owing to the acrid quality of the juice great care should be maintained both in its internal and external use. The Sanscrit authors regard it as purgative and usually administer it with other drugs of the same action to increase its effect. Ainslie states that the native herb-doctors of India give the juice in intestinal obstruction and in the œdema of malarial cachexia. The dose is 1.25 grams in 24 hours given in 300 cc. of sweetened water in divided doses. This dose is, in my opinion, dangerous; 40–60 centigrams a day is more prudent.

BOTANICAL DESCRIPTION.—A small tree, from 5 to 6° high. Trunk erect, jointed, 5-sided, at the angles 2 rows of thorns. Leaves spatulate, fleshy. Flowers yellowish. Calyx bell-shaped, 5-lobed. Corolla, numerous imbricated, spatulate petals with ravelled or fringed ends. Stamens in groups. Styles 3. Stigma coarse. Seed vessel, 3 carpels on a stalk.

HABITAT.—In all parts of Luzon.

Euphorbia Tirucalli, L.

NOM. VULG.—*Consuelda*, Sp.-Fil.; *Katwit, Suelda*, Tag.

USES.—The milky juice of this species is very caustic. It is used chiefly in India mixed with oil as an embrocation for rheumatism; given internally it is regarded as an antisyphilitic. Dr. J. Shortt states that it is an excellent alterant in syphilis in dose of 30 centigrams, morning and evening. It is further employed in malarial hypertrophy of the spleen, in asthma and as a purgative; in a word the same virtues are attributed to it as to the foregoing species.

BOTANICAL DESCRIPTION.—Small trees, 9–12° high. Trunk erect. Branches cylindrical, stumpy (not tapering), several very small leaves at the ends. Flowers yellowish, in umbels. Calyx, 5 rounded, fleshy sepals. Corolla, 5 groups of woolly hairs on the divisions of the calyx. Stamens 5, inserted on the sepals, with double or irregular anthers. Seed vessel, 3 carpels each with one seed.

HABITAT.—Very common, especially in the suburbs of Manila where they serve as hedges.

Phyllanthus reticulatus Müll. (*Cicca decandra*, Blanco.)

NOM. VULG.—*Tinatinaan, Tintatintahan, Malinta,* Tag.; *Suĝot-olaĝ,* Vis.

USES.—The natives eat the little berries of this species, which are dark purple before and black after maturity, and use their juice for ink. The leaves are diuretic and refreshing; the bark alterant. In the bazaars of India the bark is sold commonly in pieces 1° long and as thick as the wrist; its taste is slightly sweet, color dark and the alterative dose of its decoction is 120–150 grams a day. In Concan they make a compound pill of the leaf-juice, powdered cubebs and camphor, to be dissolved in the mouth for ulcerated, bleeding or scorbutic gums. The juice is also given internally for urticaria.

BOTANICAL DESCRIPTION.—Small trees, 12° or more high, with leaves pinnate, oval, entire, alternate, glabrous, downy when young. Common petiole, 2 stipules at the base. Flowers monœcious. Staminate: calyx, 5 colored sepals; no corolla; filaments 4, coarse, somewhat shorter than the calyx, the middle one thicker and 2-parted; anthers 10, 4 on the middle filament and two on each of the others. Pistillate: calyx and corolla same as staminate; nectary, 5 glandules on the base of the ovary. Fruit, a black berry seated within the calyx, crowned with 2 erect styles, 6 or 8 compartments each with a single seed.

HABITAT.—Grows everywhere and is well known.

Phyllanthus Niruri, L.

P. urinaria, L.

NOM. VULG.—*Hierba de San Pablo, de San Pedro,* Sp.

USES.—This species is not used medicinally in the Philippines, but in India is given for its diuretic effect and has great repute in the treatment of genito-urinary diseases, dropsy and gonorrhœa. The infusion of the leaves of *P. Niruri* with

Fenugreek seeds is a highly prized remedy for chronic dysentery, mentioned by Ainslie. The leaves are bitter and tonic and in Bombay they are in common use in gonorrhœa to correct the acidity of the urine. Bruised and mixed with salt they make a sort of jelly frequently used as an application for itch; without salt the same is used for contusions.

The dose of the leaf juice of both species, for internal use, is 15 grams a day in divided doses.

A decoction of the entire plant well dried and powdered, is given for jaundice in doses of 5 grams a day.

The milky juice of the stem is useful in the local treatment of ulcers. The bruised root is employed in Concan for neuralgia.

Botanical Description.—*P. Niruri* is an herb with straight stem. Leaves alternate, pinnate with stylet in place of the odd leaflet. Leaflets nearly oval, glabrous, 2 stipules at the base. Flowers monœcious, greenish, axillary; the staminate growing along the common petiole above the pistillate. Staminate: Calyx, 5 lanceolate, entire sepals; no corolla; 1 filament with 1 anther. Pistillate: Calyx and corolla as above; ovary free, 3 biovulate cells; style with 2 stigma-bearing branches. Fruit capsular, globose.

P. urinaria may be distinguished by its sessile flowers and reddish stem.

Habitat.—Very common in Manila and all over Luzon.

Jatropha Curcas, L.

Nom. Vulg.—*Tuba*, Tag.; *Kasla*, Vis.; *Tawatawa*, Iloc. (Seeds called "English Physic Nuts" in India.)

Uses.—The milky juice of the trunk and branches is a drastic purgative, too active for safety as a physic. Mixed with water it is used as a wash for atonic ulcers.

The seeds yield 25–30 per cent. of a yellowish oil, more active than castor oil as a purgative but less certain. Ten or twelve of the former equal in effect 30 to 40 drops of the latter. Its density is 0.919, and it differs from castor oil in being only slightly soluble in absolute alcohol. In some parts of the Philippines it is used for purposes of illumination, and it is exported to Europe to adulterate soaps and candles. It contains a little stearin which begins to be deposited at 9° and is entirely solidified at 0°.

The fruit is strongly purgative, and this action is not due to the oil but to a peculiar resin so active that 3 fruits produce drastic effects. Whatever purgative action the oil possesses is due to the resin which it contains in solution. It seems, therefore, preferable to treat the seeds with alcohol, thus dissolving the resin, and use the tincture thus obtained in place of the oil.

The natives use the plant to intoxicate the fish in ponds and sluggish streams.

The seeds of the species *J. multifida*, L., also called *tuba* in Tag., and *mana*, are likewise purgative in their action. Dr. Waring saw a case of poisoning with the fruit; the patient, a young man, suffered violent vomiting, intense pain in the stomach and head, and marked prostration. He recovered under the use of lime juice and stimulants.

BOTANICAL DESCRIPTION.—The *J. Curcas* is a small tree growing as high as 9°. Leaves alternate, cordate, glabrous, 3–5 cut-lobed. Flowers yellowish-green, monœcious, in terminal umbels, staminate and pistillate flowers mingled without order. Staminate: Calyx, 5 unequal sepals; corolla bell-shaped, 5 petals, woolly within, a small notch at the end, bent downward; stamens 10, in 2 whorls of 5. Pistillate: Calyx and corolla as above; several tongue-like staminodes replace the stamens; ovary free, oblong, 3-celled, 1 ovule in each cell; style 3-branched. Seed vessel fleshy, of 3 capsules, each bearing 1 oval, coriaceous seed.

HABITAT.—Luzon and Visayas.

Aleurites Moluccana, Willd. (*A. triloba,* Forst. and Blanco.)

Nom. Vulg.—*Lumbán, Kapili,* Tag.; *Belgaum* or *Indian Walnut,* Indo-Eng.

Uses.—The kernels are rich in oil which is used for illumination and the manufacture of soap. For industrial purposes it is superior to linseed oil, according to the report of the Madras Drug Committee.

Dr. O'Rocke states that in doses of 1–2 ounces it acts as a gentle and sure purgative, producing copious bilious evacuations after 3–6 hours, without causing nausea, colic or other similar effects. The municipal physician of Sampaloc, Señor Xerez, states that he has frequently used this oil in Manila, as a purgative, and he agrees perfectly with Dr. O'Rocke as to its effect.

D. Anacleto del Rosario, the distinguished Filipino chemist, tells me that he once witnessed a case of poisoning by the fruit of the *lumbán,* the patient being a native boy. Doubtless the milky juice, so active in all the Euphorbiaceæ, was the cause of the symptoms. It is true that the kernel causes colic and copious alvine discharges.

Nellino's chemical analysis of the seeds is as follows:

Water	5.25
Fatty matter	62.97
Cellulose	28.99
Mineral matter	2.79

The ashes contain the following matters:

Lime	28.69 %
Magnesia	6.01 "
Potash	11.23 "
Phosphoric acid	20.30 "

The oil is yellow, syrupy, transparent, odorless, insipid.

Botanical Description.—A tree with leaves bunched or clustered, 3–5 lobulate with as many nerves. Petioles about as long as the leaves. Flowers white, terminal in panicles, the pistillate mixed with the more numerous staminate flowers. Staminate: Calyx monophyllous, cylindrical, 2-toothed; corolla, 5 linear petals twice as long as the calyx; stamens 20 or more, joined in a column at their bases. Pistillate: Calyx and corolla as above; ovary of 2 or 3 uniovulate locules, encircled by a disk; style 2- or 3-branched. Seed vessel large, ovate, compressed, fleshy, 2 sutures at right angles, 2 compartments, in each a hard nut.

HABITAT.—Grows all over Luzon and is well known to the natives.

Croton Tiglium, L. (*C. glandulosum*, *C. muricatum*, Blanco.)

NOM. VULG.—*Tuba kamaisa*, Tag.; *The Purging Croton*, Eng.

USES.—The fruit is used by the Filipinos to intoxicate the fish in ponds and sluggish streams. The seeds contain an oil that is official in all Pharmacopœias as one of the most powerful hydragogue cathartics. As it is intensely irritating it should never be administered alone but combined with other substances, such as castor oil, or in pill form. The internal dose is 1 to 2 drops. It is considered a specific for lead colic and is indicated when not only purgation but active irritation of the digestive canal is desired.

Applied to the skin it is a strong irritant causing rapid and painful vesication. Great care should be exercised not to raise the hands to the eyes after touching the oil, as serious inflammation might result.

BOTANICAL DESCRIPTION.—A small tree, 8–9° high, with rough trunk. Leaves alternate, ovate, acute, minutely serrate, both surfaces beset with sharp hairs. Flowers yellowish-white, monœcious. Staminate: Fewer than the pistillate, growing above them; calyx 5-toothed; corolla, 5 woolly petals; stamens 16, joined in the center. Pistillate: Calyx 5-toothed;

corolla much less developed than in the staminate; ovary free, 3 uniovulate locules; styles 3, bifid. Seed vessel dry, with thin envelope bristling with stiff hairs; 3 carpels each containing a seed.

HABITAT.—Common in Luzon.

Acalypha Indica, L. (*A. Caroliniana*, Blanco.)

NOM. VULG.—Not known.

USES.—This plant is not used medicinally in the Philippines, but is very common in India. Dr. G. Bidie, of Madras, states that the expressed juice of the leaves is in great repute, wherever the plant grows, as an emetic for children and is safe, certain and speedy in its action. Like ipecacuanha it seems to have little tendency to act on the bowels or depress the vital powers, and it decidedly increases the secretion of the pulmonary organs. Probably an infusion of the dried leaves or an extract prepared from the green plant would retain all its active properties. The dose of the expressed juice for an infant is a teaspoonful.

Dr. A. E. Ross speaks highly of its use as an expectorant, ranking it in this respect with senega; he found it especially useful in the bronchitis of children. He also makes favorable report of a cataplasm of the leaves as a local application to syphilitic ulcers and as a means of relieving the pain attendant on the bites of venomous insects.

The alleged purgative action of the root noticed by Ainslie is confirmed by Dr. H. E. Busteed, who reports having used the expressed juice of the root and leaves as a laxative for children.

Langley, a military surgeon, states that in Canara the natives employ the leaf juice in congestive headache, soaking pledgets of cotton with it and introducing them into the nasal fossæ; the resultant nose bleed relieves the headache. The powder of the dry leaves is dusted on ulcers and putrid sores. In asthma and bronchitis, both of children and adults, Langley has used this plant with good results, and he recommends 1.25–3.50 grams of the tincture (100 grams of the fresh plant to 500 of alcohol, 90°) repeated several times a day; the effect is expectorant, nauseant and, in large doses, emetic.

It must be noted that only the young, growing plants are active.

The flowers of another species, *A. hispida*, Burm., called *bugos* in Tag. and Vis., is used in India for the dysentery.

BOTANICAL DESCRIPTION.—A little plant, about 3° high. Leaves alternate, broad, lanceolate, 5-nerved, serrate from middle to apex. Petioles much longer than the leaves, 2 stipules at their bases. Flowers greenish, monœcious in axillary spikes, pedunculate, as long as the leaves, crowned by a prolongation of the axis in the form of a cross. Staminate: Numerous, in upper part of spike; calyx 4 parts; no corolla; stamens 8–16, small, free. Pistillate: Less in number, at the base of the spike; perianth of 3 imbricated leaflets; ovary, 3 uniovulate locules; style, 3 branches which also subdivide. Capsule 3-celled, each cell containing a globose seed with cicatrix.

HABITAT.—Luzon, Panay and Mindanao. Blooms in October.

Echinus Philippensis, H. Baillon. (*Croton Philippense*, Lamk.; *Rottlera tinctoria*, Roxb.; *Mallotus Philippensis*, Müll.)

NOM. VULG.—*Banato*, Tag.; *Buas, Vuas*, Iloc.; *Monkey-face Tree, Kamela* or *Kamala Dye*, Indo-Eng.

USES.—The capsular fruit of this plant is thickly beset with reddish glands and hairs, which, when brushed off and gathered in powder form, constitute the *kamala dye* of the Hindoos. It was mentioned by the Arabian physicians of the tenth century under the names of *Kanbil* and *Wars*. In India the powder is highly valued as a yellow dye-stuff for silk. Medicinally it is used as an anthelmintic, the English physician Mackinnon, of the Bengal Hospital, having been the first to scientifically prove this property; he reported that it was successful in expelling the tape-worm. It is now official in the Pharmacopœia of India and also in the U. S. P. as an anthelmintic and purgative; in Switzerland it is commonly given to expel the bothriocephalus which abounds there, the lake fish acting as hosts.

The dose recommended by the Pharmacopœia of India is 8–12 grams, divided in 3 or 4 doses. This amount sometimes causes nausea and colic; in the third or fourth stool the tænia is commonly expelled in a lifeless condition. Dujardin-Beaumetz advises a dose of 30 grams of castor oil in case the tænia has not been expelled 2 hours after the last dose of kamala. The powder is efficacious but the tincture seems to be surer; the dose is 6 grams for children and 20 for adults, given in divided doses in aromatic water every hour for 6 hours. This tincture is prepared by macerating 200 grams of kamala in 500 cc. alcohol for 7 days; then filtering with expression and adding enough alcohol to complete the 500 cc.

The powder is also used in India as a local application in herpes circinata. It is insoluble in water; in ether and alcohol it yields 80% of a red resin. Anderson noted that a concentrated ethereal solution of kamala after a few days formed a solid crystalline mass, yellow, very soluble in ether; this substance he named *rottlerin*, $C_{11}H_{10}O_3$.

Botanical Description.—A tree, 6–8 meters high, covered with stellate groups of short yellow hairs. Leaves alternate, petiolate, rhomboid-oval or lanceolate, acuminate, 3-nerved, entire or slightly dentate, upper surface glabrous, lower surface covered with woolly hairs and powdery red glands. Flowers yellowish-green, small, diœcious, apetalous, in spikes. Staminate: By 3's in the axil of each bract; perianth, 3 or 5 deeply cut, lanceolate lobules; stamens 15–25, free, inserted in the center of the flower. Pistillate: In the axil of each bract;

ovary, 3 locules each with 1 ovule, covered like the leaves with hairs and yellow, granular glands. Seed vessel globose, 3-celled, like ovary covered with hairs and glands.

HABITAT.—Mountains of Morong, San Mateo, Tarlak, Bosoboso, Ilocos Norte, Albay and Batangas.

Ricinus communis, L. (Variety *microcarpus*, Müll.)

NOM. VULG.—*Tuĝantaĝan*, *Liĝasina*, Tag.; *Taĝantaĝan*, *Tawatawasiĝa*, Iloc.; *Castor Oil Plant*, Eng.

USES.—A purgative oil is expressed from the seeds, called "Aceite de Ricino" (castor oil). It operates mechanically in the intestinal tract and its action is rapid and is indicated whenever it is desired simply to empty the intestines without producing any irritating effect; it is, therefore, a purgative indicated in diseases of children, in pregnancy, and in hemorrhoidal congestions where a non-irritating evacuation of the rectum is desired. It is an anthelmintic, though not ordinarily given alone, but in combination with other drugs of a purely anthelmintic action, the object being to expel the worms which have been attacked by the specific.

Oil extracted simply by expression is less purgative than that obtained by treating the seeds with bisulphide of carbon and absolute alcohol; also less purgative than the seeds themselves, because it contains only a very small proportion of a drastic principle existing exclusively in the seeds; this principle is completely dissolved in the oil extracted by chemical process.

It is pale yellow in color, very viscid, with a characteristic mouldy odor. The purgative dose is 10–30 grams. A small dose may purge as actively as a larger one provided that the patient drink abundantly after the administration of the drug. The best method of disguising its taste is by giving it in half a cup of very strong, hot coffee. Just before the dose, take a swallow of coffee to disguise the taste even more effectually.

Castor oil enters into the composition of elastic collodion (simple collodion, 30 grams, castor oil, 2 grams). The leaves pounded and boiled are applied as a poultice to foul ulcers.

Botanical Description.—There are two forms of this variety in the Philippines, possessing the same properties and known by the same common name: *R. viridis*, Müll. (*R. communis*, Blanco) and *R. subpurpurascens*, Müll.; the former is the more common and has a glabrous, fistular stem. Leaves peltate, palmately cleft in 7 or 9 lobules, lanceolate, serrate. Petioles long. Flowers greenish, monœcious, the staminate ones in large panicled clusters below the pistillate. Filaments numerous, subdivided into several anther-bearing branches. Pistillate flowers, 3 sepals, 3 styles. Seed vessel, 3 prickly capsules, containing solitary seeds.

The *R. subpurpurascens* is distinguished from the former by bearing 2 glandules at the base of the leaves, the mulberry color of which latter suggests its common name, *Taĝantaĝan na morado*, Tag., Vis.

Habitat.—Very common in Luzon, Mindanao and other islands.

URTICACEÆ.

Nettle Family.

Artocarpus integrifolia, Willd.

Nom. Vulg.—*Naĝka*, Tag.; *Jack Fruit Tree*, Eng.

Uses.—The huge fruit of this tree is well known to the Filipinos and well liked by them as an article of food, eaten fresh or in sweet preserves. The arils and pulpy envelopes of the seeds are the parts eaten, also the seeds themselves, boiled or roasted. According to Padre Mercado the roasted seeds have an aphrodisiac action.

The heated and powdered leaves are applied to wounds and given internally for congestions. The resin of the trunk is a useful application to ulcers and in India they give it internally to cure la melena, the dose, one "tola" mixed with the same amount of *manga* resin and a little lime water. The same resin if heated makes an excellent cement for broken china.

Botanical Description.—A tree, 20° or more in height, with abundant milky sap. Leaves alternate, oval, acute at both ends, slightly wavy and revolute borders, tough, glabrous and dark green upper surface; light green, slightly rough under surface. Petioles short. Flowers greenish, monœcious, growing on root, trunk and branches. Calyx very small, monophyllous, of about 7 deciduous lobules. Staminate: On a club-shaped receptacle, 3′ or 4′ long, bristling with the stamens; filaments very short, anthers 2-celled. Pistillate: On a common, oblong receptacle which ripens to the great fruit; style 1, short; rarely 2 divergent styles; stigmas acute. Fruit about size and shape of a small watermelon, beset with many sharp eminences, containing many seeds enveloped in thick arils.

Habitat.—It grows in all parts of the Archipelago and is commonly known.

Laportea gaudichaudiana, Wedd. (*Urtica umbellata, U. ferox*, Blanco.)

Nom. Vulg.—*Liĝaton, Lipa, Apariagua* (?), Tag., Vis.; *Lipaĝdoton*, Pam.

Uses.—The Padre Mercado writes as follows concerning the properties of this plant: "The leaves, applied with salt in the form of a plaster, purify dog bites, foul, putrid, malignant and cankerous ulcers; they cure boils, contusions and all abscesses; mixed with wax they may be applied for obstruction of the spleen; mashed with the juice and inserted in the nose they arrest nose-bleed; cooked with snails they soften the stomach, excite the secretion of urine and dissipate flatus; the juice given as a gargle aborts inflammation of the epiglottis. The seeds mixed with wine are a sexual excitant and "clear out" the womb; taken with syrup they relieve dyspnœa, pain in the side and inflammation of the lungs and force up the humors from the chest; it may be mixed with medicines that corrupt the flesh (sic). The grated root drunk with wine relieves painful flatulence. I myself (continues the Padre Mercado) have experimented with a woman who suffered with painful flatulence and this remedy relieved her."

We repeat that all the foregoing is copied from the writings of Padre Mercado and we offer it as a therapeutic curiosity.

P. Blanco states that merely to touch the leaves causes an intolerable itching.

Botanical Description.—A small tree, 12–15° high, trunk richly branched. Leaves opposite, bunched at the ends of the branches, notched at the base, long, ovate, serrate, hairy on both surfaces. Flowers yellowish-white, diœcious. Staminate: In compound racemes; calyx 4 parts; corolla none; stamens 4, inserted on the base of the calyx. Pistillate: Flowers in 2-forked umbel, flat, very large; calyx, none; stamens none; stigma 1; seed heart-shaped.

Habitat.—Very common in all the fields and in the mountains. Blooms in June.

CASUARINEÆ.

Beefwood Family.

Casuarina Sumatrana, Jung. (*C. equisetifolia*, Blanco.)

Nom. Vulg.—*Agoho*, Tag.; *Malabohok*, *Agoho*, Vis.; *Aro*, *Karo*, *Agoó*, Iloc.

Uses.—The bark is astringent by virtue of the large quantity of tannin it contains. Its principal use is in decoction in the treatment of diarrhœa, dysentery and hæmoptysis; it is also given in amenorrhœa, though it is apt to increase the pain. Externally it is used as a wash for contusions and ulcers.

19

Another species, *C. equisetifolia*, Forst., confounded with the former species by the natives, has the same therapeutic applications.

Botanical Description.—A tree with stellately arranged straight branches. Leaves stellate, long, narrow, linear, 4-grooved. They have been compared to the tail of a horse and the tail of a certain bird—the casobar. Staminate and pistillate flowers greenish, on different parts of the same stalk. Staminate, in small aments. Pistillate on small globose aments; calyx proper of the floweret, a coarse scale; corolla none; ovary conical; styles 2, flattened, divergent; stigmas acute. Fruit: Each floweret produces a woody seed-vessel, bivalved, ovate, glabrous, with a small seed ending in an oval wing; all these seed vessels joined form a small cone about 1′ long.

Habitat.—Very common in Ilocos, Tarlak, Binangonang of Lampong and N. Ecija.

MONOCOTYLEDONS.

MUSACEÆ.

Banana Family.

Musa paradisiaca, L.

M. sapientum, L.

NOM. VULG.—*Plátano*, Sp.; *Sagiĝ*, Tag., etc.; *Banana*, Eng.

USES.—The fruit produced by the various varieties of the banana plant constitutes one of the most wholesome and delicious of foods, appreciated by natives and Europeans alike. According to Boussingaul its nutritive value is greater than that of the potato and it may be used constantly without ill effects. Bananas contain a large percentage of sugar and mucilage. In India they dry them in the sun, as figs and grapes are treated in other countries and thus preserve them for long voyages by sea or land; eaten in conjunction with animal food they are a strong preventive of scurvy. If eaten when thoroughly ripe they have a laxative effect.

The young and tender leaves are used in the Philippines as a protective dressing for ulcers, dermatitis, burns and cantharidal or other artificial blisters. Before applying to the affected surface the leaf is heated to make it more flexible and coated with a thin layer of cocoanut oil or other fatty substance.

In the dispensaries of India they also use the leaves in this way, thus protecting and at the same time maintaining the moisture of the part. Dr. Waring recommends the practice and Dr. Van Someren follows it in the application of water dressings, having substituted banana leaves for gutta-percha.

In Mauritius the fruit is used for dysentery, and the flowers, together with an equal quantity of those of *Spilanthes Acmella*, are made into a decoction and prescribed for dropsy.

Botanical Description.—The banana plant with its huge waving leaves and succulent stem is universally familiar. The flower stalk rises through the center developing a drooping spike, the flowers in short rows in the axils of its large purplish bracts. According to Blanco there are 57 varieties of this plant in the Philippines, the following being the most common edible varieties: *bug̃ulag̃, lakatan, letondag̃, obispo, higo, morado, butuan, bentikohol, sabá, tampuhig̃.*

Habitat.—Common everywhere in the islands.

ZINGIBERACEÆ.

Ginger Family.

Zingiber officinale, L. (*Amomum zingiber*, L. and Blanco.)

Nom. Vulg.—*Ajengibre, Jengibre*, Sp.; *Luya*, Tag.; *Laya*, Bic.; *Ginger*, Eng.

Uses.—The rhizome is used principally as a condiment in the Philippines. Its flavor is extremely agreeable, much appreciated in Europe by the English who are the greatest consumers of the condiment. In the Philippines a decoction is made of ginger and brown sugar, called *tahu* by the Chinese who drink it regularly as we do coffee in the early hours of the morning. It is an excellent drink, aromatic, tonic, stomachic and stimulant, and would probably be highly useful as well as economical as a part of the ration of European and native troops in the field. Hot *tahú* or *tahu* is an active diuretic, and during the last epidemic of cholera in Manila some physicians used it with very satisfactory results.

Ginger is a good carminative and is official in the pharmacopœias of Europe, America and India. It is used with good effect in flatulent colic, atonic diseases of the intestines so common in the Philippines and in chronic rheumatism.

The tincture is given in doses of 2–4 grams. The official infusion 30–60 grams.

The rhizome contains a volatile oil[1] (25 per cent.), a pale yellow liquid, specific gravity 0.878, the odor like that of the rhizome but lacking its strong and piquant taste. Its reaction is not acid; it dissolves slowly in alcohol. The burning taste is due to a resin that produces protocatechuic acid when melted with potassa.

Botanical Description.—The only part employed is the rhizome, well known all over the islands and found in all their pharmacies and shops.

Several stems rise 2–3° directly from the peculiar, branched rhizome; long-lanceolate, acuminate, entire, glabrous, alternate leaves diverge stiffly from the sides of the stem; petiole proper very short, its broader extension ensheathing the stem; general appearance of a single stem is much like that of the Solomon's seal so familiar in the U. S.

Curcuma longa, L.

Nom. Vulg.—*Dilaw*, Tag.; *Dulaw*, *Kalawaga*, *Kinamboy*, Vis.; *Ågay*, Pam.; *Turmeric Plant*, Eng.

Uses.—The yellow rhizome called by some *azafrán* (saffron), is used as a condiment; its odor is remotely suggestive of vanilla. The Philippine herb-doctors give it internally for hæmoptysis, externally as a plaster or in infusion for acute dermatitis. The juice is prescribed in doses of 30–60 grams in bronchial catarrh. In India they inhale the fumes of burning turmeric paper for coryza, and with good effect according to the testimony of Dr. Waring.

The drug is official in the Pharmacopœia of India. It is carminative, stimulant and probably antiseptic. Its decoction is used as an eye-wash in catarrhal and purulent conjunctivitis. The Mohammedans of Decan use it for jaundice upon the

[1] European analyses make the amount 1–2.2 per cent.

theory that the yellow color of the skin in that disease is an indication for a remedy of the same color. The juice is also used in many parts of India to stain the face, nails and other parts of the body.

The tincture is prepared by macerating 30 grams of bruised rhizome in 200 cc. alcohol for seven days, then filtering. Turmeric paper is prepared by impregnating unsized paper with this tincture, and then drying. Both tincture and paper are used to test for alkalies.

The rhizomes contain a pigment called curcumin, an essential oil and fæcula. Curcumin ($C_{14}H_{14}O_4$) is crystalline, yellow by direct light and blue by reflected light; it was studied by Jackson and Menke.

In the Philippines it is used extensively as a diaphoretic and emmenagogue and in icterus, intestinal colic and dysmenorrhœa; externally for skin diseases, contusions and atonic ulcers.

Gubler regards it as a diffusible stimulant. Its use is more extensive in England than in France and Spain; in India it forms an ingredient of *curry*, called *carí* in Manila. Curcumin is eliminated by the urine, which it colors yellow, and if at the same time an alkali be taken by the patient, especially a salt of calcium, the urine becomes red and may communicate this stain to the clothes. This fact should be borne in mind to avoid embarrassing mistakes in diagnosis or prognosis. Dose of powder, 2–5 grams.

Botanical Description.—Leaves 2–4° long, rising in bush-like bunches directly from the rhizome, broad-lanceolate, acuminate, gradually tapering down the long petioles; numerous prominent nerves give a ribbed appearance to the blade. Rhizome cylindrical, irregular, bright yellow within.

Elettaria Cardamomum, White.

Nom. Vulg.—*Lag̑kuas, Lag̑kawas*, Vis.; *Cardamon*, Eng.

USES.—This plant, though official in several pharmacopœias, is not used as a medicine in the Philippines, probably on account of its scarcity here. The seeds are used as a condiment; they are stimulant and carminative and yield good results in atonic dyspepsia, nervous depression and spasmodic or flatulent affections of the intestine. The dose of the powdered seeds is from 0.60–1.50 grams in pill form; the tincture is, however, more convenient and is given in doses of from 4 to 8 grams.

BOTANICAL DESCRIPTION.—A plant with a scaly rhizome and adventitious roots from which spring the stems, some of which bear leaves and others flowers. The leaves are alternate, in pairs; extended, lanceolate blade, with a short petiole. Branches bearing flowers, short, flexible and scaly. The flowers spring from the sheaths of the leaves. Calyx tubular, 3-toothed; second calyx with limb divided into 3 unequal lobules. Stamens 3. Ovary inferior, 3 many-ovuled compartments. Style simple. Stigma rounded. Fruit an oblong, ovoid capsule, 3-celled, trivalvate. Seeds blackish, albuminous.

HABITAT.—Visaya Islands.

AMARYLLIDACEÆ.

Amaryllis Family.

Crinum Asiaticum, L. (*C. giganteum*, Blanco.)

NOM. VULG.—*Bakoĝ*, Tag.

USES.—The decoction of the leaves is used in the Philippines as an expectorant. The plant is official in the Pharmacopœia of India as an emetic and in small doses is nauseant and diaphoretic. As an emetic the dose of the fresh juice of the root is 8–16 grams every 10 minutes till vomiting occurs. Dr. W. O'Shaughnessy, writing from Bengal, states that this is the only indigenous and abundant emetic plant of which he has experience, which acts without producing griping, purging, or other unpleasant symptoms. In a communication to Dr. Waring he remarks that it is a good emetic and diaphoretic whenever ipecacuanha is not at hand but that it should be regarded not so much as a substitute for that article as a resource in case of need.

The leaf juice is used in India to drop into the ears for disease of these organs.

One of the infinite remedies used by the Filipinos under the name of "contrapoisons," without specifying or knowing what poison, is the powdered root of *Crinum*, given internally with a little water. They also use the leaves locally for the itch, bruising them and rubbing the affected parts energetically with them. I may note here in passing, what I have written before: that the Filipinos have from time immemorial been familiar with the sarcopt of scabies (Kahaw) which they pick out with a needle or spine of some fish or vegetable.

BOTANICAL DESCRIPTION.—A plant with globose, scaly root. Leaves keeled or ridged. Flowers white, on a flattened stalk, on a spathe of 2 leaflets and several dry threads enclosing 4 flowerets. Corolla funnel-form, tube long and triangular; limb cut in 6 horizontal lanceolate lobes. Stamens 6, shorter than corolla. Anthers long. Stigma with 3 points. Seed vessel inferior, 3-celled, each cell containing a seed.

HABITAT.—Very common on the seashore and in groves of mangrove trees. Blooms in July.

LILIACEÆ.

Lily Family.

Aloes Barbadensis, Mill. (*A. humilis*, Blanco; *A. vera*, L.; *A. vulgaris*, Banck.; *A. Indica*, Royl.)

NOM. VULG.—*Sabila*, Tag.; *Dilaĝ boaya*, Vis.; *Aloes*, Eng.

USES.—This species is one of those which produce the substance known in pharmacy as *aloes*, which is the juice of the leaf evaporated to the consistency of an extract. It is official in all pharmacopœias and its properties are known to the Filipino herb-doctors. They use the fresh juice of the leaves as a stimulant of the scalp in baldness and locally in contusions. Aloes is a slow purgative and its irritating action on the lower portion of the large intestine extends to the genito-urinary organs. It is, therefore, an emmenagogue and its prolonged use causes hemorrhoids, especially in man. It is contra-indicated where there is disease of the genito-urinary organs or rectum. As it increases the secretion of bile it is useful in certain hepatic diseases. It is used in small doses as a tonic in dyspepsia. The tonic dose is $\frac{1}{2}$–20 centigrams; purgative, 15–50 of the extract, preferably in pill form. It is customary to associate it with other purgatives.

BOTANICAL DESCRIPTION.—A stemless plant, the leaves springing immediately from the root as in the pineapple, joined at the base, straight, ligulate, very fleshy and becoming thinner toward the end, with stiff thorns along the edges. Flowers between yellow and red outside and straw-colored inside, in racemes on a cylindrical scape 3° or more high, sometimes ramose, peduncles very short. Corolla cylindrical, somewhat incurved, cleft to the middle in 6 parts, 3 external, acute and superposed on the others, obtuse at the apex and of different color. Stamens 6, inserted at the nectiferous base of the ovary and of the same length as the corolla. Anthers erect. Ovary cylindrical with 6 furrows. Stigma obtuse, with raveled edges. The seed vessel ovoid, 3-valved, 3-celled, with 2 seeds in each, furnished with 3 spongy wings.

HABITAT.—Common in gardens.

Allium sativum, L.

NOM. VULG.—*Ajo*, Sp.; *Bawaĝ*, Tag.; *Garlic*, Eng.

Allium Cepa, L.

NOM. VULG.—*Cebolla*, Sp.; *Lasuna*, *Sibuyas*, Tag.; *Onion*, Eng.

USES.—The garlic and the onion are used to excess as condiments in Philippine as well as Spanish cooking. Both are difficult of digestion and communicate a very disagreeable odor to the breath, intolerable to those who are unaccustomed to it. Garlic possesses the singular property, familiar to many students and soldiers, of inducing a transient fever if introduced within the anus. When bruised and applied to the skin it has a counter-irritant action which makes it useful in the treatment of rheumatism, but the odor is so disagreeable that it is not worth while to use it for that purpose when we have so many other medicines which produce the same effect without being objectionable. It is also used locally for the bites of venomous animals.

The onion is used cooked as a poultice over the bladder and internally for various catarrhs. It is better to abstain from the therapeutic and culinary use of products so indigestible and so malodorous.

BOTANICAL DESCRIPTION.—These plants are so well known in all parts of the world that a description of them would be superfluous.

PALMÆ.

Palm Family.

Areca Catechu, L.

NOM. VULG.—*Boĝa*, Tag.; *Betel-nut Palm*, *Areca*, Eng.

USES.—The seeds form part of a masticatory very common throughout the extreme Orient, known as *Buyo* and composed of a betel leaf, a little slaked lime, and a slice of the fruit of the bonga, known as *Siri* in Indo-China and among the Malays. It is so common that it is hard to find a man or woman who does not use it. The saliva of those who use it is red and of a strong odor, and its careless use in time blackens the teeth and makes the breath extremely disagreeable. Habitual chewers consider it a tonic of the mouth and stomach and a general stimulant as well. It probably does possess these properties but they are reversed in the case of persons who use it immoderately for they lose appetite, become salivated, and the whole organism degenerates. The carbonized and powdered fruit is used as a dentifrice but its virtues are doubtless identical with those of any vegetable charcoal, *i. e.*, absorbent and antiseptic.

One unaccustomed to the use of bonga and chewing it for the first time, usually experiences a most disagreeable combination of symptoms; constriction of the œsophagus, a sensation of heat in the head and face, the latter becoming red and congested; at the same time dizziness and precordial distress are experienced. The same phenomena occur in certain persons after eating palmito salad or the tender central portion of the bonga and of other palms.

The flowers are eaten in salad like the above-mentioned *palmito*. The seed is astringent and tænifuge; for the latter purpose it is given internally as a powder in a dose of from 16 to 24 grams. Its action is uncertain. The catechu which is obtained in India from the Bonga differs from that obtained from the *Acacia Catechu* and is a tonic analogous to rhatany and cinchona.

The seeds contain about 14% of a fatty crystalline material which melts at 39°, and after saponification yields a crystalline, fatty acid that may be regarded as a mixture of lauric and muriatic acids. They also contain about 14% of a red, amorphous tonic material which, after drying, is but slightly soluble in cold or hot water.

The lower part of the petiole of the leaves is thin and broad, ensheathing the trunk, is as tough as pasteboard when dry and is used in the Philippines as wrapping paper; Dr. Bholanauth Bose and other physicians of India use it as a material for splints in fractures, a practice which might well be imitated in Manila and especially in the country.

BOTANICAL DESCRIPTION.—A well-known palm with slender stem, surrounded by many circles; it grows to about the same height as the coco-nut palm or less. The flowers spring in bunches of long, thread-like spikes from the trunk a little below the crown of leaves at the base of the long, smooth, green, sheath-like petioles which clasp the trunk; each spike bears many staminate and a few pistillate flowers. The fruit is about the size and shape of a hen's egg, the husk tow-like or filamentose, the kernel pinkish or light red.

HABITAT.—Grows throughout the islands.

Cocos nucifera, L.

NOM. VULG.—*Coco*, Sp.-Fil.; *Niog*, Tag.; *Coco-nut Palm*, Eng.

USES.—This plant is, perhaps, the most useful in the Philippines. Without it and the bamboo plant the people of the Archipelago would not know how to live. It produces vinegar, an alcoholic drink called *tuba* or *coco-wine*, an oil, an edible nut, and its leaves are used instead of nipa to roof the huts.

Tuba is an opaline, slightly sweet liquid, with an agreeable taste, which rapidly becomes acid under the influence of the heat. A flowering or fruit-bearing stalk, which has not been incised before, is chosen and encircled with several rings of rope or rattan. The stalk is then cut and a bamboo vessel called a *bombón* is hung to receive the sap which escapes during the night. This liquid is valuable as a drink for those who are debilitated, suffering from pulmonary catarrh, and even for consumptives, who are accustomed to drink it every morning, sometimes with marvelous results, according to reports. The heat of the day rapidly ferments the tuba, converting it into a mild vinegar, which is widely used for domestic purposes in the Philippines. When fermented and distilled it produces a weak alcohol of disagreeable taste called coco-wine.

The ripe fruit contains a rather soft and savory meat which is generally eaten mixed with the clear, sweet coco-nut milk. Later the meat becomes firmer and is used as a food and an oil much used in the islands is extracted from it. To extract the oil the meat is grated and pressed until all the juice is extracted. This is called the milk and when boiled is converted almost completely into oil. Cocoanut milk has an agreeable taste and may in some cases take the place of cow's milk. It is apt to produce diarrhœa, however, which action may be bad for some but on the other hand good for others, such as the habitually constipated. Both the meat and the milk are widely used by the natives in making sweets.

In the greater part of the islands it is the only oil used for illumination. As a medicine it is employed internally as a purgative and externally in the treatment of scores of troubles in which the good results obtained are due, not to the oil but to the massage used in rubbing it in. It has the reputation of stimulating the growth of the hair and all the natives and some Europeans use it lavishly as a hair ointment. When fresh its odor is agreeable, but it easily becomes rancid and assumes a most disagreeable odor. In the Visayan Islands they make an oil of a nauseous odor which they call in Manila *Caracoa.* It is used only for illumination and by the poor.

At a temperature of 20° or more the oil remains liquid; it is colorless when fresh and properly extracted. It solidifies at 18° and two kinds of soap are made of it; one soft and exceedingly cheap called "Quiapo"; the other hard, white, of a high quality, but as a rule containing an excess of lime which in time is deposited in a fluorescent film on its surface.

In India the root is employed in the treatment of dysentery.

Botanical Description.—A tree most familiar to every one.

Habitat.—Common in all parts of the Archipelago.

Nipa fruticans, Wurmb.

NOM. VULG.—*Nipa,* Sp.-Fil.; *Sasa,* Tag.

USES.—The dry leaves of this palm are generally used in the villages of Manila Province, Pampanag, Bulacan and other provinces in the construction of roofs and walls of houses, which are therefore called "nipa houses." The decoction of the fresh leaves is used as a lotion for indolent ulcers, and a popular preserve is made from the fruit.

Like the coco and following the same process the nipa yields a liquid also called tuba and possessing properties identical with those of the former plant. The weak alcohol distilled from it has some repute in the treatment of conjunctivitis, for which purpose a few drops are mixed with a small quantity of water and the eyes are washed with it several times a day. This alcohol, improperly called wine of nipa, has a characteristically unpleasant odor which makes it impracticable for medicinal or industrial use. Several chemists have attempted to remove the characteristic odor from nipa alcohol, but their results had always been negative because the odorous principle was distilled over at the same temperature as the alcohol. Finally a distinguished Filipino chemist, D. Anacleto del Rosario, perfected a process of producing from the nipa tuba an absolute alcohol perfectly free from the characteristic odor; an alcohol, in fact, possessing all the qualities of chemically pure alcohol, and of such a high grade that it was awarded the first prize at the last World's Fair in Paris.

BOTANICAL DESCRIPTION.—A palm about 6° high with long, pinnate leaves with leaflets which separate, at maturity, like those of the coco palm. Flowers monœcious, in a spathe. Fruit, many pyramidal drupes joined together, but easily separable. The outer covering of each drupe is hard, the inner part tow-like; seed enveloped in a sort of fleshy white meat.

HABITAT.—Salt water marshes, especially in Pampanga and the Visayan Islands.

CYPERACEÆ.

Sedge Family.

Cyperus rotundus, L.

Nom. Vulg.—*Mutha*, Tag.; *Botobotones*, Vis.; *Mota*, *Malaapolid*, *Sursur*, *Onoran*, *Kusuĝ*, *Omadiuĝ*, *Galonalpas*, Pam.; *Nutgrass* or *Coco-grass*, Eng.

Uses.—The root possesses stimulant, diaphoretic, diuretic and emmenagogue properties. In the Philippines it is used internally for dysentery, and in India for the same purpose and as a vermifuge. It is given as a tonic in gastro-intestinal diseases, and General Hardwick has reported good results with it in cholera; as he reported only two cases, his testimony is not of much value.

The Chinese use the dry or roasted root, especially in inflammation of the viscera and uterine diseases. They also attribute to it diuretic, emmenagogue and anthelmintic properties. In Java and India they use it for gonorrhœa, and in Mauritius as a diaphoretic and astringent. In the Philippines the bruised root is applied to the face for toothache.

Botanical Description.—The root is ovoid, ranging in size from that of a hazel-nut to that of a walnut, composed of a white, spongy substance. Leaves sword-shaped, ensheathing the stem. Flowers in a compound umbel on the end of the stalk which is naked, long and triangular. The umbellets are alternate, awl-shaped, with distinct flowers. Calyx universal, with 2 sword-shaped leaflets. Calyx proper, a very small, ridged scale. Corolla none. Stamens 3. Filaments long, inserted on the base of the ovary. Anthers long and straight. Style 1. Stigmas 3, simple, revolute. Fruit 1. Seed oblong, 3-sided, glabrous.

Habitat.—Common in Luzon and Panay. Blooms in June and July.

GRAMINEÆ.

Grass Family.

Zea Mays, L.

NOM. VULG.—*Maíz*, Sp.; *Maize, Corn*, Eng.

USES.—Corn is an extensive article of diet in the Philippines, but has the reputation of being indigestible. This is true when it is eaten in the grain, but in the form of meal it is easily digested and highly nutritious. The tassels have been used in the Philippines from time immemorial in decoction as a diuretic, for which property they received notice in the *Medical World* of Paris about the year 1876. The entire plant is diuretic and the natives give the decoction of the stalk for various diseases of the bladder and kidneys. An extract of the tassels has been put on the market, but it is better to administer a decoction made from 20 grams of tassel to 1 liter of water to be taken at will during the day. Rademaker and Fischer give the following chemical composition:

Fixed oil	5.25
Resin, crystalline matter and chlorophyl	3.25
Maizenic acid	2.25
Sugar and gum	19.50
Albuminoids	3.50
Salts and extracts	5.50
Cellulose	37.00
Water	20.00

The fixed oil is bright yellow, saponifiable by potash, soluble in chloroform and ether, insoluble in alcohol, solidifies at 10°.

HABITAT.—Very common in all parts of the islands.

Andropogon Schoenanthes, L.

NOM. VULG.—*Salay, Tag̃lad*, Tag.; *Paja de Meca*, Sp.-Fil.; *Baliyoko*, Vis.; *Geranium Grass*, Eng.

Uses.—The Filipino women use the leaves to perfume their gogo hair-wash. The decoction of the leaves is used internally as a diuretic (10 grams to a liter of water) and also to bathe pregnant women. The roots also are diuretic.

A Manila pharmacist, D. Rosendo García, has obtained a good quality of the fixed oil of this plant. In India they call this essence *rusa*, *geranium* and *gin-gembre* (nimar oil, Eng.); the annual export from Bombay is over 40,000 English pounds. It is dextrogyrous and its formula is C_5H_4.

Another species, the *A. nardus*, L., commonly called "raiz de mora" (mulberry root), "citronella," Eng., possesses the same therapeutic properties as the former. It also possesses an agreeable perfume and yields an essential oil, which, like rusa, is used to adulterate Attar of Roses.

The dried root is widely used in the Philippines and in Europe as well, to preserve clothing from moths and other destructive insects, at the same time giving them a sweet odor. In India the decoction is used internally, 10 grams to a liter of water, in the treatment of rheumatism and as a diuretic.

Botanical Description.—An indigenous grass with sword-shaped leaves about 4° high, tapering at the base, possessing a sweet odor. Root thick, irregular, rough, formed by the union of several small rootlets.

Saccharum officinarum, L.

Nom. Vulg.—*Cañamiel*, *Caña de azúcar*; *Caña dulc*, Sp.; *Tubo*, Tag.; *Sugar Cane*, Eng.

Uses.—The Filipinos are very fond of the fresh cane. The juice, which is extracted by means of primitive wooden presses, is used as a drink mixed with lemon juice or vino and is sold in markets and public places as a popular beverage on hot days. A tepid juice, extracted from heated cane is given for catarrhal troubles. This use of the juice is the only one peculiar to the Philippines. Its general use and properties are universally familiar and are amply treated in the materia medica.

Botanical Description.—This plant is so universally familiar that it is unnecessary to describe it. More than 20 varieties are found in the Philippines.

Habitat.—Throughout the islands, especially in the Island of Negros and the Luzon Provinces of Pampanga, Bulacan and Nueva Ecija.

Oriza, L.

Nom. Vulg.—*Arroz*, Sp.; *Palay*, Tag. (the plant and the unhusked rice); *Bigas*, Tag. (the husked rice); *Rice*, Eng.

Uses.—All the people of Indo-China, China, Japan and the greater part of the Indian Archipelago eat rice as Europeans do bread.

In the Philippines an immense variety of rice grows and in the World's Fair at Paris, in 1889, Señor D. Regino García, of Manila, presented a unique collection of 147 varieties. The rice grown in high lands above irrigation is called "arroz de secano" and mountain rice, and that grown in low and irrigated land is called "arroz de sementera" and swamp rice. The two kinds are equally valuable as food.

The proportion of starch in rice is large, but it contains but a small amount of gluten, and therefore a large amount must be eaten in order to obtain sufficient nutritive elements.

Water	5.00
Starch	85.07
Parenchyma	4.80
Nitrogenous matter	3.68
Crystallizable sugar	0.29
Gummy matter	1.71
Oil	0.13
Phosphate of lime	0.40
Chloride of potash, phosphate of potash, acetic acid, calcareous vegetable salt, salt of potash, sulphur	Traces.

In the Filipino therapeutics rice has an extensive use, especially in the form of a decoction called *cange*, which is commonly given in the treatment of diarrhœa and dysentery, with good results. Cooked as a sort of mush it may be used as a substitute for linseed poultices and has the great advantage of not becoming rancid. Roasted and powdered it is dusted upon wounds or abrasions of the skin and forms a dry and absorbent covering under which they heal rapidly.

It has lately been claimed that beriberi is due to a microorganism found in rice under certain abnormal conditions; this claim is not yet firmly established and beriberi is still one of the many problems in medicine which are awaiting solution.

HABITAT.—All parts of the Archipelago.

BAMBUSEÆ.

Bamboo Family.

NOM. VULG.—*Caña*, Sp.; *Bamboo*, Eng.

Linnæus and Blanco include in the genus *Bambus* all the different species of bamboo to which the Spaniards have given the general name of *caña*. The plant is of incomparable value to the natives of the Philippines; they build their houses of it, make agricultural and industrial instruments of it, use it in all the varied apparatus of their fisheries and for a multitude of household utensils and furniture.

The variety *B. arundinacea*, Retz. (*B. arundo*, Blanco), *Kawayag-totóo*, Tag., is the largest and most generally employed in making houses and furniture. The tender shoots prepared in lime water are edible but have the deserved reputation of being difficult of digestion.

The variety *Schizostachyum acutiflorum*, Munro (*B. diffusa*, Blanco), *Osiw, Bokawy*, Tag., is less used. The shoots are used to treat opacity of the cornea, for which purpose they are cut when about a palm in height, the outer leaves removed, and the center soaked over night with a little sugar candy. The following day the water in the bottom of the jar is collected and used to paint the cornea.

The variety *Dendrocalamus sericens*, Munro (*B. mitis*, Blanco), *Taywanak*, Tag., is also used in medicine. Its abundant sap is given internally in the treatment of phthisis.

All of the above species and the *Dendrocalamus flagellifer*, Munro (*B. levis*, Blanco), *Boho*, Tag., produce at their joints a hard porcelain-like substance, friable, of opaline color, called "bamboo stone" or "tabashir" in India, where, as well as in the Philippines and Indo-China, it has great repute among the popular remedies. It is given in venereal diseases, hiccough, hemorrhage, fevers and other diseases. As a matter of fact, it is an almost inert substance, the imaginary virtues of which originated, doubtless, in the apparently remarkable fact that a stone (?) was produced inside of a vegetable.

The analysis of M. Guibourt is as follows:

Silicon	96.04
Water	2.94
Lime and potassium	0.13
Organic material	Traces.

INDEX OF PLANTS

ACCORDING TO THERAPEUTIC PROPERTIES.

Alteratives.—Anona muricata.—Tinospora crispa.—Raphanus sativus.—Bombax malabaricus.—Oxalis corniculata.—Citrus acida and C. Bigaradia.—Mangifera Indica.—Pongamia glabra.—Lawsonia alba.—Hydrocotyle Asiatica.—Alangium Lamarkii.—Oldenlandia corymbosa.—Calotropis gigantea.—Ehretia buxifolia.—Solanum nigrum.—Cassytha filiformis—Euphorbia Tirucalli.—Phyllanthus reticulatus.

Anthelmintics.[1] — Cleome viscosa. — Pangium edule. — Ruta graveolens.—Melia Azedarach.—Dysoxylum Blancoi.—Mangifera Indica.—Anacardium occidentale.—Mucuna pruriens.—Quisqualis Indica.—*Punica Granatum.*[2]—Jussiæa suffruticosa.—Carica Papaya.—Trichosanthes anguina and T. cucumerina.—Lagenaria.—Momordica.—Hydrocotyle Asiatica.—Sphæranthus Indicus.—Calotropis gigantea.—Tectona grandis.—Clerodendron infortunatum.—Chenopodium ambrosioides.—Echinus Philippinensis.—Cyperus rotundus.—*Rhinacanthus communis.*

Antispasmodics.—Sida carpinifolia.—Hibiscus Abelmoschus.—Ruta graveolens.—Citrus acida and C. Bigaradia.—Cedrela Toona.—Celastrus paniculata.—Cassia occidentalis.—Carum copticum.—Blumea balsamifera.—Artemisia vulgaris.—Solanum nigrum.—Datura alba.—Nicotiana Tabacum.—Adhatoda vasica.—Chenopodium ambrosioides.—Chloranthus officinalis.

Antiseptics.—Ruta graveolens.—Citrus acida and C. Bigaradia.—Mangifera Indica.—Anacardium occidentale.—Erythrina Indica.—Pongamia glabra.—Entada scandens.—*Coffea Arabica.*—Blumea balsamifera.—Spilanthes Acmella.—Nerium odorum.—Solanum nigrum.—Nicotiana Tabacum.—Tectona grandis.—Ocimum.—Piper Betle.—*Cinnamomum.*—Acalypha Indica.—Curcuma longa.—Areca Catechu.—Nipa fruticans.

[1] Including tænifuges.

[2] Names in italics are considered of especial importance by the author.

Astringents.—Tetracera macrophylla.—Michelia Champaca.—Anona squamosa, A. reticulata and A. muricata.—Nelumbium nucifera.—Bixa Orellana.—Garcinia mangostana, G. Cambogia.—Ochrocarpus pentapetalus.—Sida carpinifolia.—Thespesia populnea.—Bombax malabaricus.—Sterculia fœtida.—Murraya exotica.—Ægle decandra.—Feronia elephantum.—Melia Azedarach.—Sandoricum Indicum.—Caropa Moluccensis.—Rhamnus Wightii.—Mangifera Indica.—Odina Wodier.—Pterocarpus.—Cæsalpinia Sappan.—Acacia Farnesiana.—Terminalia Catappa and T. Chebula.—Psidium pomiferum.—Melastoma malabatrichum.—Punica Granatum.—Hymenodictyon Indicum.—Tectona grandis.—Achyranthes obtusifolia.—Artocarpus integrifolia.—Casuarina Sumatrana.—Areca Catechu.—Cyperus rotundus.

Acids or Refrigerants.—Oxalis corniculata.—*Averrhoa Bilimbi* and *A. Carambola.*—*Citrus acida* and *C. Bigaradia.*—Feronia elephantum.—Amaranthus spinosus.—Phyllanthus reticulatus.—*Tamarindus Indica.*

Balsams.—Calophyllum Inophyllum.—Dipterocarpus turbinatus. Garuga pinnata.—Canarium commune.

Carminatives.—Illicium anisatum.—Cleome viscosa.—Helicteres Isoara.—Abroma fastuosa.—Feronia elephantum.—Terminalia Chebula.—Carum copticum.—Fœniculum vulgare.—Plumbago Zeylanica.—Coleus aromaticus.—Rosmarinus officinalis.—Aristolochia Indica.—Zingiber officinale.—Curcuma longa.—Elettaria Cardamomum.

Convulsives.—*Strychnos Ignatii.*

Cosmetics.—Eriodendrum anfractuosum.—Cocos nucifera.

Diaphoretics.—Cissampelos Pareira.—Sida carpinifolia.—Hibiscus Rosa-Sinensis.—Gossypium herbaceum.—Ruta graveolens.—Xanthoxylum oxyphyllum.—Celastrus paniculata.—Hydrocotyle Asiatica. Eupatorium Ayapana.—Blumea balsamifera.—Plumbago Zeylanica. Calotropis gigantea.—Tylophora asthmatica.—Oroxylum Indicum.—Barleria Prionitis.—Justicia Gendarussa.—Ocimum.—Anisomeles ovata.—Crinum Asiaticum.—Cyperus rotundus.—Andropogon Schoenanthus and A. nardus.

Digestives.—*Carica Papaya.*

Diuretics.—Cissampelos Pareira.—Abutilon Indicum.—Anacardium occidentale.—Abrus precatorius.—Erythrina Indica.—Clitoria ternata.—Cassia occidentalis.—Hydrocotyle Asiatica.—Pæderia fœtida.—Spilanthes Acmella.—Achras Sapota.—Ipomœa pes-capræ.—Solanum nigrum.—Limnophila Menthastrum.—Sesamum Indicum.—

Lippia nodiflora.—Tectona grandis.—Vitex.—Amaranthus spinosa. —*Achyranthes obtusifolia.*—Chenopodium ambrosioides.—Phyllanthus reticulatus and P. Niruri.—Allium Cepa.—Cyperus rotundus.—Zea Mays.—Andropogon Schoenanthus.

Emmenagogues.—Michelia Champaca.—Artabotrys odoratissimus. Anamirta Cocculus.—Cissampelos Pareira.—Hibiscus Rosa Sinensis. —Gossypium herbaceum.—Abroma fastuosa.—Ruta graveolens.—Dysoxylum Blancoi.—Cæsalpinia Sappan and C. pulcherrima.—Citrullus Colocynthis.—Morinda citrifolia.—Blumea balsamifera.—Artemisia vulgaris.—Plumbago Zeylanica.—Plumeria acutifolia.—Sesamum Indicum.—Vitex.—Chenopodium ambrosioides.—Aristolochia Indica.—Casuarina Sumatrana.—Aloes Barbadensis.—Cyperus rotundus.

Emetics.—Hibiscus tiliaceus. — Dysoxylum Blancoi. — Moringa pterygosperma.— Clitoria ternatea. — Entada scandens. — Trichosanthes anguina.—Lagenaria.—Alangium Lamarkii.—Randia dumetorum.—Pæderia fœtida.—Allamanda cathartica.—Thevetia neriifolia.—Cerbera Odallam.—Calatropis gigantea. — Tylophora asthmatica.—Justicia Gendarussa.—*Acalypha Indica.* — *Crinum Asiaticum.*

Emollients.—Sida carpinifolia.—Abutilon Indicum.—Urena sinuata.— Hibiscus Rosa-Sinensis.—Gossypium herbaceum. — Eriodendron anfractuosum.—Helicteres Ixora.—Biophytum sensitivum.—Zizyphus Jujuba.—Abrus precatorius.—Clitoria ternata.—Cæsalpinia pulcherrima.—Lawsonia alba. — Luffa Ægyptiaca. — Ipomœa pescapræ.—Sesamum Indicum.—Acanthus ilicifolius.—Lippia nodiflora. —Plantago erosa.—Musa paradisiaca and M. sapientum.—Curcuma longa.—Allium Cepa.—Cocos nucifera.—Oriza.

Stimulants.—Illicium anisatum. — Artabotrys odoratissimus. — Brassica juncea. — Raphanus sativus. — Mesua ferrea. — Hibiscus Abelmoschus.—Helicteres Ixora.—Ruta graveolens.—Xanthoxylum oxyphyllum.—Citrus acida.—Celastrus paniculata.—Moringa pterygosperma.—Cæsalpinia pulcherrima.—Hydrocotyle Asiatica.—Carum copticum. — Fœniculum vulgare. — *Coffea Arabica.* — Eupatorium Ayapana.—Blumea balsamifera.—Sphæranthus Indicus.—Spilanthes Acmella. — Artemisia vulgaris. — Mimusops Elengi. — Jasminum Sambac.—*Capsicum fastigiatum.*—Ocimum.—Rosmarinus officinalis. —Chenopodium ambrosioides.—Piper Betle and P. nigrum.—Chloranthus officinalis.—*Cinnamomum.*—*Zingiber officinale.*—Curcuma longa. —Allium sativum and A. Cepa.—Cyperus rotundus.—Andropogon Schoenanthus and A. nardus.

Expectorants.—Hibiscus Rosa-Sinensis.—Biophytum sensitivum. —Trichosanthes cucumerina.—Blumea balsamifera.—Tylophora asthmatica.—Acanthus ilicifolius.—Barleria Prionitis.—Adhatoda vasica.—Vitex.—Ocimum.—*Acalypha Indica.*—*Crinum Asiaticum.*

Febrifuges.—Michelia Champaca.—Tinospora crispa.—Anamirta Cocculus.—Sida carpinifolia.—Melia Azedarach.—Dysoxylum Blancoi.—Carapa Moluccensis.—Cedrela Toona.—Erythrina Indica.—Cæsalpinia Bonducella and C. pulcherrima.—Cassia occidentalis.—Ammannia vesicatoria.—Trichosanthes cucumerina.—Hymenodictyon excelsum.—Ixora coccinea.—Morinda citrifolia.—Achras Sapota. —Mimusops Elengi.—Thevetia neriifolia.—Plumeria acutifolia.—Alstonia scholaris.—Vitex.—Clerodendron infortunatum.—Anisomeles ovata.—Aristolochia Indica.—Piper nigrum.—Chloranthus officinalis.

Galactagogues.—Gossypium herbaceum.

Antigalactagogues.—Jasminum Sambac.—Piper Betle.

Hemostatics.—Portulaca oleracea.—Tetracera macrophylla.—Mangifera Indica.—Pterocarpus.—Cæsalpinia Sappan.—Euphorbia pilulifera.

Narcotics (*sedatives and anodynes*).—Anamirta Cocculus.—Argemone Mexicana.—Pangium edule.—Cassia occidentalis.—Solanum nigrum.—*Datura alba.*—Nicotiana Tabacum.—Vitex.

Nutritive Plants.—*Anona squamosa,* A. reticulata and A. muricata. —Nelumbium nucifera.—Pangium edule.—Portulaca oleracea.—Garcinia mangostana and G. Cambogia.—Sterculia fœtida.—*Theobroma Cacao.*—*Averrhoa Bilimbi, A. Carambola.*—Feronia elephantum.—Garuga pinnata.—Canarium commune.—Sandoricum Indicum.—Zizyphus Jujuba.—*Mangifera Indica.*—Anacardium occidentale.—Moringa pterygosperma.—Agati grandiflora.—*Tamarindus Indica.*—Bauhinia malabarica.—Parkia Roxburghii.—Psidium pomiferum.—Eugenia Jambolana.—Trichosanthes.—Lagenaria.—Momordica.—Achras Sapota.—Solanum nigrum.—Sesamum Indicum.—Artocarpus integrifolia.—*Musa paradisiaca* and *M. sapientum.*—Areca Catechu. —*Cocos nucifera.*—*Zea Mays.*—*Saccharum officinarum.*—*Oriza.*—Bambuseæ.

Purgatives.—Argemone Mexicana.—Garcinia Morella.—Mesua ferrea.—Agati grandiflora.—Erythrina Indica.—Clitoria ternatea.—Cæsalpinia pulcherrima.—Cassia fistula and C. alata.—Tamarindus Indica.—Entada scandens.—Terminalia Chebula.—Jussiæa suffruticosa.—Carica Papaya.—Trichosanthes anguina and T. cucumerina.—

Lagenaria.—Luffa Ægyptiaca.—Momordica.—*Citrullus Colocynthis.*—Trianthema monogyna.—Morinda citrifolia.—Spilanthes Acmella.—Carthamus tinctorius.—Allamanda cathartica.—Cerbera Odallam.—Plumeria acutifolia.—Calotropis gigantea.—Ipomœa hederacea.—Ipomœa Turpethum.—Solanum nigrum.—Sesamum Indicum.—Tectona grandis.—Samadera Indica.—Mirabilis Jalapa.—Amaranthus spinosus.—Euphorbia neriifolia.—Euphorbia Tirucalli.—Jatropa Curcas.—Aleurites moluccana.—Croton Tiglium.—Acalypha Indica.—*Ricinus communis.—Aloes Barbadensis.*

Sialagogues.—Carum copticum.

Bitter Tonics.—Michelia Champaca.—Tinospora crispa.—Cissampelos Pareira.—Cratæva religiosa.—Mesua ferrea—.Sida carpinifolia.—Murraya exotica.—Citrus Bigaradia.—Samadera Indica.—Melia Azedarach.—Rhamnus Wightii.—Agati grandiflora.—Cæsalpinia Bonducella.—Cassia occidentalis.—Terminalia Chebula.—Trichosanthes cucumerina.—Momordica.—Hymenodictyon excelsum.—Morinda citrifolia.—Sphæranthus Indicus.—Achras Sapota.—Mimusops Elengi.—Alstonia scholaris.—Calotropis gigantea.—*Strychnos Ignatii.*—Limnophila Menthastrum.—Oroxylum Indicum.—Vitex.—Clerodendron infortunatum.—Anisomeles ovata.—Phyllanthus Niruri.—Aloes Barbadensis.—*Areca Catechu.—Nerium odorum* (cardiac).

Aromatic Tonics.—Feronia elephantum.—Sandoricum Indicum.—Fœniculum.—*Coffea Arabica.*—Eupatorium Ayapana.—Artemisia vulgaris.—Chenopodium ambrosioides, Cinnamomum.—*Zingiber officinale.*

Vesicants.—Anacardium occidentale.—Moringa pterygosperma.—Ammannia vesicatoria.—Plumbago Zeylanica.—Calotropis gigantea.—Euphorbia Tirucalli.

Rubefacients or Revulsives.—Moringa pterygosperma.—Plumeria acutifolia.—Croton Tiglium.—Jatropha Curcas.—Allium sativum.

Stimulants.—Sterculia urens.—Argemone Mexicana.—Kleinhovia hospitata.—Celastrus paniculata.—Pongamia glabra.—Cassia alata.—Entada scandens.—Kalanchoe laciniata.—Elettaria Cardamomum.

Antiherpetics, etc.—Sterculia fœtida.—Canarium commune.—Trichosanthes palmata.

INDEX OF PLANTS

ACCORDING TO SPECIAL DISEASES.

Aphthæ, Stomatitis, Glossitis.[1]—Tetracera macrophylla.—Feronia elephantum.—Pterocarpus santalinus, Indicus and erinaceus.—Melastoma malabatrichum.—*Punica Granatum.*—Mimusops Elengi.—Calotropis gigantea.—Tectona grandis.—Ocimum.—Achyranthes obtusifolia.—Phyllanthus reticulatus.

Hemorrhoids.—Mesua ferrea.—Thespesia populnea.—Terminalia Chebula.—Punica Granatum.—Plumbago Zeylanica.—Capsicum fastigiatum.—Sesamum Indicum.—Aloes Barbadensis (for inducing the hemorrhoids).

Amenorrhœa and Dysmenorrhœa.—Abroma fastuosa.—Dysoxylum Blancoi.—Cæsalpinia Sappan.—Cæsalpinia pulcherrima.—Blumea balsamifera.—Artemisia vulgaris.—Plumeria acutifolia.—Sesamum Indicum.—Chenopodium ambrosioides.—Casuarina Sumatrana.—Aloes Barbadensis.

Anasarca.—Plumbago Zeylanicum. —Coffea Arabica.—Plumeria acutifolia.—Calotropis gigantea.—Ipomœa pes-capræ.—Solanum nigrum.—Barlonia Prionitis.—Achyranthes obtusifolia.—Euphorbia neriifolia.—Phyllanthus Niruri.—Cissampelos Pareira.

Anal Fistula.—Pterocarpus.

Asthma.—Gossypium herbaceum.—Garuga pinnata.—Dysoxylum Blancoi.—Erythrina Indica.—Cæsalpinia pulcherrima.—Entada scandens.—Trichosanthes palmata.—Coffea Arabica.—Tylophora asthmatica.—Datura alba.—Acanthus ilicifolius.—*Adhatoda vasica.* Coleus aromaticus.—*Euphorbia pilulifera.*—Euphorbia Tirucalli.—Euphorbia neriifolia.—Phyllanthus Niruri.

Spleen, Affections of.—Ammannia vesicatoria.—Lawsonia alba.—Momordica.

Beriberi.—Celastrus paniculata.—Vitex.

[1] I do not join these diseases because I consider them identical or due to the same pathogenic agent but because the plants that follow are used indifferently for the diseases.

Blenorrhœa, Gonorrhœa, Urethritis.—Nymphæa Lotus.—Argemone Mexicana.—Dipterocarpus turbinatus.—Sterculia fœtida.—Clitoria ternata.—Pterocarpus.—Trichosanthes palmata.—Mimusops Elengi.—Plumeria acutifolia.—Lippia nodiflora.—*Ocimum.*—*Amaranthus spinosus.*—Cassytha filiformis.—Cyperus rotundus.

Bronchi and Lungs, Diseases of.—Anona muricata.—Calophyllum Inophyllum.—Dipterocarpus turbinatus.—Canarium commune.—Zizyphus Jujuba.—Abrus precatorius.—Erythrina Indica.—Cæsalpinia pulcherrima.—Trichosanthes cucumerina.—Lagenaria.—Ixora coccinea.—Blumea balsamifera.—Tylophora asthmatica.—Sesamum Indicum.—Barleria Prionitis.—*Adhatoda vasica.*—Vitex.—Coleus aromaticus.—Anisomeles ovata.—*Chenopodium ambrosioides.*—*Euphorbia pilulifera.*—Acalypha Indica.—Curcuma longa.

Cholera.—Artabotrys odoratissimus.—Samadera Indica.—Carum copticum.—Eupatorium Ayapana.—*Zingiber officinale.*—Cyperus rotundus.

Colic.—(*a*) *Flatulent: Illicium anisatum.*—Argemone Mexicana.—Cleome viscosa.—Helicteres Ixora.—Dysoxylum Blancoi.—Terminalia Chebula.—*Carum copticum.*—*Fœniculum.*—Plumbago Zeylanica.—Ipomœa pes-capræ.—Ocimum.—Coleus aromaticus.—Rosmarinus officinalis.—Aristolochia Indica.—*Piper Betle.*—*Elettaria Cardamomum.*

(*b*) *Lead:* Allamanda cathartica.

Contusions.—Samadera Indica.—Plumeria acutifolia.—Aloes Barbadensis.—Casuarina sumatrana.

Heart, Diseases of.—Helicteres Ixora.—Coffea Arabica.—Cinnamomum.

Coryza (*rhinitis, nasal catarrh, ozœna*).—Agati grandiflora.—Ocimum.—Curcuma longa.

Diabetes.—Eugenia Jambolana.

Diarrhœa, Dysentery.—Anona squamosa.—Anona reticulata and A. muricata.—Nelumbium nucifera.—Bixa Orellana.—Garcinia mangostana.—Ochrocarpus pentapetalus.—Thespesia populnea.—Gossypium herbaceum.—Bombax malabaricum.—Averrhoa Bilimbi.—*Averrhoa Carambola.*—Murraya exotica.—*Ægle decandra.*—*Feronia elephantum.*—Sandoricum Indicum.—Carapa Moluccensis.—Cedrela Toona. Rhamnus Wightii.—Mangifera Indica.—Pterocarpus.—Cæsalpinia Bonducella.—Bauhinia malabarica.—Kalanchoe laciniata.—Terminalia Catappa.—Psidium pomiferum.—Eugenia Jambolana.—Punica Granatum.—Jussiæa suffruticosa.—*Carica Papaya.*—Carum copticum.

Hemoptysis. — Tetracera macrophylla. — Portulaca oleracea. — Cæsalpinia Sappan.—Casuarina Sumatrana.—Curcuma longa.

Herniæ.—Nicotiana Tabacum.

Liver, Diseases of.—Anona muricata.—Kalanchoe laciniata.—Lawsonia alba.—Lagenaria.—Momordica. — Oldenlandia corymbosa.—Sphæranthus Indicus.—Carthamus tinctorius.—Solanum nigrum.

Cephalalgia.—Portulaca oleracea.—Coffea Arabica.—Blumea balsamifera.—Vitex.—Colus aromaticus.—Acalypha Indica.

Laryngitis.—Mangifera Indica.—Capsicum fastigiatum.

Leucorrhœa. — Garcinia mangostana. — Sandoricum Indicum.—Mangifera Indica.—Pterocarpus.—Acacia Farnesiana.—Terminalia Chebula.—Punica Granatum.

Bloody Flux.—Artocarpus integrifolia.

Menorrhagia, Metrorrhagia. See "Hemorrhages."

Bites of Insects and Poisonous Animals.—Feronia elephantum.—Carapa moluccensis.—Eupatorium Ayapana.—Tylophora asthmatica.—Rhinocanthus communis.—Coleus aromaticus.—Leucas aspera.—*Aristolochia Indica.—Euphorbia neriifolia.*—Acalypha Indica.—Allium sativum.

Nervous Diseases (*chorea, epilepsy, convulsions, hysteria,* etc.).—Sida carpinifolia.—Ruta graveolens. — Blumea balsamifera. — Artemisia vulgaris.—Solanum nigrum.—Datura alba.—Nicotiana Tabacum.—Coleus aromaticus.—Chenopodium ambrosioides.

Neuralgia.—Coffea Arabica.—Acanthus ilicifolius.

Odontalgia.—Murraya exotica and M. Koenigi.—Pterocarpus.—Calotropis gigantea. — Plantago erosa. — Cyperus rotundus. (See "Ears.")

Intestinal Obstruction. — Nicotiana Tabacum. (See "Purgatives.")

Ears, Affections of.—Cleome viscosa.—Hibiscus tiliaceus.—Helicteres Isora.—Crinum Asiaticum. (See "Odontalgia.")

Eyes, Affections of.—Argemone Mexicana.—Portulaca oleracea.—Calophyllum Inophyllum.—Garuga pinnata.—Abrus precatorius.—Erythrina Indica.—Jasminum Sambac.—Rosmarinus officinalis.—Curcuma longa.

Orchitis.—Calophyllum Inophyllum.—Sterculia urens.—Vitex.

Paralysis.—Celastrus paniculata.—Acanthus ilicifolius.—Ocimum.—Rosmarinus officinalis.

Parasites (*pediculi,* etc.).—Anona squamosa.—Anamirta Cocculus.

Skin, Affections of (*lepra, itch, eczema, psoriasis*).—Argemone Mexicana. — Pangium edule. — Portulaca oleracea.—Urena sinuata.—Thespesia populnea. —Sterculia fœtida. —Kleinhovia hospitata.—Helicteres Isora. —Canarium commune. —Celastrus paniculata.—Mangifera Indica. —Anacardium occidentale. —Odina Wodier.—*Pongamia glabra* (itch).—Cassia fistula. —*Cassia alata* (herpes).—Entada scandens.—Psidium pomiferum.—Melastoma malabatrichum.—Lawsonia alba.—Carica Papaya.—Momordica.—*Hydrocotyle Asiatica.*—Alangium Lamarkii.—Oldenlandia corymbosa.—Ixora coccinea.—Spilanthes Acmella.—Plumbago Zeylanica.—Plumeria acutifolia.—Nerium odorum.—Calotropis gigantea.—Solanum nigrum.—Rhinacanthus communis.—Tectona grandis.—Leucas aspera.—Amaranthus spinosus.—Echinus Philippinensis.—Curcuma longa.

Burns.—Eriodendron anfractuosum.—Lawsonia alba.

Rectum, Prolapsed.—Pterocarpus.—Acacia Farnesiana.—Psidium pomiferum.

Rheumatism.—Tinospora crispa.—Cratæva religiosa.—Ochrocarpus pentapetalus.—Mesua ferrea. —Sida carpinifolia. —Samadera Indica.—Celastrus paniculata.—Erythrina Indica.—Pongamia glabra.—Momordica.—Alangium Lamarkii.—Pæderia fœtida.—Blumea balsamifera.—Spilanthes Acmella.— Plumeria acutifolia. — Calotropis gigantea.—Ipomœa pes-capræ.—Datura alba.—Oroxylum Indicum.—Acanthus ilicifolius.—Justicia Gendarussa.—Vitex.—Ocimum.—Rosmarinus officinalis.—Anisomeles ovata.—Euphorbia Tirucalli.—Zingiber officinale.—Allium sativum.—Andropogon Schoenanthus and A. nardus.

Kidneys, Affections of.—Sida carpinifolia.—*Zea Mays.*

Syphilis.—Tinospora crispa.—Erythrina Indica.—Hydrocotyle Asiatica.—Alangium Lamarkii.—Nerium odorum.—Calotropis gigantea.—Ehretia buxifolia.—Cassytha filiformis.—Euphorbia Tirucalli.—Acalypha Indica.

Tæniæ. (See "Anthelmintics.")

Phthisis.—Garuga pinnata.

Tumors.—Trichosanthes palmata.—Sphæranthus Indicus.—Ipomœa pes-capræ.

Ulcers, Wounds, Sores, etc.—Tinospora crispa.—Dipterocarpus turbinatus.—Hibiscus tiliaceus.—Sterculia fœtida.—Canarium commune.—Melia Azedarach.—Cedrela Toona.—Mangifera Indica.—Anacardium occidentale.—Odina Wodier.—Erythrina Indica.—Pongamia glabra.—Kalanchoe laciniata.—Terminalia Catappa and T. Chebula.—Psidium pomiferum.—Melastoma malabatrichum.—Hydrocotyle

Asiatica.—Morinda citrifolia.—Eupatorium Ayapana.—Blumea balsamifera.—Spilanthes Acmella.—Artemisia vulgaris.—Mimusops Elengi.—Ipomœa pes-capræ.—Solanum nigrum.—Nicotiana Tabacum.—Tectona grandis.—Phyllanthus Niruri.—Acalypha Indica.—Ricinus communis.—Artocarpus integrifolia.—Casuarina Sumatrana.—Nipa fruticans.—*Carica Papaya.*

Urticaria.—Phyllanthus reticulatus.

Bladder, Affections of.—*Cissampelos Pareira.*—Portulaca oleracea.—Dipterocarpus turbinatus.—Urena sinuata.—Abrus precatorius.—Clitoria ternata.—Pterocarpus.—Lawsonia alba.—Pæderia fœtida.—Spilanthus Acmella.—Allium sativum.—Zea Mays.

Vermes. (See "Anthelmintics.")

ALPHABETICAL INDEX

OF SYSTEMATIC AND COMMON NAMES OF PLANTS